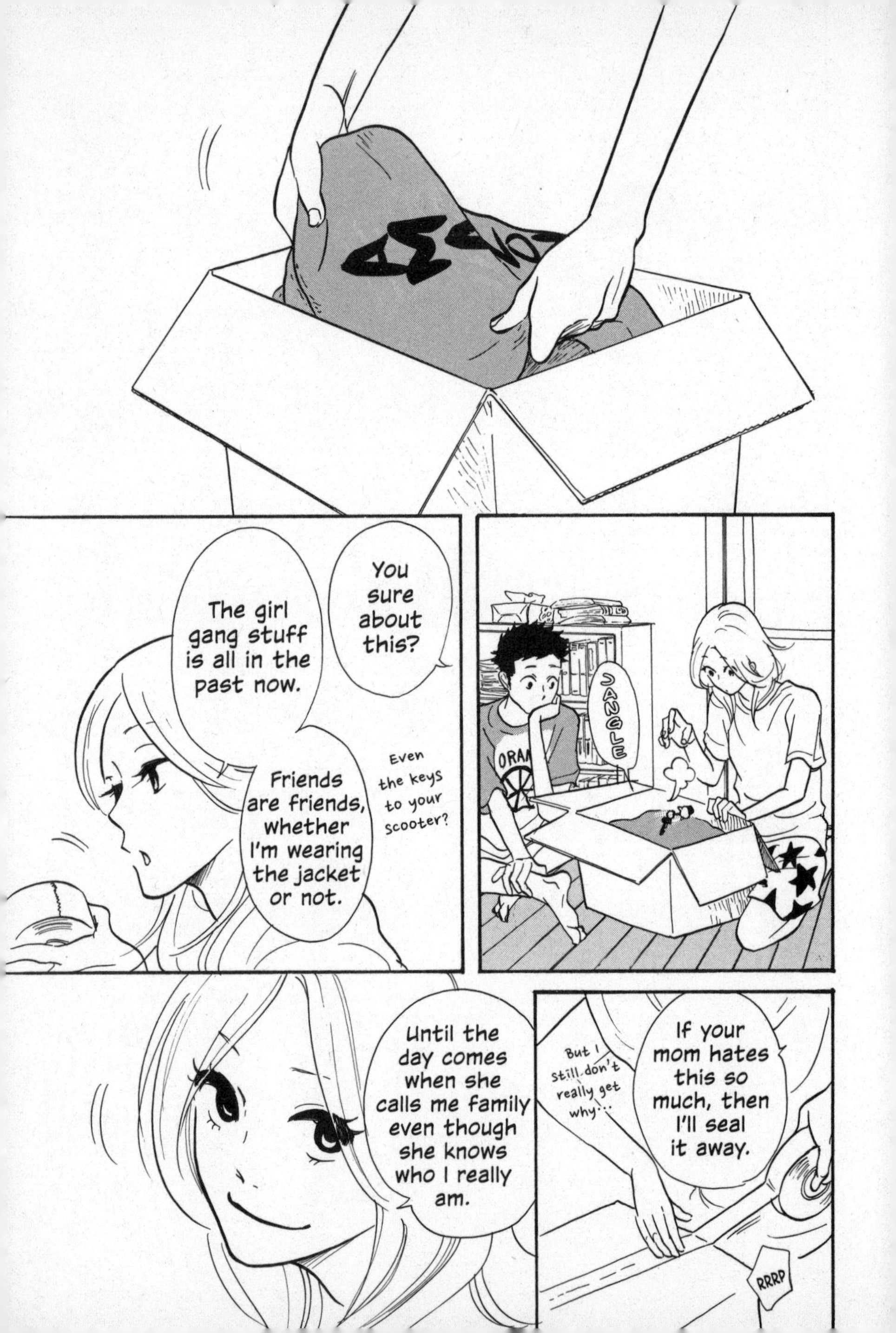
JANGLE
You sure about this?
The girl gang stuff is all in the past now.
Even the keys to your scooter?
Friends are friends, whether I'm wearing the jacket or not.
If your mom hates this so much, then I'll seal it away.
But I still don't really get why...
RRRP
Until the day comes when she calls me family even though she knows who I really am.

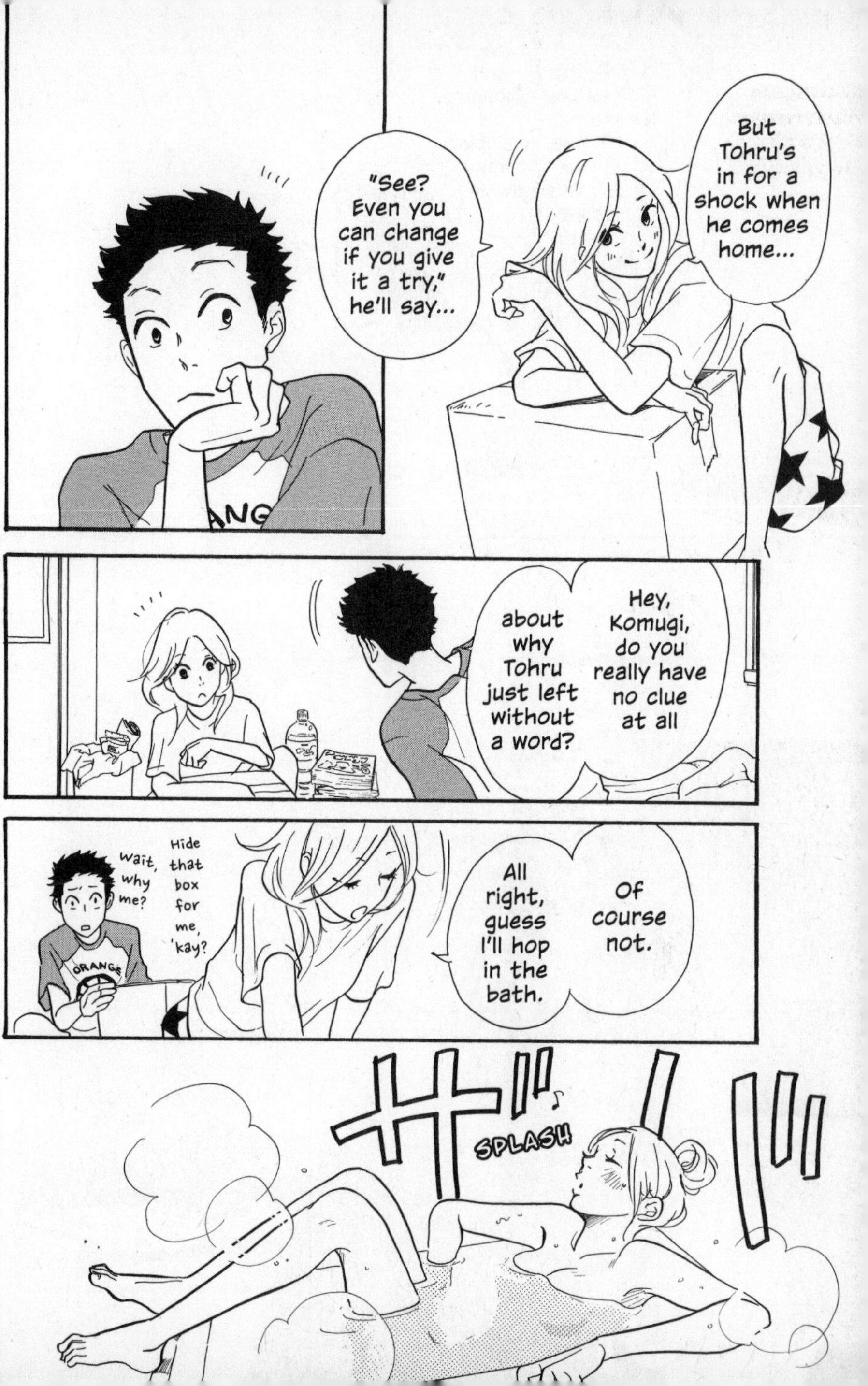
But Tohru's in for a shock when he comes home...
"See? Even you can change if you give it a try," he'll say...
Hey, Komugi, do you really have no clue at all
about why Tohru just left without a word?
Of course not.
All right, guess I'll hop in the bath.
Hide that box for me, 'kay?
Wait, why me?
ORANGE
SPLASH

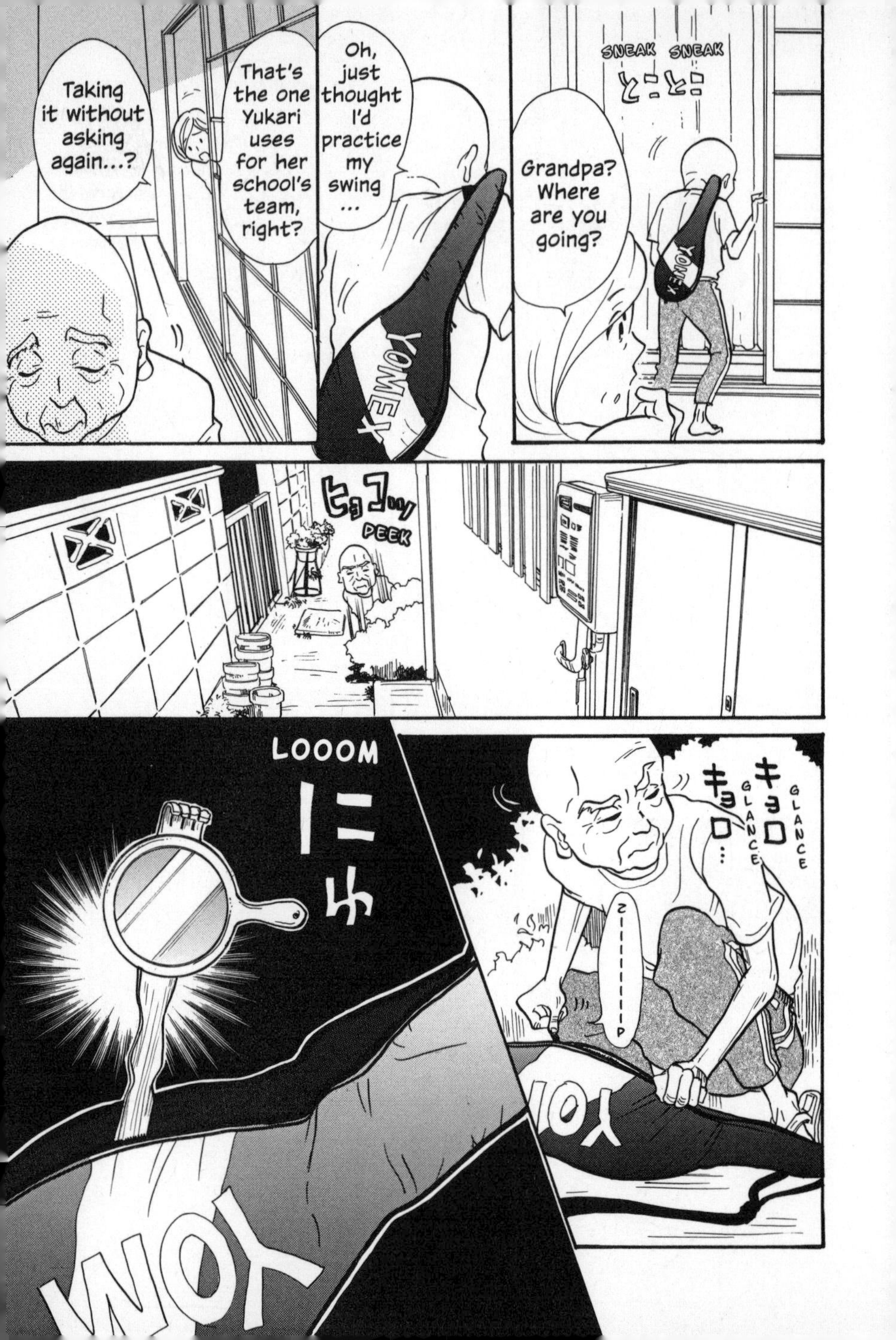
SNEAK SNEAK
Grandpa? Where are you going?
Oh, just thought I'd practice my swing ...
That's the one Yukari uses for her school's team, right?
Taking it without asking again...?
PEEK
GLANCE GLANCE
LOOOM

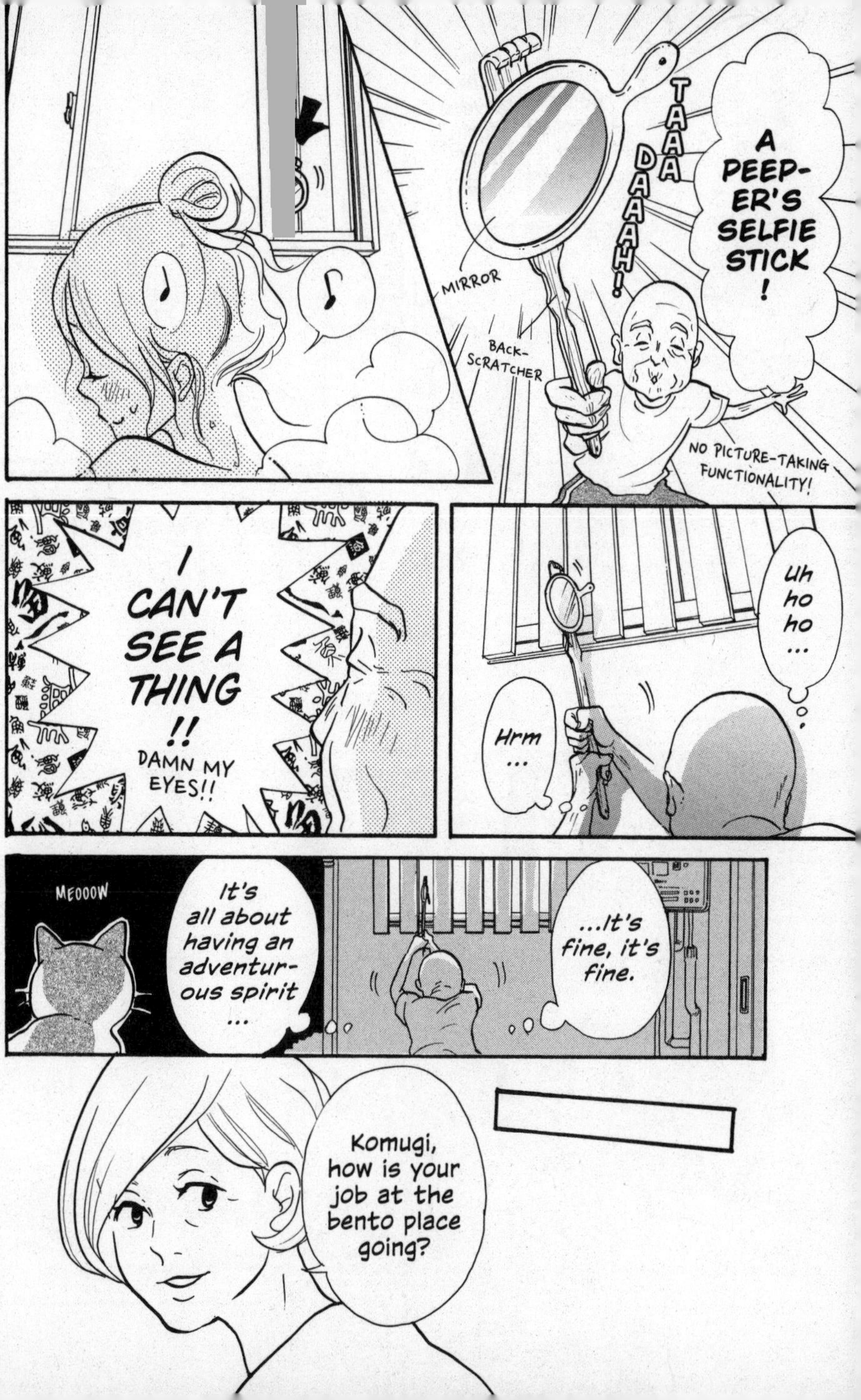
TAAA DAAAAH!
A PEEPER'S SELFIE STICK!
MIRROR
BACK-SCRATCHER
NO PICTURE-TAKING FUNCTIONALITY!
Uh ho ho...
Hrm...
I CAN'T SEE A THING!!
DAMN MY EYES!!
...It's fine, it's fine.
It's all about having an adventurous spirit...
MEOOOW
Komugi, how is your job at the bento place going?

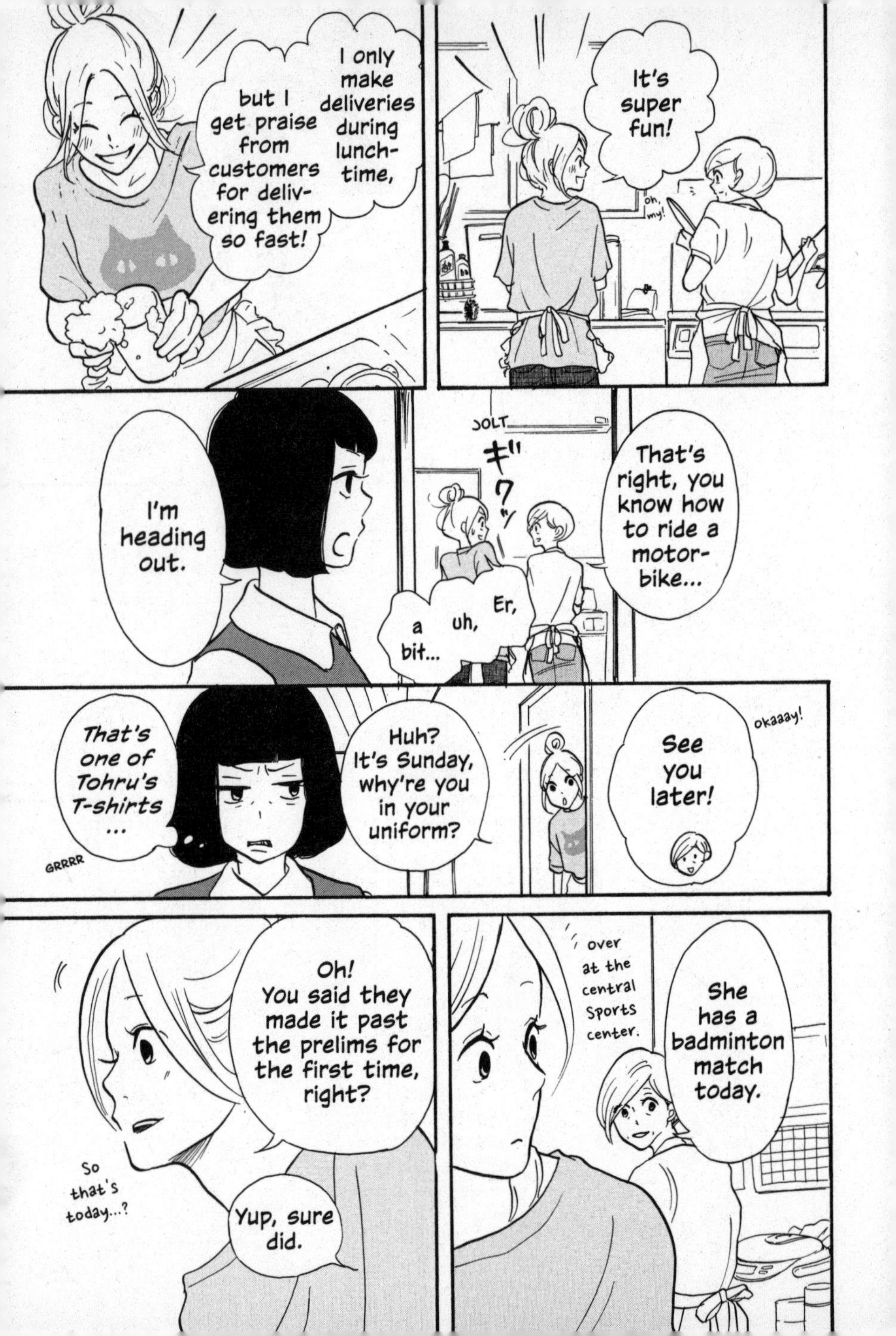
It's super fun!
Oh, my!
I only make deliveries during lunch-time,
but I get praise from customers for deliv-ering them so fast!
That's right, you know how to ride a motor-bike...
JOLT
Er, uh, a bit...
I'm heading out.
See you later!
Okaaay!
Huh? It's Sunday, why're you in your uniform?
That's one of Tohru's T-shirts ...
GRRRR
She has a badminton match today.
over at the central Sports center.
Oh! You said they made it past the prelims for the first time, right?
So that's today...?
Yup, sure did.

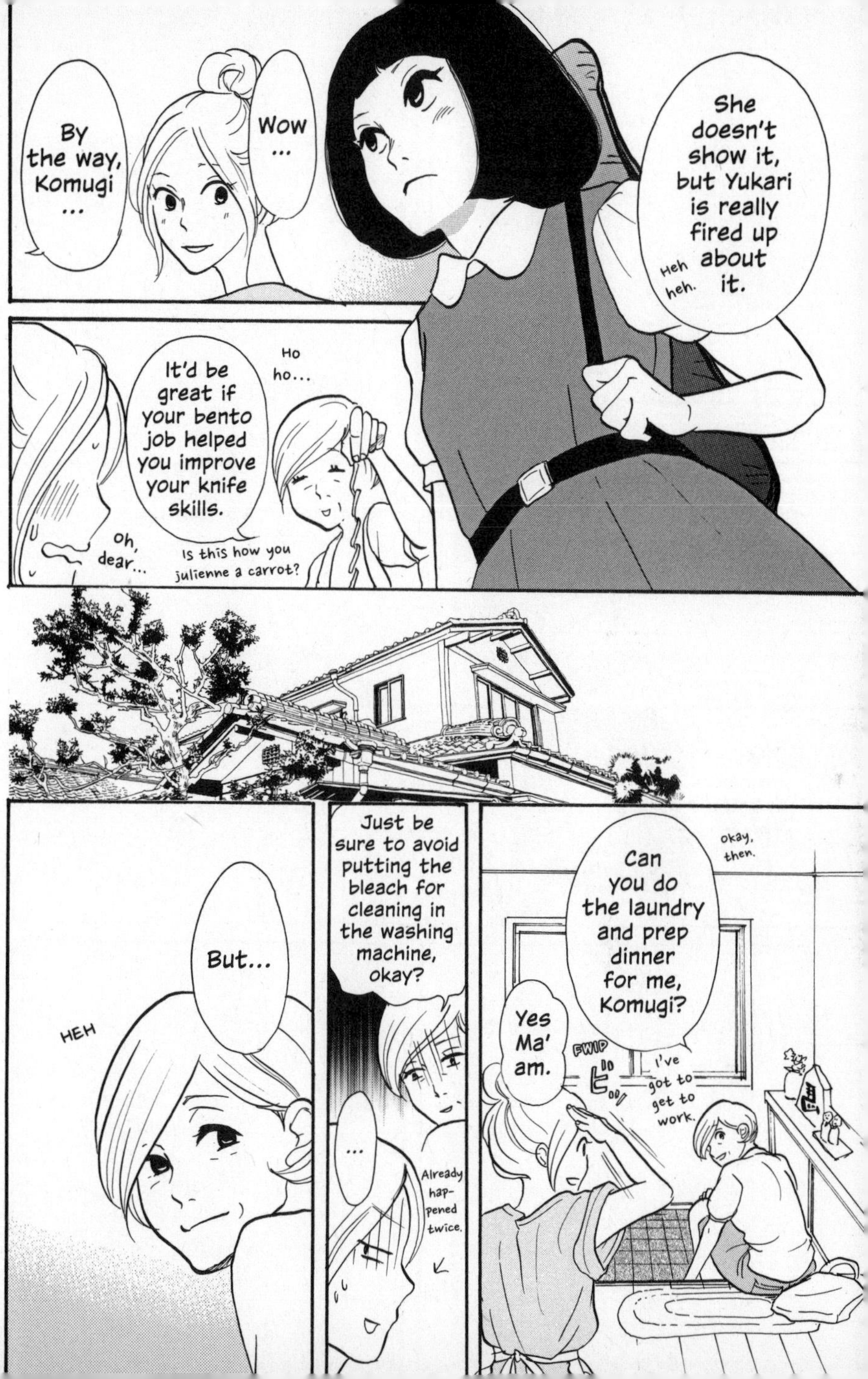
She doesn't show it, but Yukari is really fired up about it.
Heh heh.
Wow ...
By the way, Komugi ...
Ho ho...
It'd be great if your bento job helped you improve your knife skills.
Is this how you julienne a carrot?
Oh, dear...
Okay, then.
Can you do the laundry and prep dinner for me, Komugi?
I've got to get to work.
FWIP
Yes Ma' am.
Just be sure to avoid putting the bleach for cleaning in the washing machine, okay?
...
Already hap-pened twice.
But...
HEH

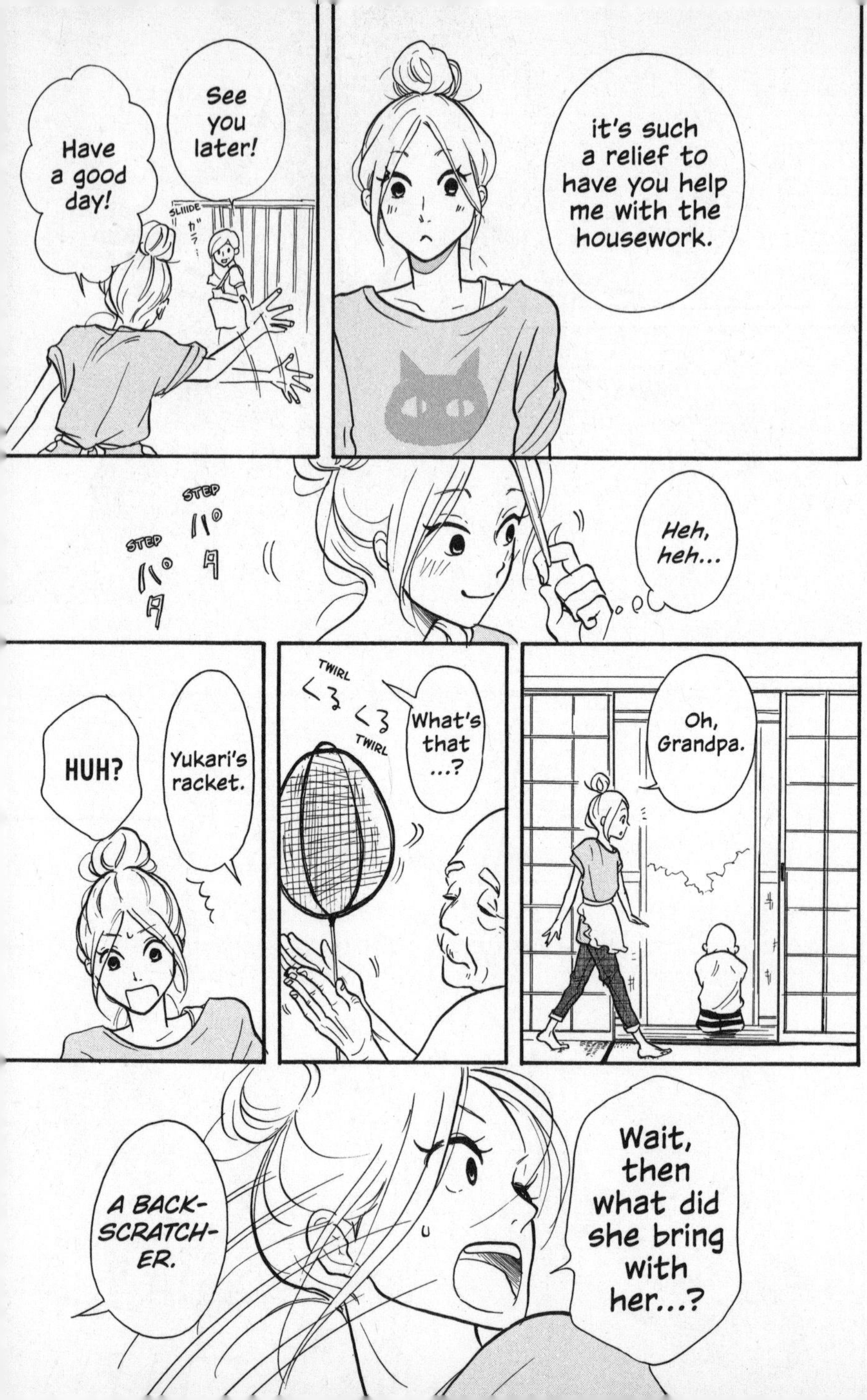
it's such a relief to have you help me with the housework.
See you later!
SLIIIDE
ガラ
Have a good day!
Heh, heh...
STEP
パタ
STEP
パタ
Oh, Grandpa.
What's that ...?
TWIRL
くる
くる
TWIRL
Yukari's racket.
HUH?
Wait, then what did she bring with her...?
A BACK-SCRATCH-ER.

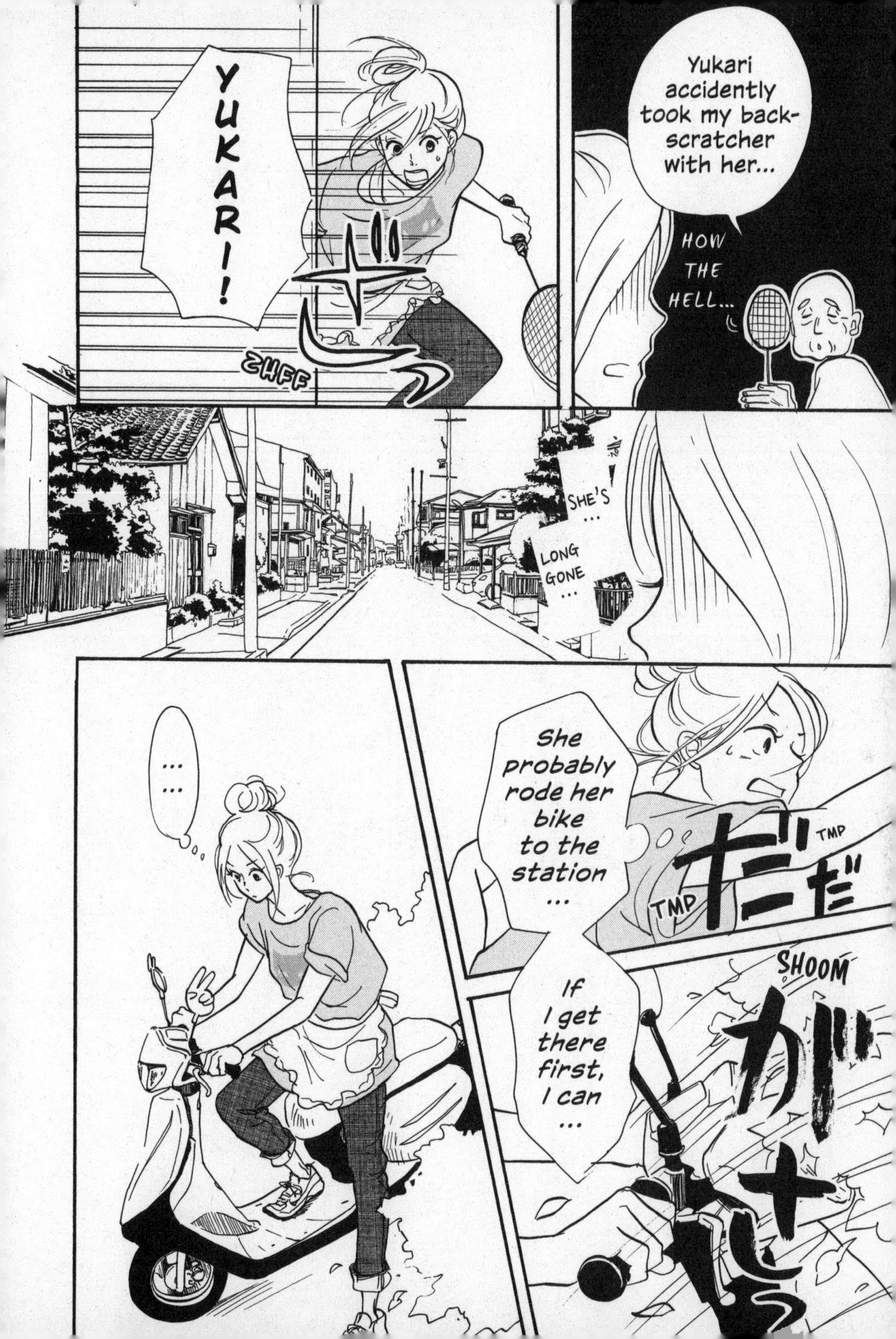
Yukari accidently took my back-scratcher with her...
HOW THE HELL...
YUKARI!
ZHFF
SHE'S ...
LONG GONE ...
She probably rode her bike to the station ...
TMP
TMP
SHOOM
If I get there first, I can ...
... ...

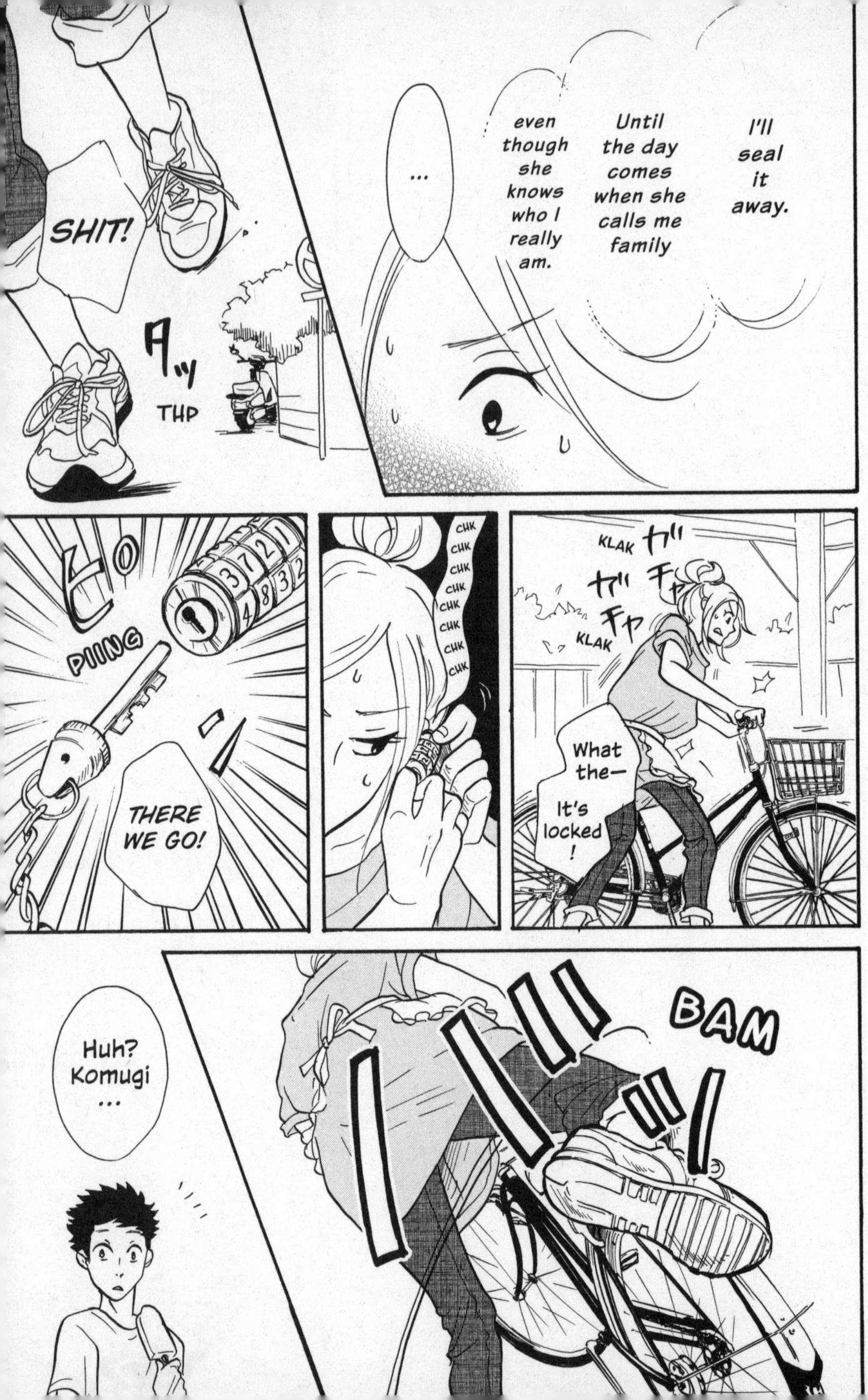
I'll seal it away.
Until the day comes when she calls me family
even though she knows who I really am.
...
SHIT!
アッ
THP
KLAK
KLAK
What the—
It's locked!
CHK CHK CHK CHK CHK CHK CHK CHK
PIING
THERE WE GO!
BAM
Huh? Komugi...

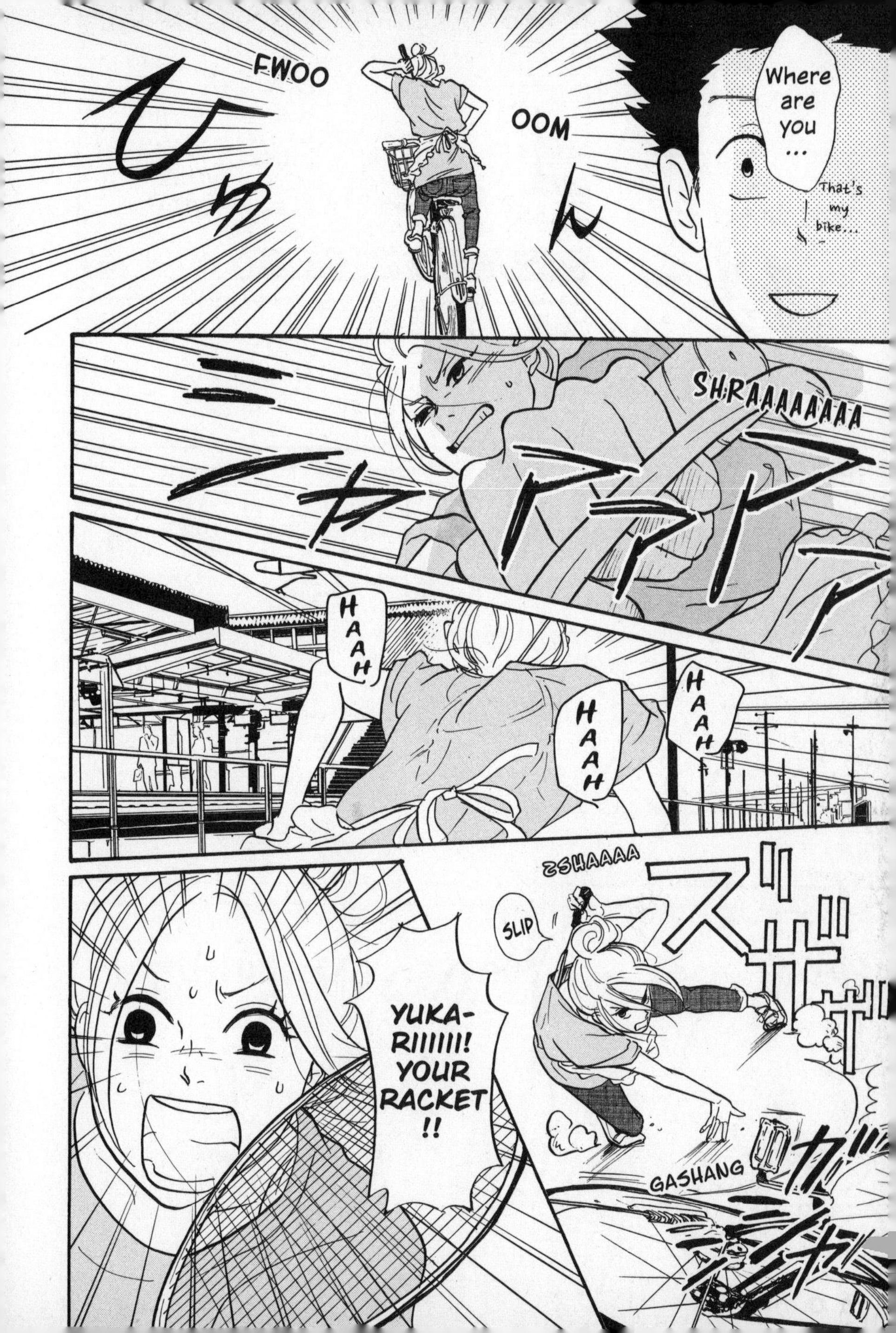
Where are you ...
That's my bike...
FWOO
OOM
SHRAAAAAAAA
HAAAH
HAAAH
HAAAH
ZSHAAAA
SLIP
GASHANG
YUKA-RIIIIIII! YOUR RACKET !!

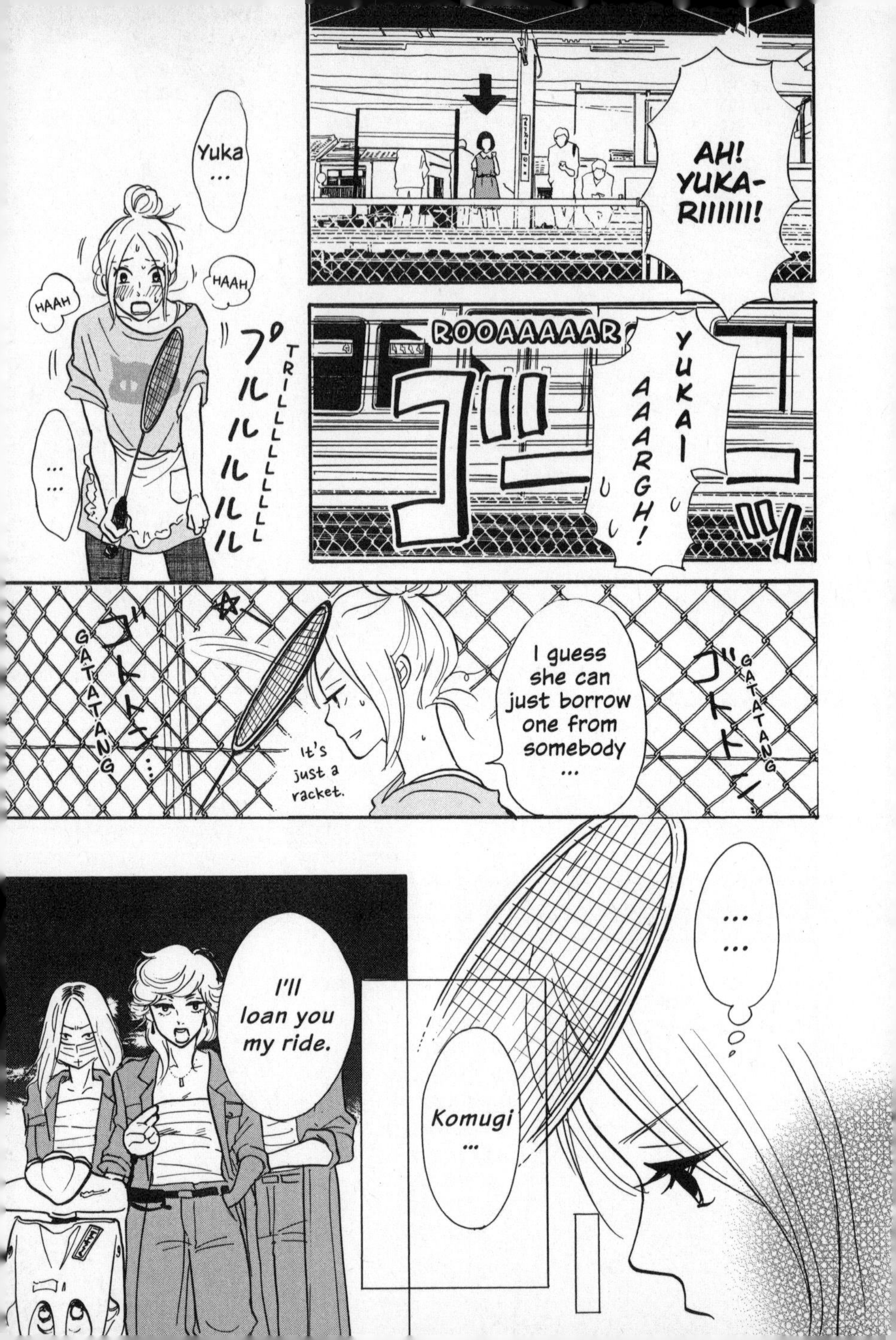

AH! YUKA-RIIIIIII!
ROOAAAAAR
ゴーーッ
YUKAI AAAARGH!
Yuka ...
HAAH
HAAH
ブルルルルル
TRILLLLLLLLL
... ...
ゴトトン
GATATANG
I guess she can just borrow one from somebody ...
It's just a racket.
ガタトン...
GATATANG
... ...
Komugi ...
I'll loan you my ride.

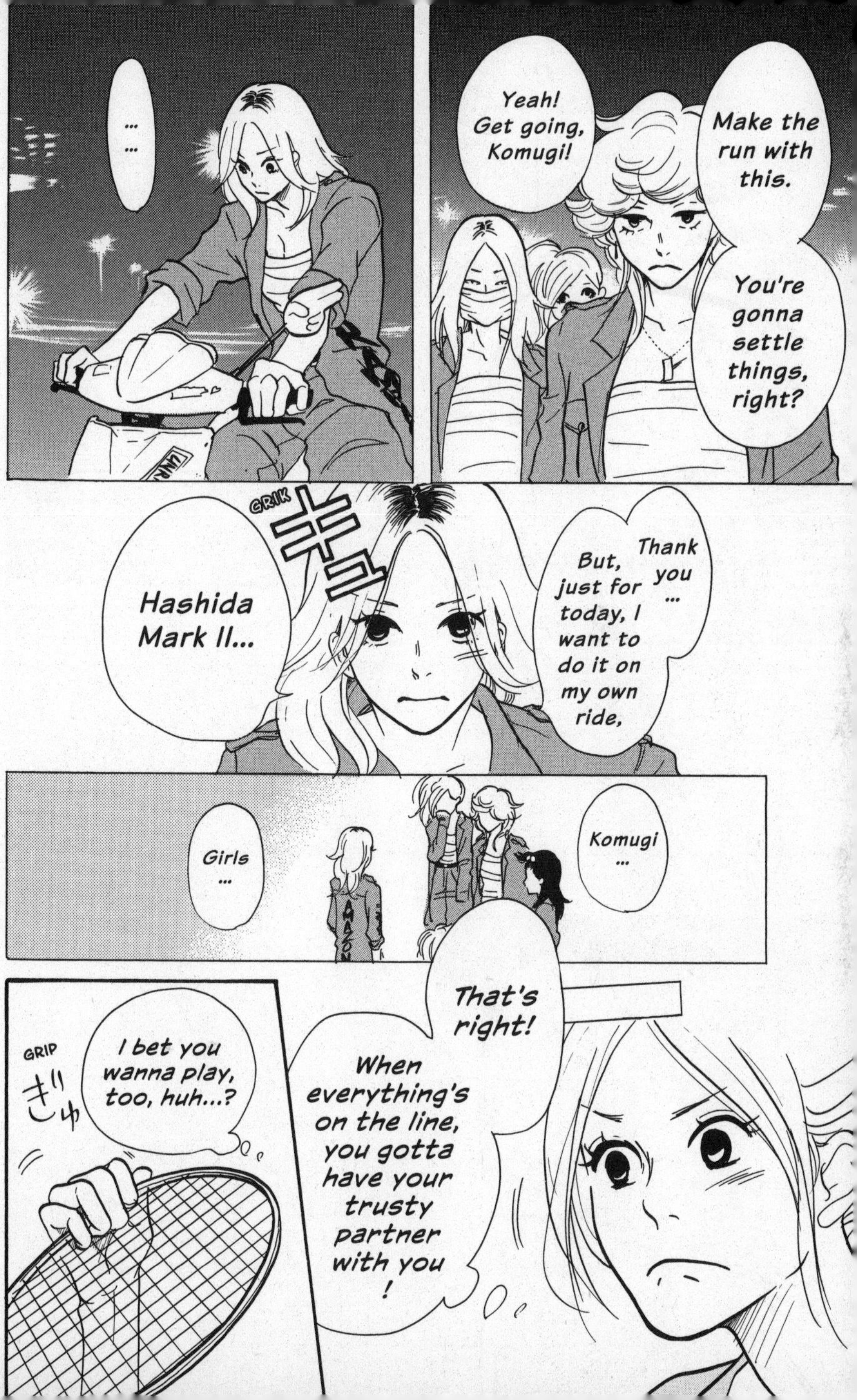
Make the run with this.
Yeah! Get going, Komugi!
You're gonna settle things, right?
...
...
Thank you ...
But, just for today, I want to do it on my own ride,
GRIK
Hashida Mark II...
Komugi ...
Girls ...
That's right!
When everything's on the line, you gotta have your trusty partner with you!
GRIP
I bet you wanna play, too, huh...?

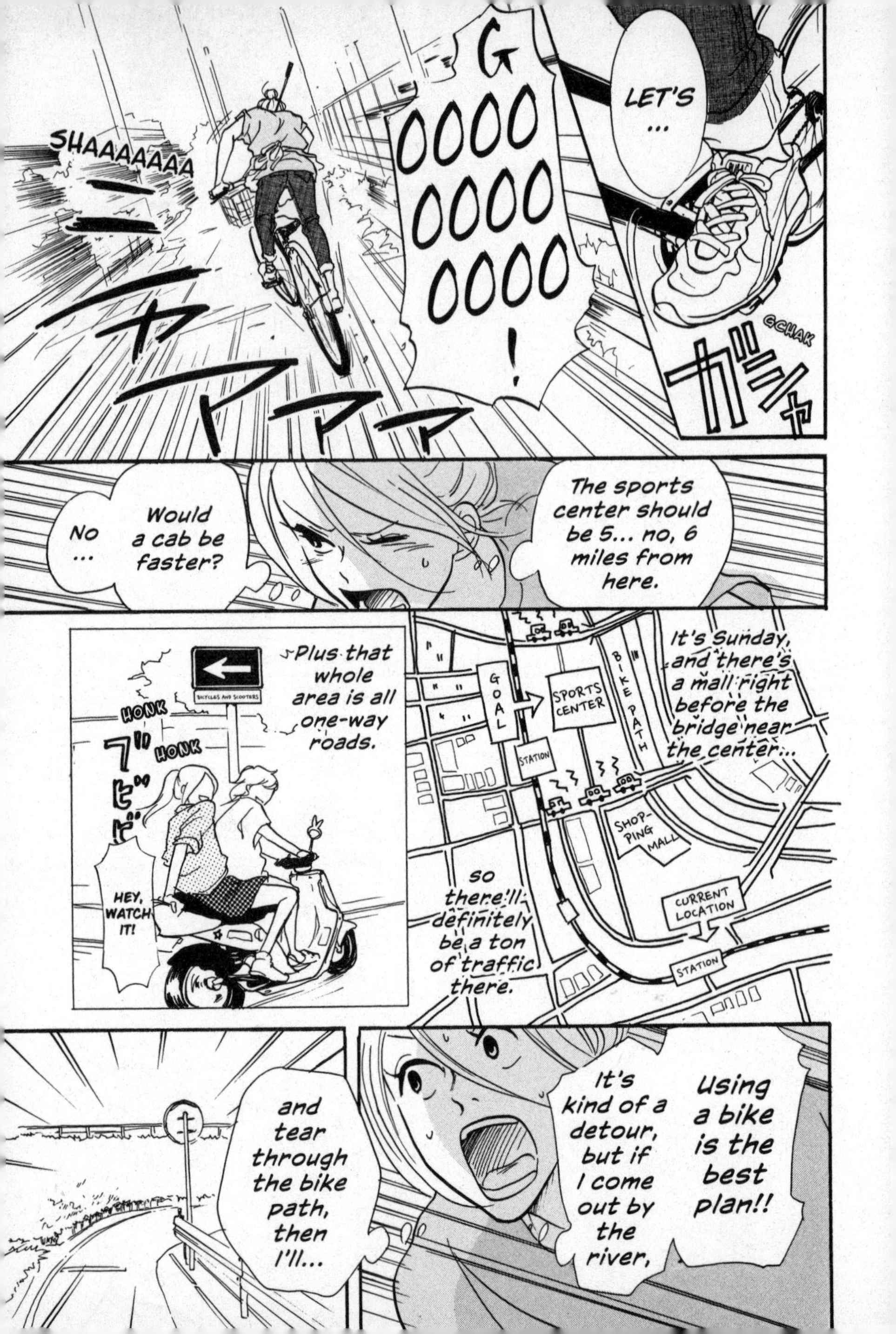
LET'S ...
GCHAK
GOOOOOOOOOOOOOOOO!
SHAAAAAAA
The sports center should be 5... no, 6 miles from here.
Would a cab be faster?
No ...
It's Sunday, and there's a mall right before the bridge near the center...
so there'll definitely be a ton of traffic there.
GOAL
SPORTS CENTER
BIKE PATH
STATION
SHOPPING MALL
CURRENT LOCATION
STATION
Plus that whole area is all one-way roads.
BICYCLES AND SCOOTERS
HONK
HONK
HEY, WATCH IT!
Using a bike is the best plan!!
It's kind of a detour, but if I come out by the river,
and tear through the bike path, then I'll...

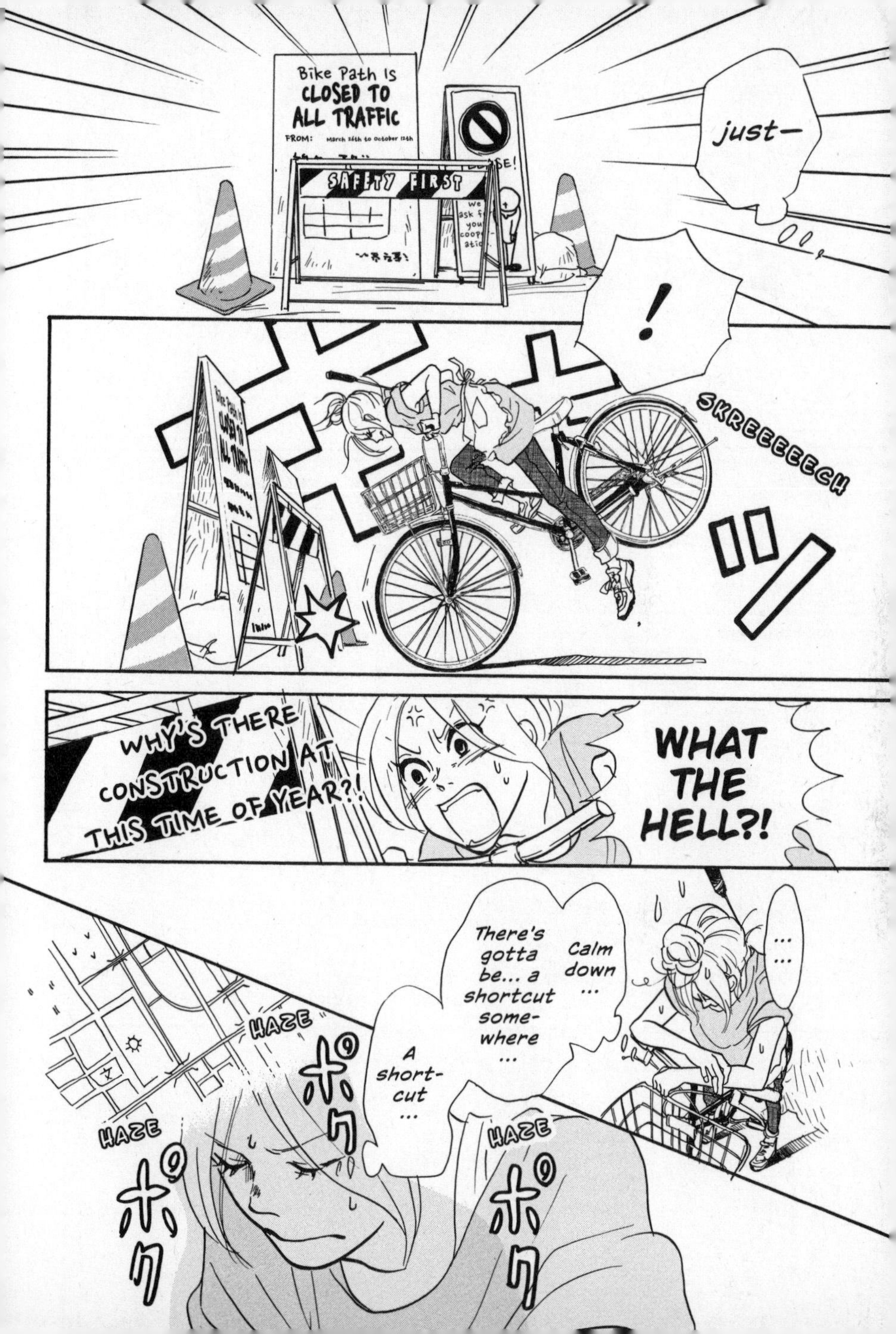
just—
Bike Path Is
CLOSED TO
ALL TRAFFIC
FROM: March 26th to October 12th
SAFETY FIRST
we
ask f
you
coop-
atio.
!
SKREEEEEECH
WHAT THE HELL?!
WHY'S THERE CONSTRUCTION AT THIS TIME OF YEAR?!
......
Calm down...
There's gotta be... a shortcut some-where...
A short-cut...
HAZE
HAZE
HAZE

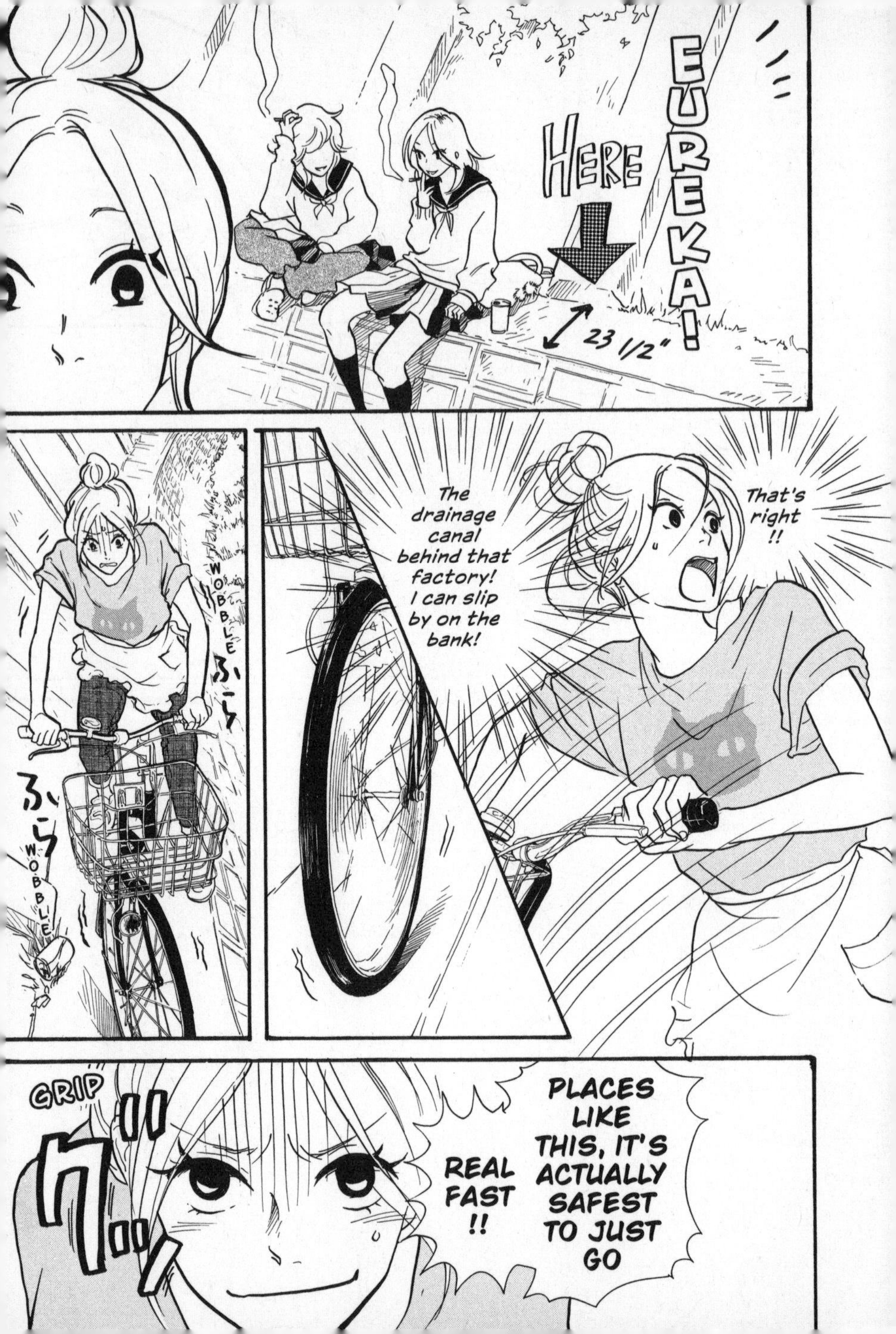
EUREKA!
HERE
23 1/2"
That's right !!
The drainage canal behind that factory! I can slip by on the bank!
WOBBLE ふーら
ふーら WOBBLE
PLACES LIKE THIS, IT'S ACTUALLY SAFEST TO JUST GO
REAL FAST !!
GRIP

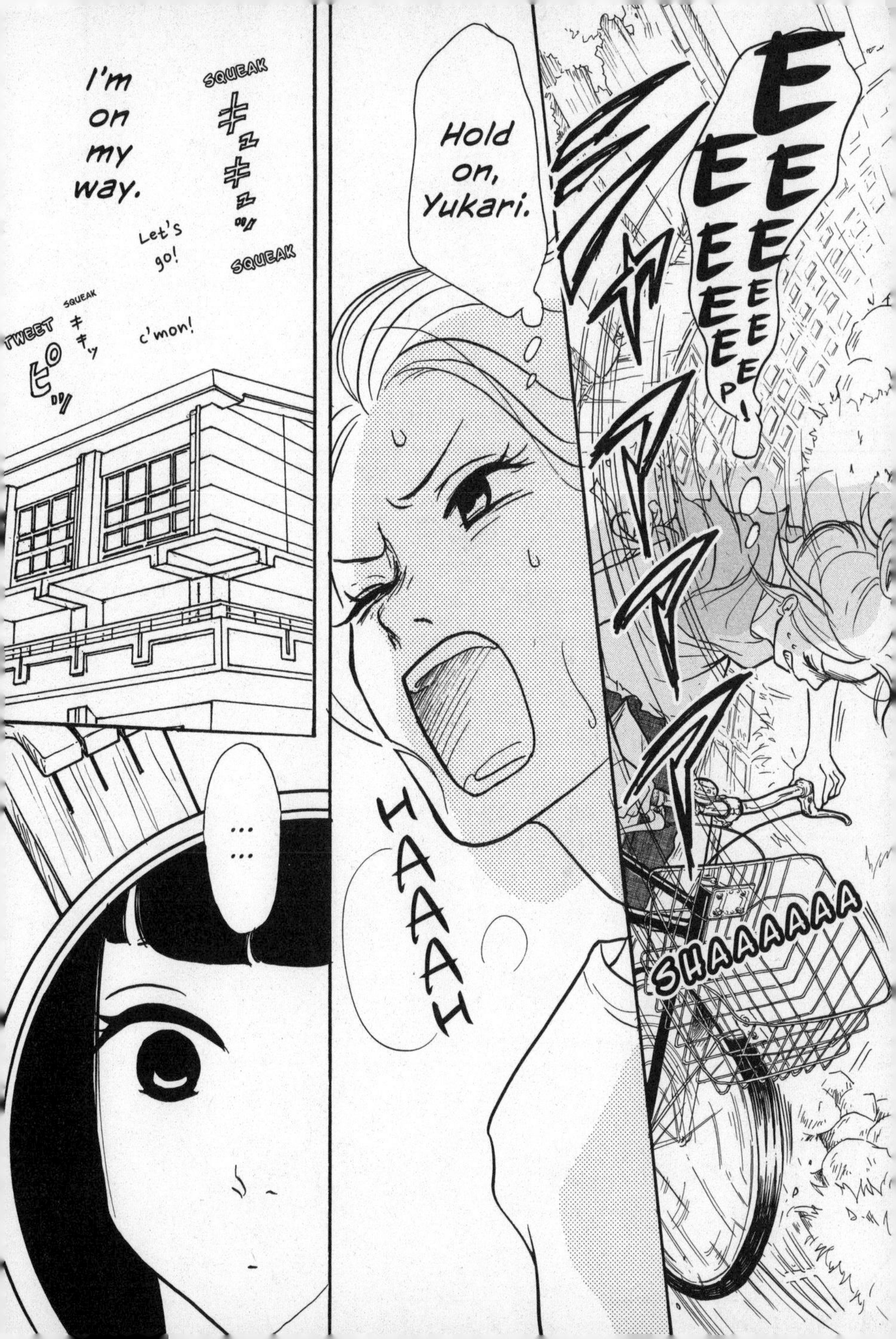
EEEEEEEEEEEEEP!
SHAAAAAAA
Hold on, Yukari.
HAAAH
I'm on my way.
SQUEAK
SQUEAK
Let's go!
SQUEAK
TWEET
c'mon!
......

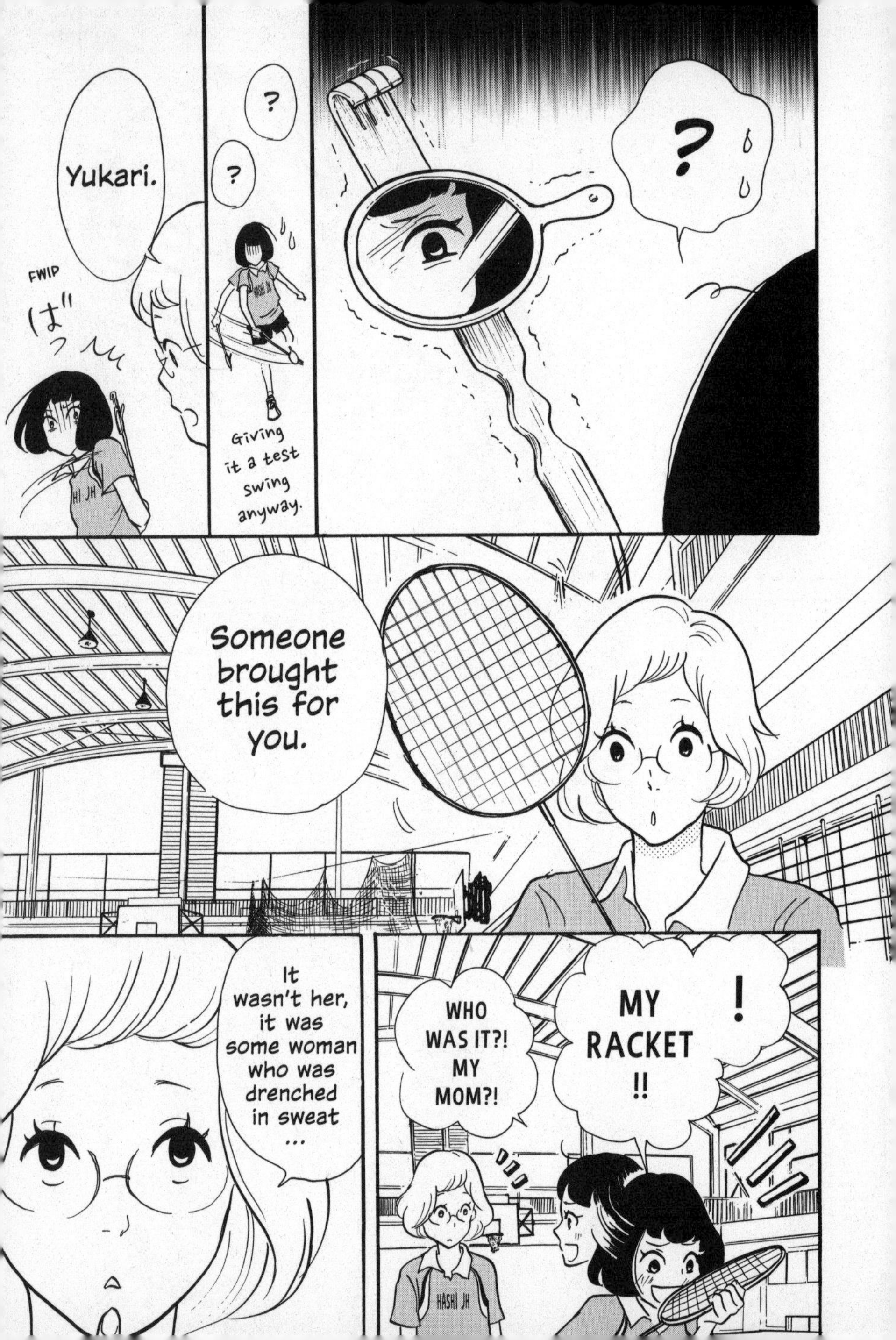
?
?
?
Giving it a test swing anyway.
Yukari.
FWIP
ばっ
Someone brought this for you.
!
MY RACKET !!
WHO WAS IT?! MY MOM?!
It wasn't her, it was some woman who was drenched in sweat ...

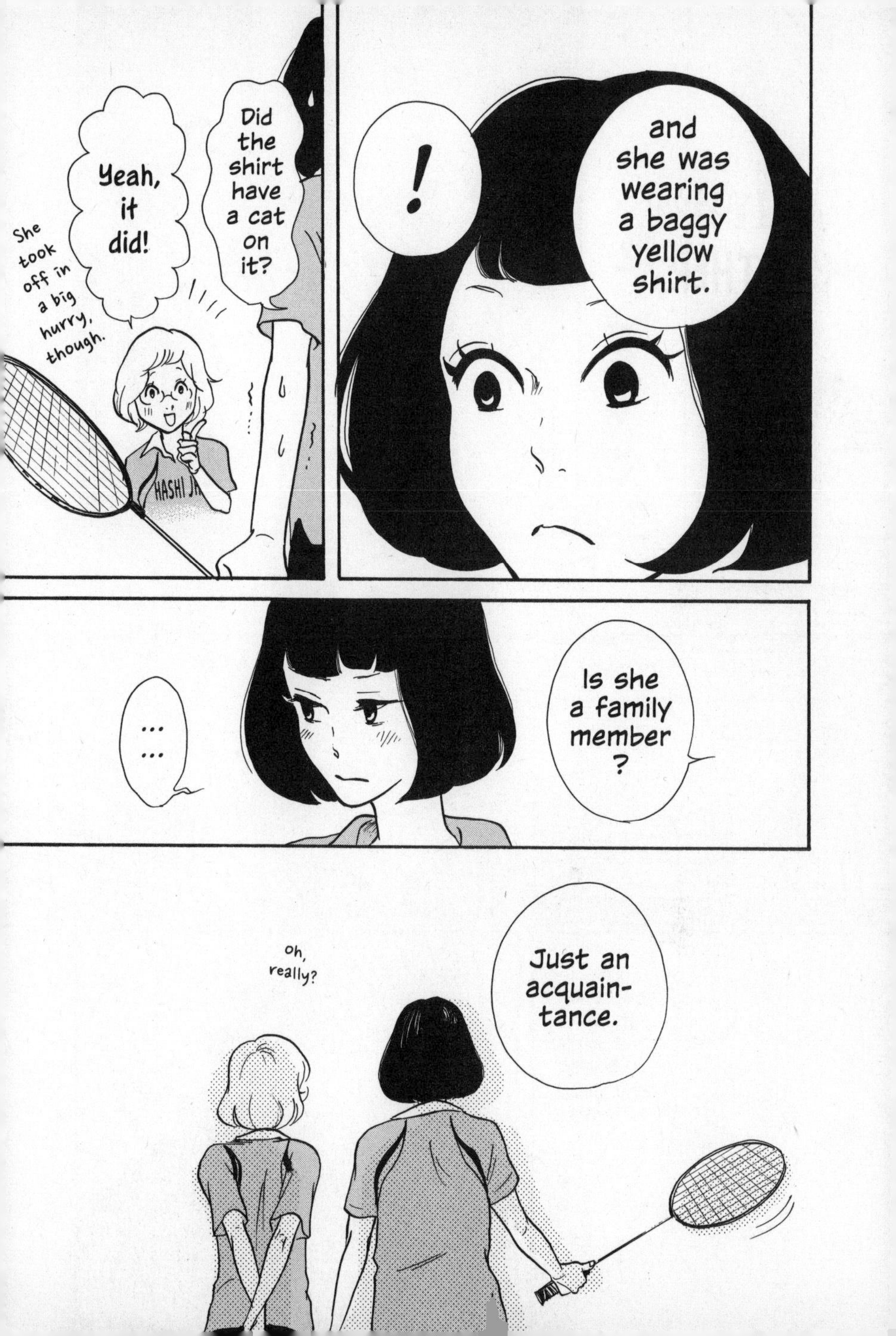
and she was wearing a baggy yellow shirt.
!
Did the shirt have a cat on it?
Yeah, it did!
She took off in a big hurry, though.
Is she a family member?
……
Just an acquaintance.
Oh, really?

13

A LITTLE BROTHER, OR SOMETHING

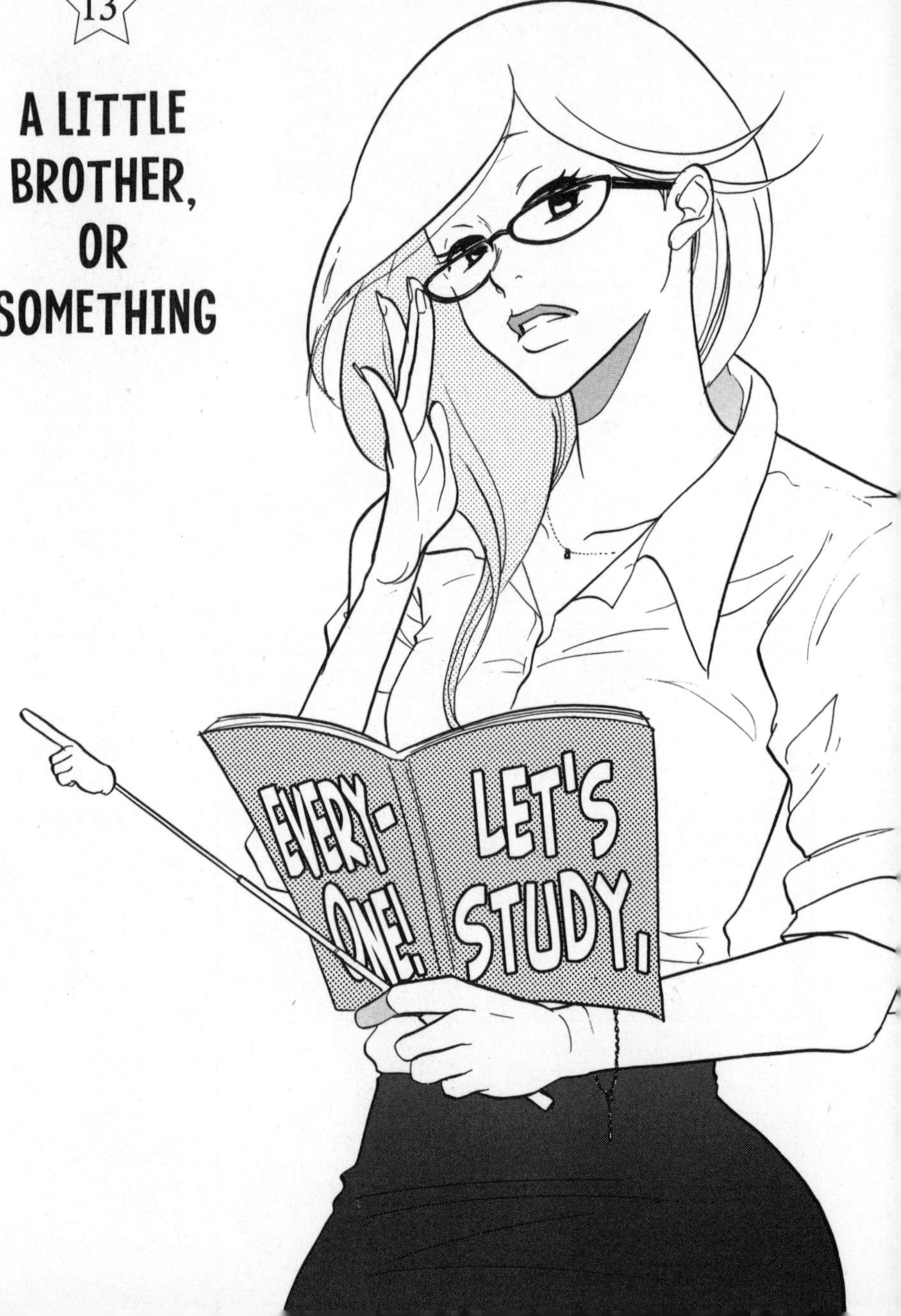
EVERY-ONE!
LET'S STUDY.

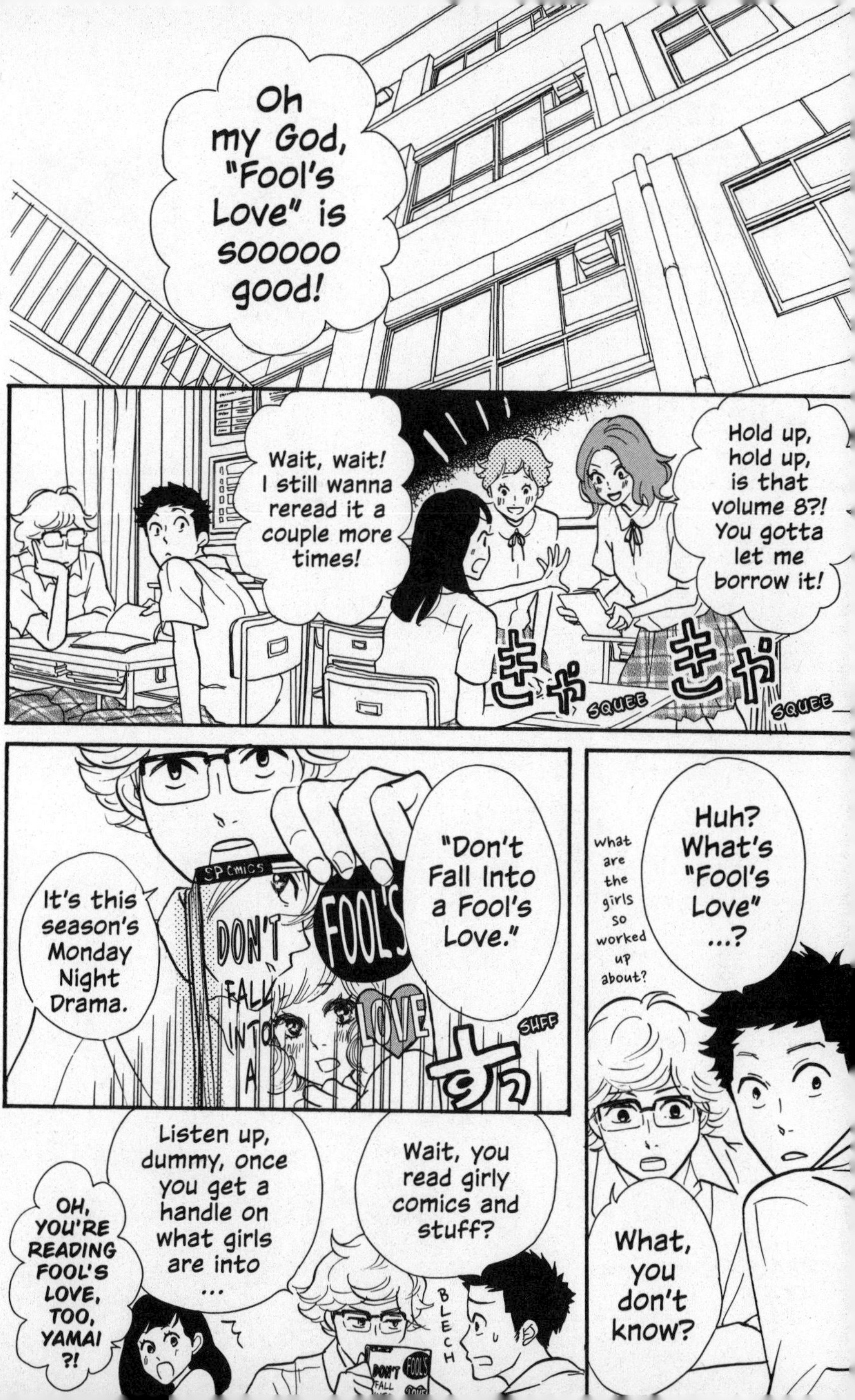
Oh my God, "Fool's Love" is sooooo good!
Hold up, hold up, is that volume 8?! You gotta let me borrow it!
Wait, wait! I still wanna reread it a couple more times!
きゃ SQUEE
きゃ SQUEE
Huh? What's "Fool's Love" ...?
what are the girls so worked up about?
What, you don't know?
"Don't Fall Into a Fool's Love."
It's this season's Monday Night Drama.
SP COMICS
DON'T FALL INTO A FOOL'S LOVE
すっ SHFF
Wait, you read girly comics and stuff?
Listen up, dummy, once you get a handle on what girls are into ...
OH, YOU'RE READING FOOL'S LOVE, TOO, YAMAI ?!
BLECH

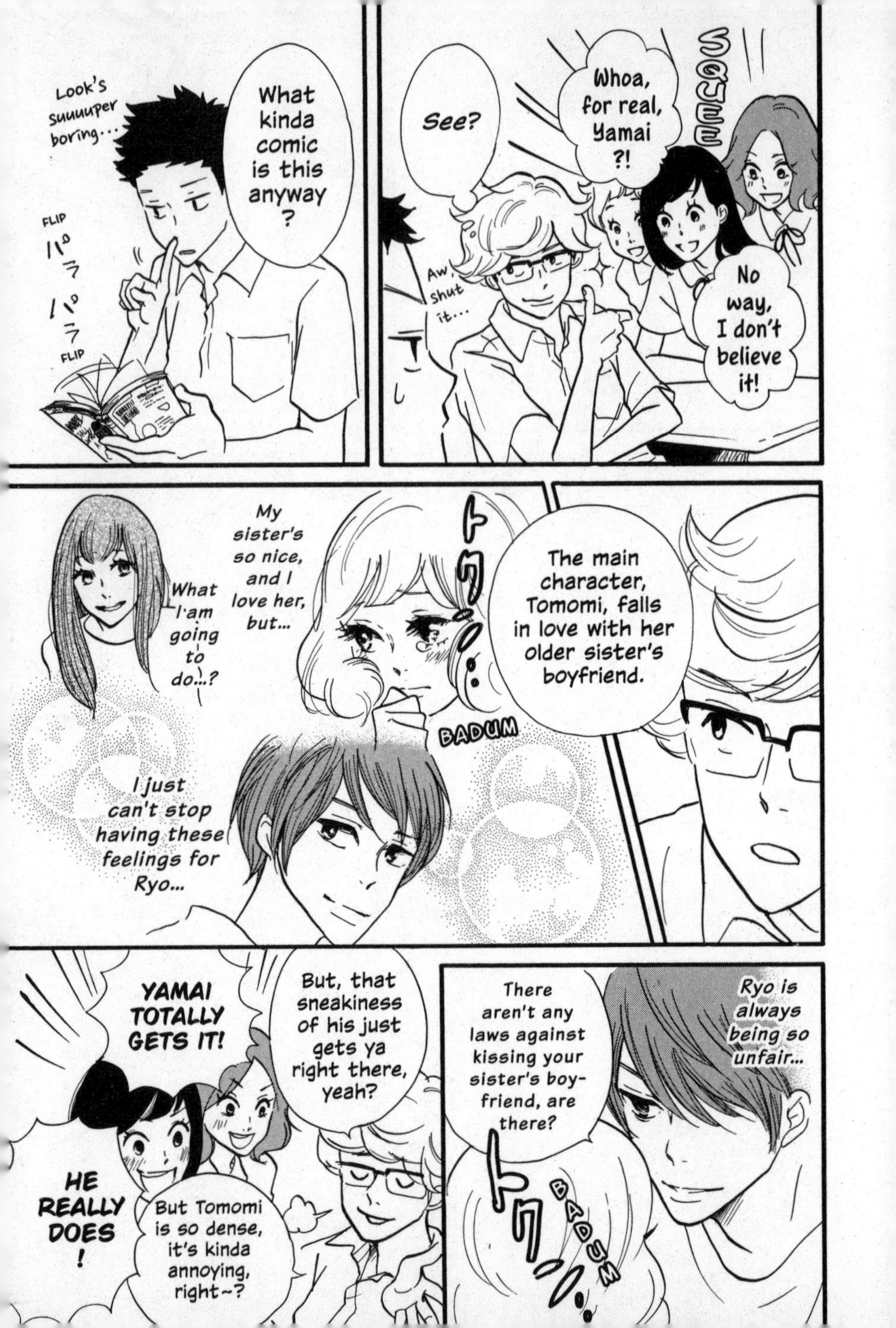
SQUEE
See?
Whoa, for real, Yamai?!
No way, I don't believe it!
Aw, shut it...
What kinda comic is this anyway?
Look's suuuuper boring...
FLIP
FLIP
The main character, Tomomi, falls in love with her older sister's boyfriend.
My sister's so nice, and I love her, but...
What I am going to do...?
BADUM
I just can't stop having these feelings for Ryo...
Ryo is always being so unfair...
There aren't any laws against kissing your sister's boyfriend, are there?
BADUM
But, that sneakiness of his just gets ya right there, yeah?
YAMAI TOTALLY GETS IT!
HE REALLY DOES!
But Tomomi is so dense, it's kinda annoying, right~?

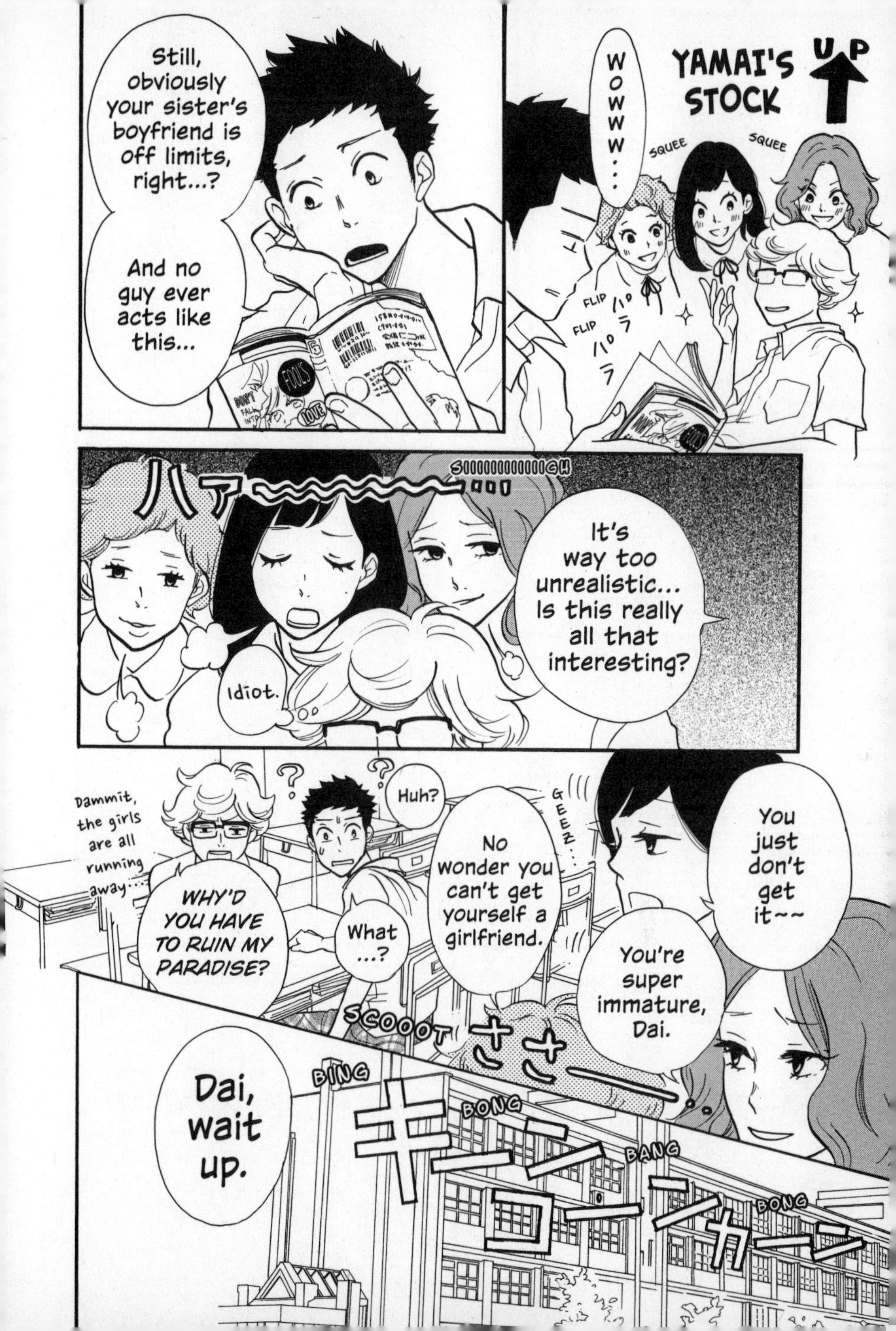
YAMAI'S STOCK UP
WOWWW...
SQUEE
SQUEE
FLIP
FLIP
パラパラ
Still, obviously your sister's boyfriend is off limits, right...?
And no guy ever acts like this...
ハア〜〜〜
SIIIIIIIIIIIIIGH
It's way too unrealistic... Is this really all that interesting?
Idiot.
You just don't get it~~
You're super immature, Dai.
GEEZ...
No wonder you can't get yourself a girlfriend.
Huh?
What...?
Dammit, the girls are all running away...
WHY'D YOU HAVE TO RUIN MY PARADISE?
SCOOOT
さー
BING
BONG
BANG
BONG
キーンコーンカーン
Dai, wait up.

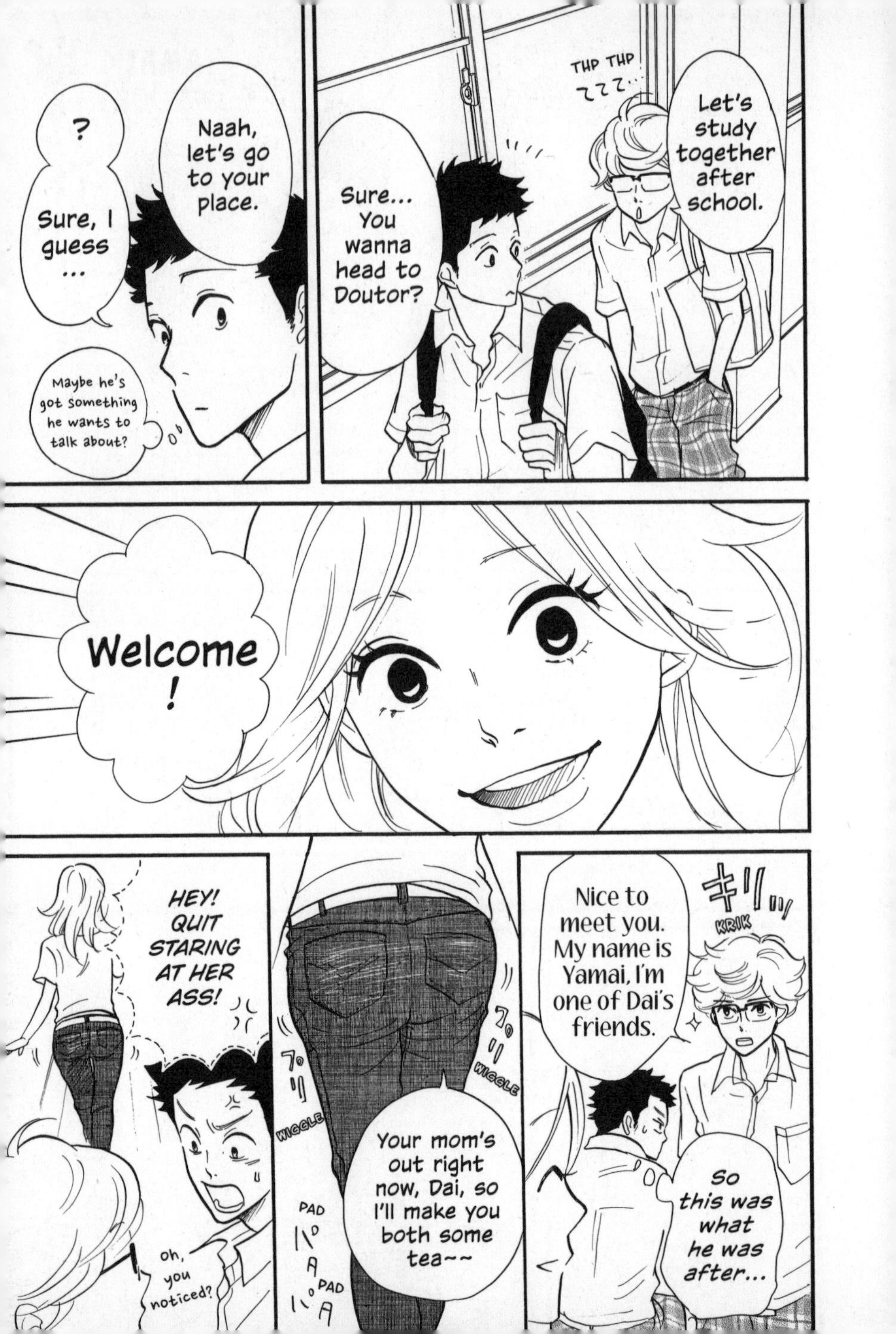
THP THP
Let's study together after school.
Sure... You wanna head to Doutor?
Naah, let's go to your place.
?
Sure, I guess ...
Maybe he's got something he wants to talk about?
Welcome!
KRIK
Nice to meet you. My name is Yamai, I'm one of Dai's friends.
So this was what he was after...
WIGGLE
WIGGLE
Your mom's out right now, Dai, so I'll make you both some tea~~
PAD
PAD
HEY! QUIT STARING AT HER ASS!
oh, you noticed?

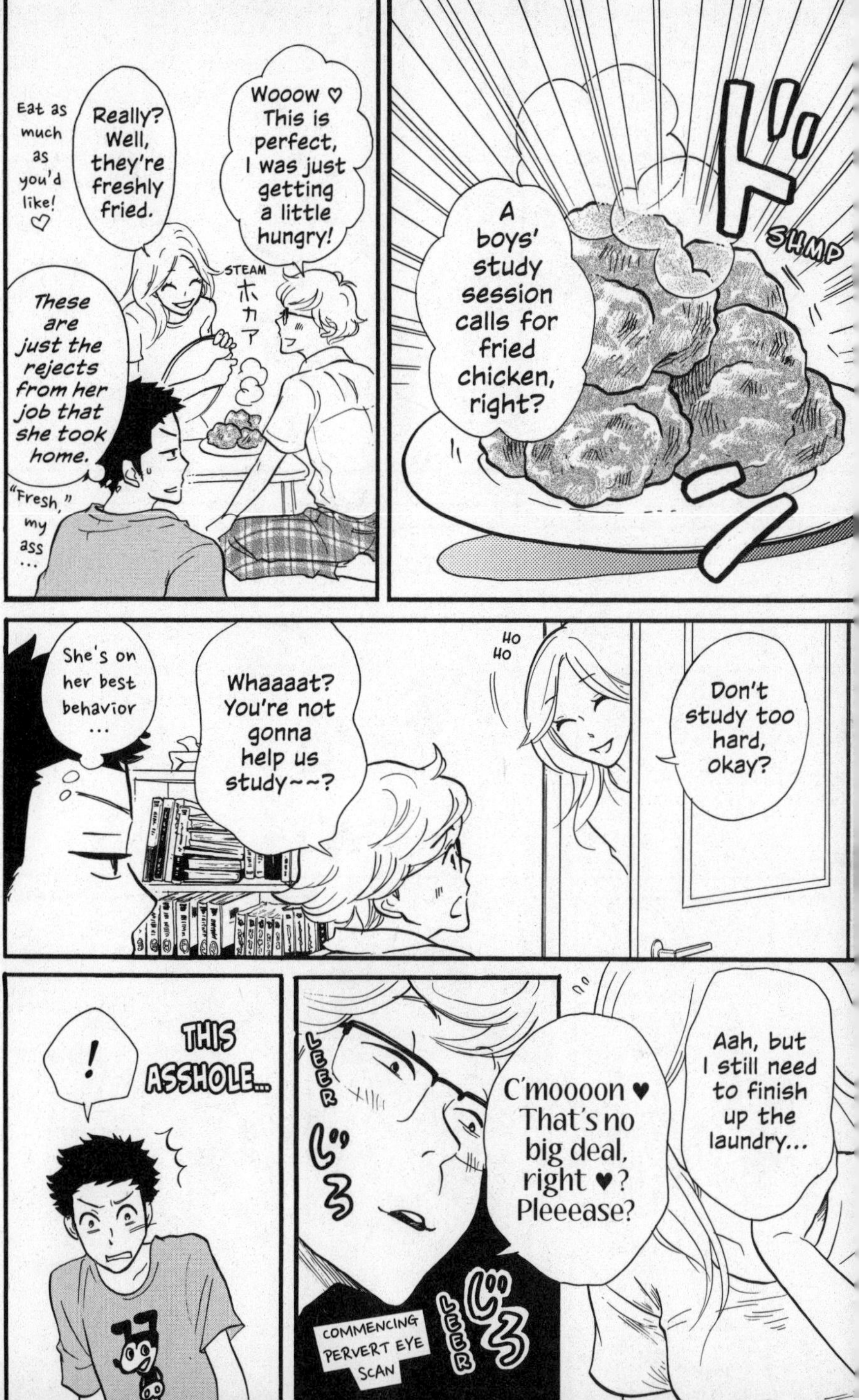
A boys' study session calls for fried chicken, right?
ド
SHMP
Wooow ♡ This is perfect, I was just getting a little hungry!
Really? Well, they're freshly fried.
Eat as much as you'd like! ♡
STEAM
ホカァ
These are just the rejects from her job that she took home.
"Fresh," my ass ...
Don't study too hard, okay?
HO HO
Whaaaat? You're not gonna help us study~~?
She's on her best behavior ...
Aah, but I still need to finish up the laundry...
C'moooon ♥ That's no big deal, right ♥? Pleeease?
LEER
じろ
LEER
じろ
COMMENCING PERVERT EYE SCAN
THIS ASSHOLE...
!

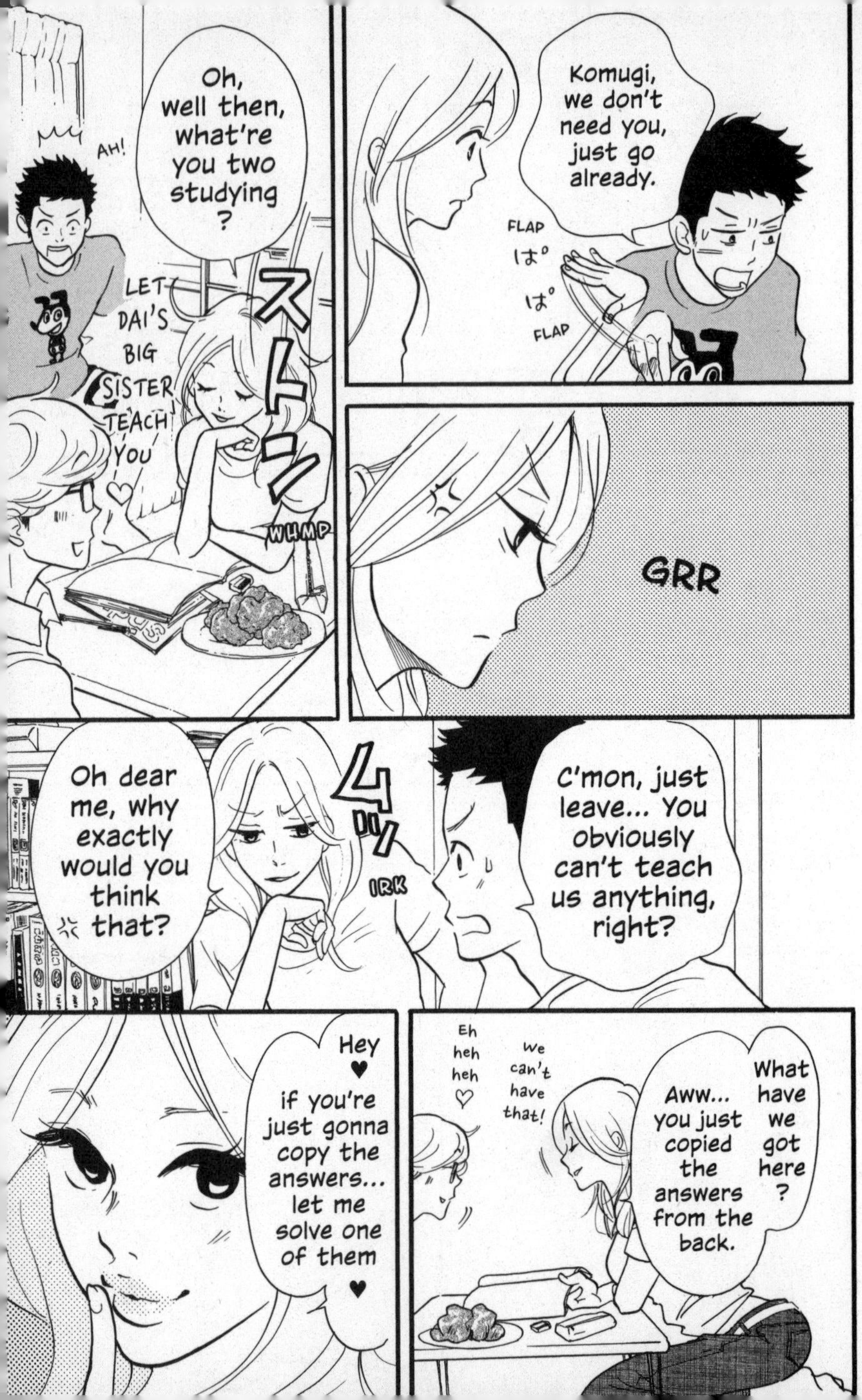
Komugi, we don't need you, just go already.
FLAP
ぱ
ぱ
FLAP
GRR
Oh, well then, what're you two studying?
AH!
LET DAI'S BIG SISTER TEACH YOU ♡
ストン
WHMP
C'mon, just leave... You obviously can't teach us anything, right?
ム
IRK
Oh dear me, why exactly would you think that?
What have we got here?
Aww... you just copied the answers from the back.
We can't have that!
Eh heh heh ♡
Hey ♥ if you're just gonna copy the answers... let me solve one of them ♥

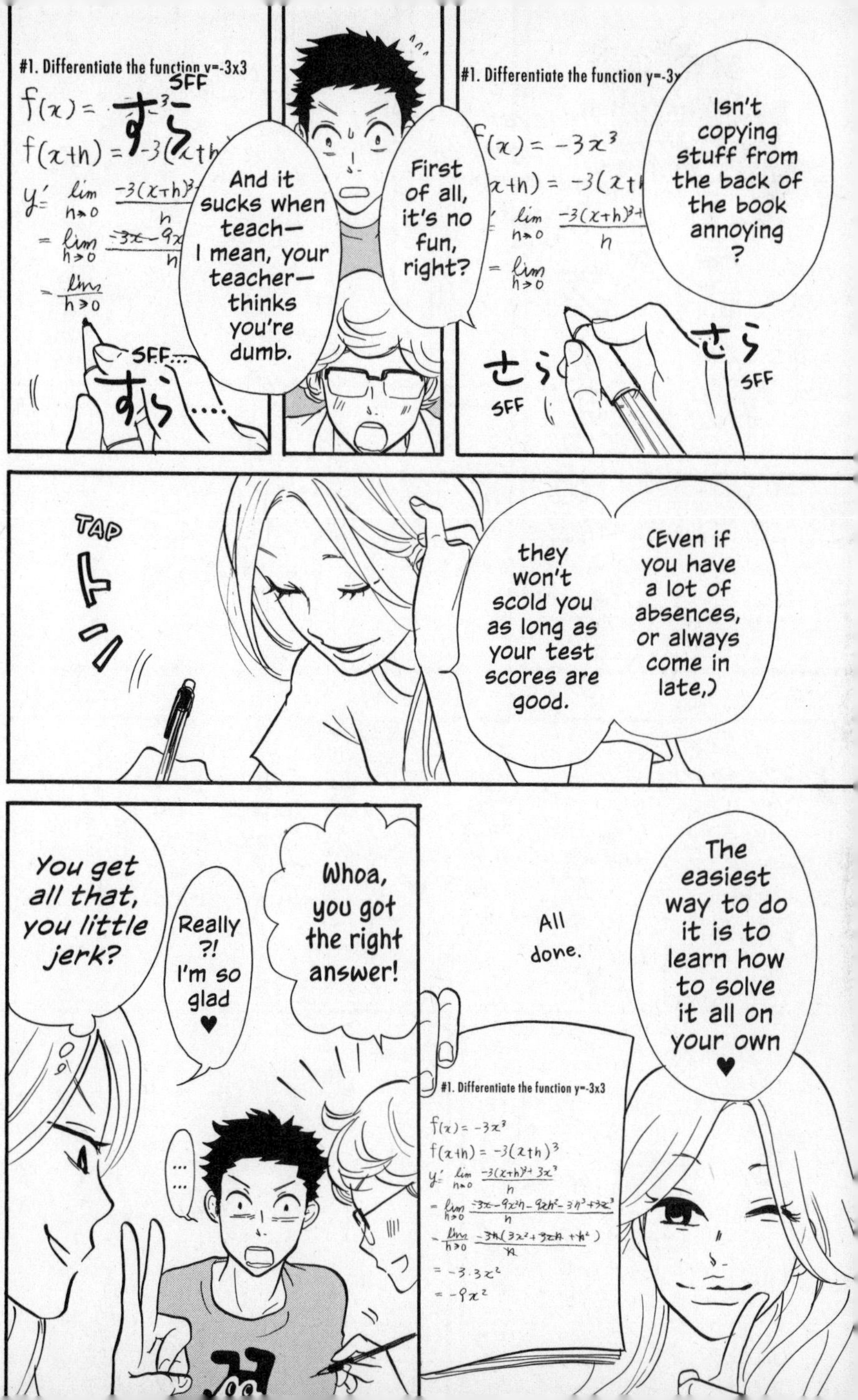
#1. Differentiate the function y=-3x
Isn't copying stuff from the back of the book annoying?
SFF
SFF
First of all, it's no fun, right?
And it sucks when teach— I mean, your teacher— thinks you're dumb.
#1. Differentiate the function y=-3x3
SFF
SFF...
(Even if you have a lot of absences, or always come in late,)
they won't scold you as long as your test scores are good.
TAP
The easiest way to do it is to learn how to solve it all on your own ♥
All done.
#1. Differentiate the function y=-3x3
Whoa, you got the right answer!
Really?! I'm so glad ♥
You get all that, you little jerk?
......

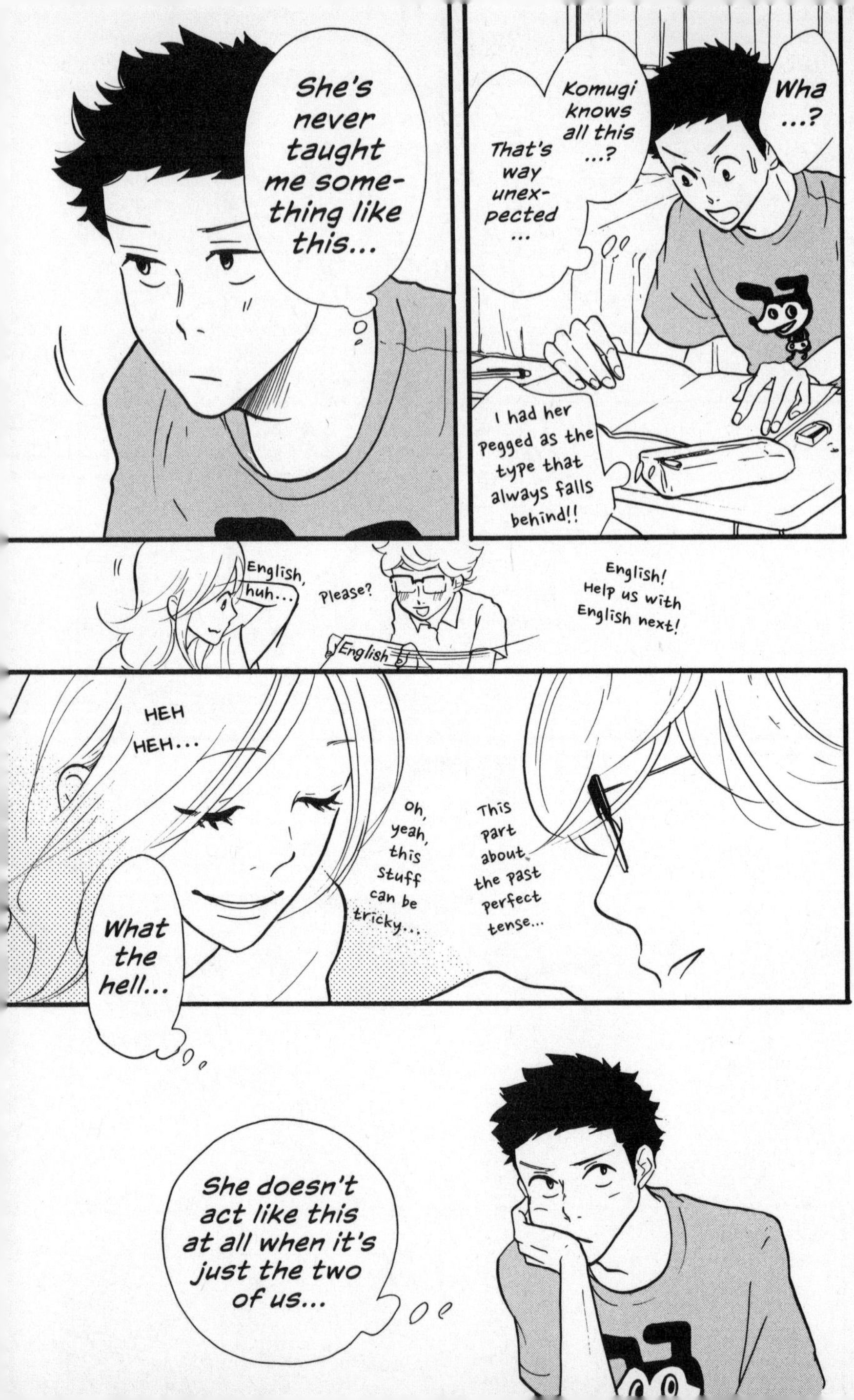
Wha ...?
Komugi knows all this ...?
That's way unexpected ...
She's never taught me something like this...
I had her pegged as the type that always falls behind!!
English! Help us with English next!
Please?
English, huh...
English
This part about the past perfect tense...
Oh, yeah, this stuff can be tricky...
HEH HEH...
What the hell...
She doesn't act like this at all when it's just the two of us...

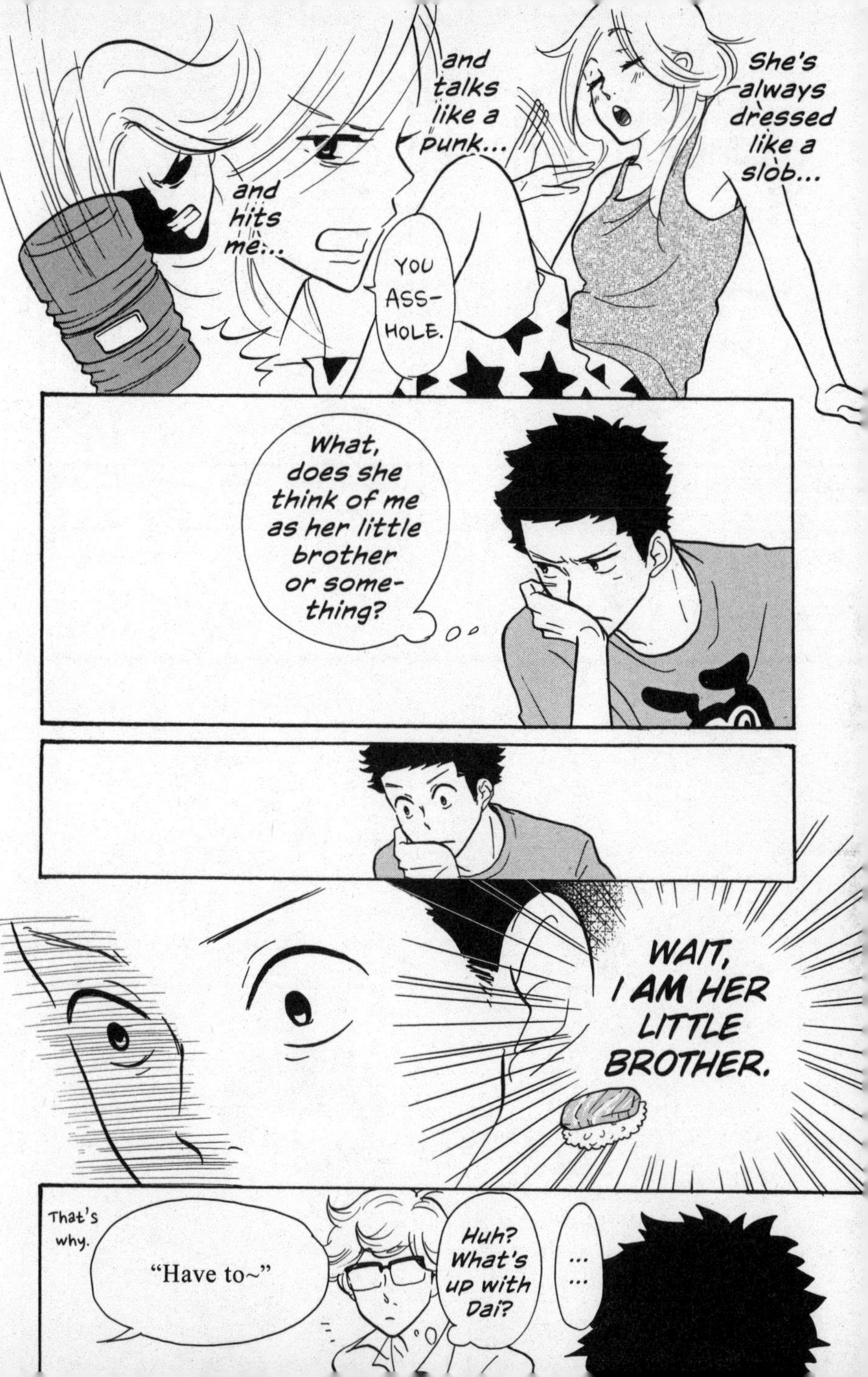
She's always dressed like a slob...
and talks like a punk...
and hits me...
YOU ASS-HOLE.
What, does she think of me as her little brother or some-thing?
WAIT, I AM HER LITTLE BROTHER.
......
Huh? What's up with Dai?
That's why.
"Have to~"

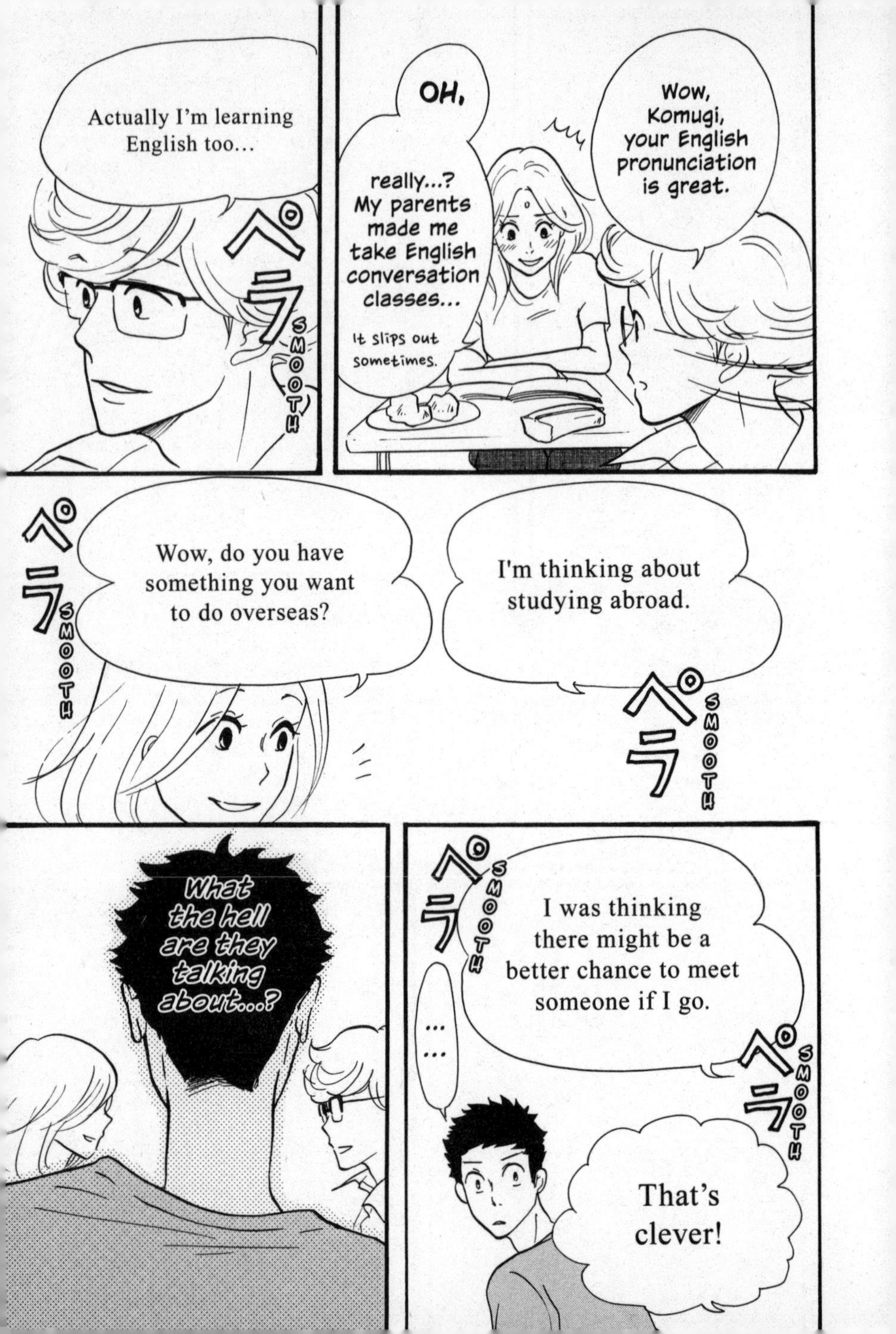
Wow, Komugi, your English pronunciation is great.
OH,
really...? My parents made me take English conversation classes...
It slips out sometimes.
Actually I'm learning English too...
ペラ
SMOOTH
I'm thinking about studying abroad.
ペラ
SMOOTH
Wow, do you have something you want to do overseas?
ペラ
SMOOTH
ペラ
SMOOTH
I was thinking there might be a better chance to meet someone if I go.
......
ペラ
SMOOTH
That's clever!
What the hell are they talking about...?

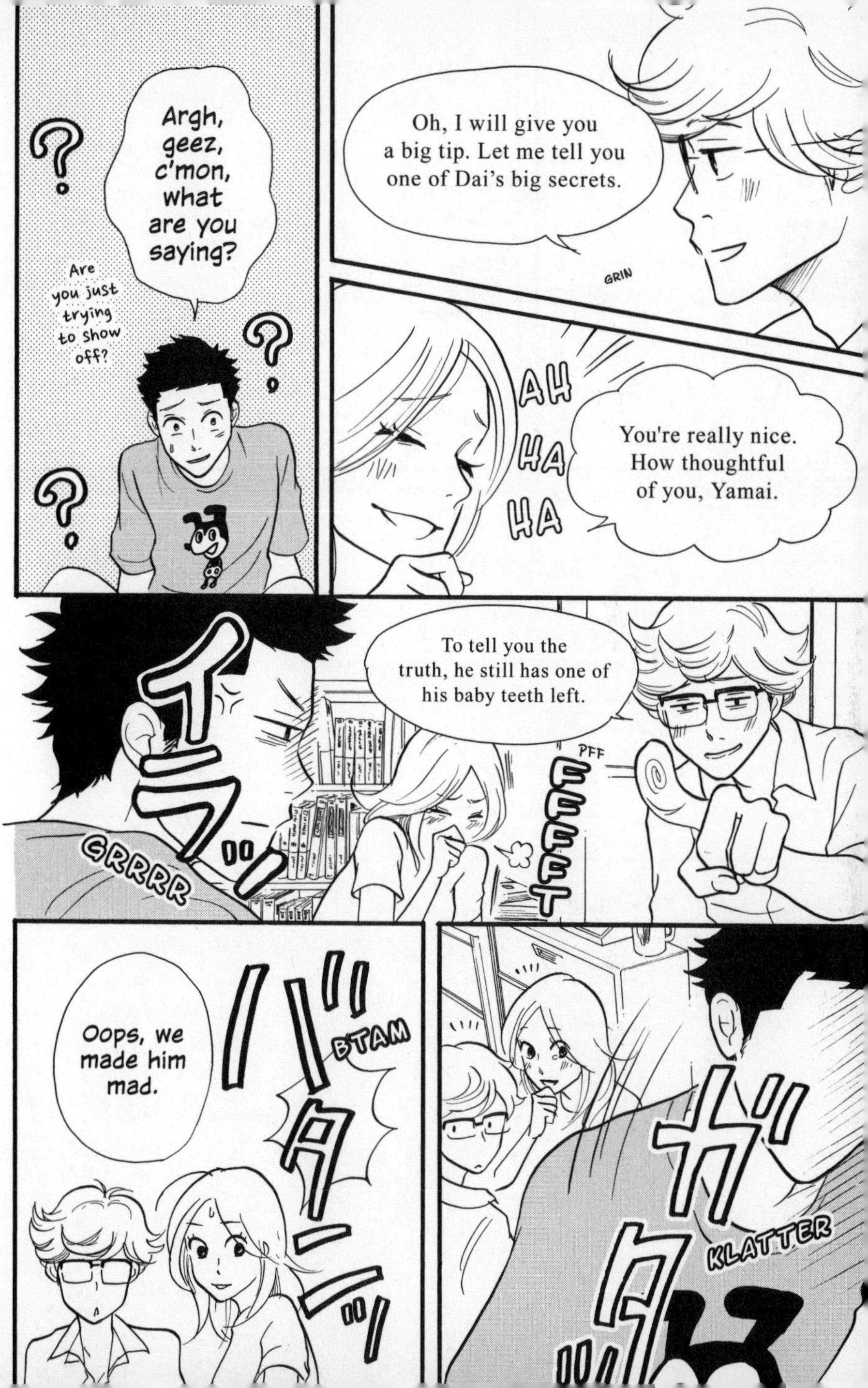
Oh, I will give you a big tip. Let me tell you one of Dai's big secrets.
GRIN
AH HA HA
You're really nice. How thoughtful of you, Yamai.
Argh, geez, c'mon, what are you saying?
Are you just trying to show off?
To tell you the truth, he still has one of his baby teeth left.
PFF
FFFFFFT
GRRRRR
KLATTER
Oops, we made him mad.
BTAM

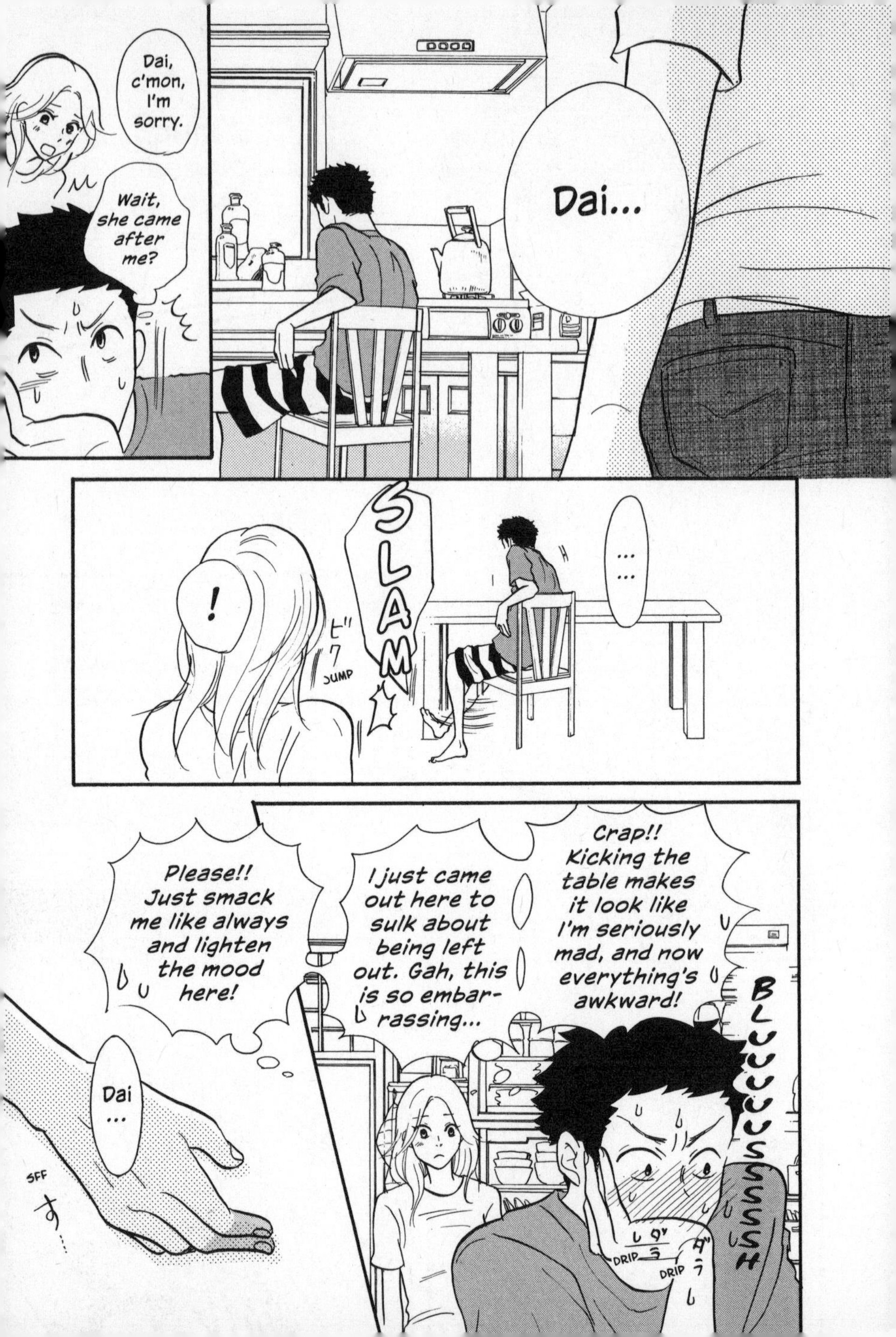
Dai...
Dai, c'mon, I'm sorry.
Wait, she came after me?
......
SLAM
ビク
JUMP
!
Crap!! Kicking the table makes it look like I'm seriously mad, and now everything's awkward!
I just came out here to sulk about being left out. Gah, this is so embarrassing...
Please!! Just smack me like always and lighten the mood here!
BLUUUUUSSSSSH
DRIP
DRIP
Dai...
SFF
す...

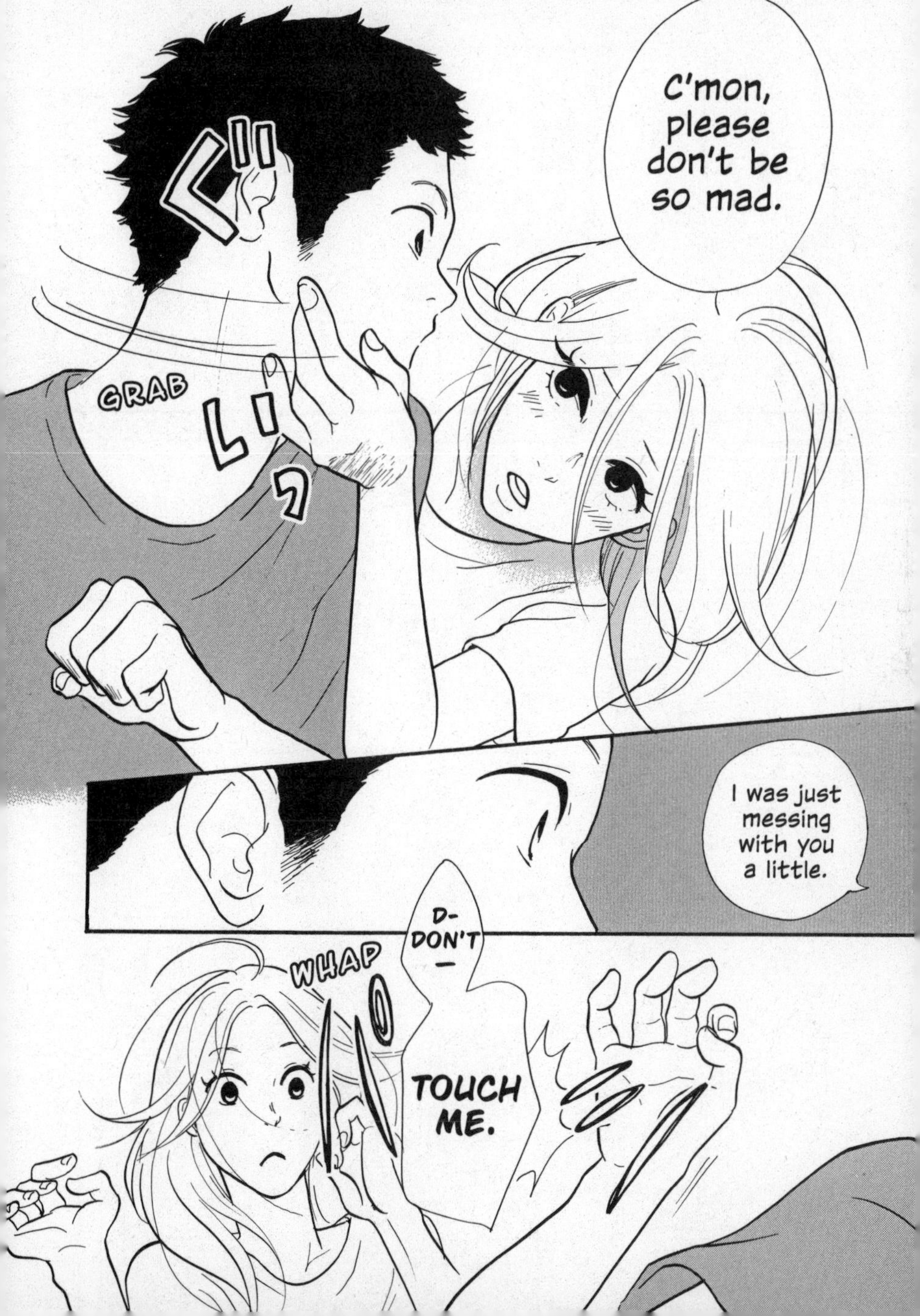
C'mon, please don't be so mad.
GRAB
I was just messing with you a little.
D-DON'T—
TOUCH ME.
WHAP

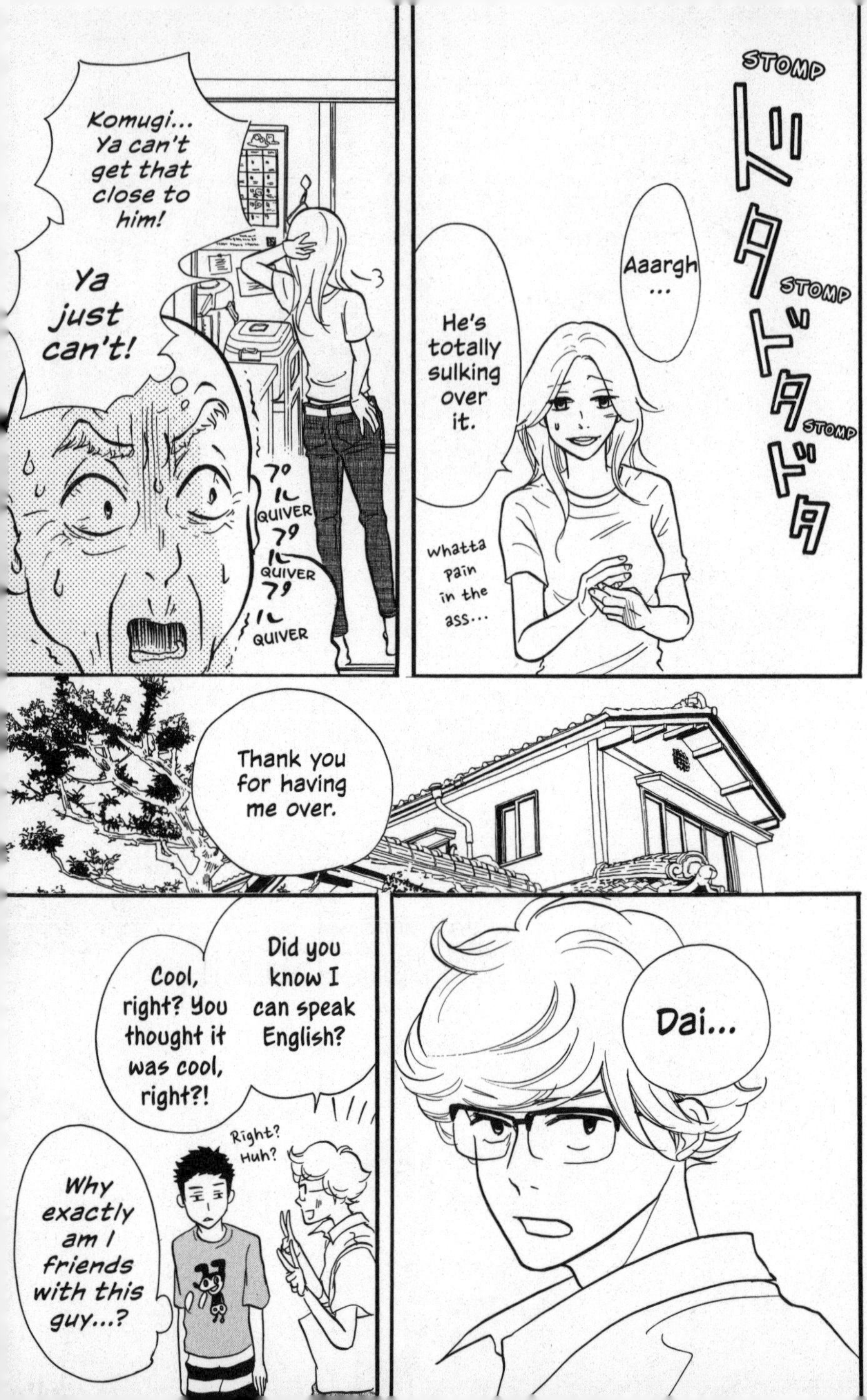

STOMP
ドタドタドタ
STOMP
STOMP
Aaargh...
He's totally sulking over it.
whatta pain in the ass...
Komugi... Ya can't get that close to him!
Ya just can't!
QUIVER
QUIVER
QUIVER
Thank you for having me over.
Dai...
Did you know I can speak English?
Cool, right? You thought it was cool, right?!
Right? Huh?
Why exactly am I friends with this guy...?

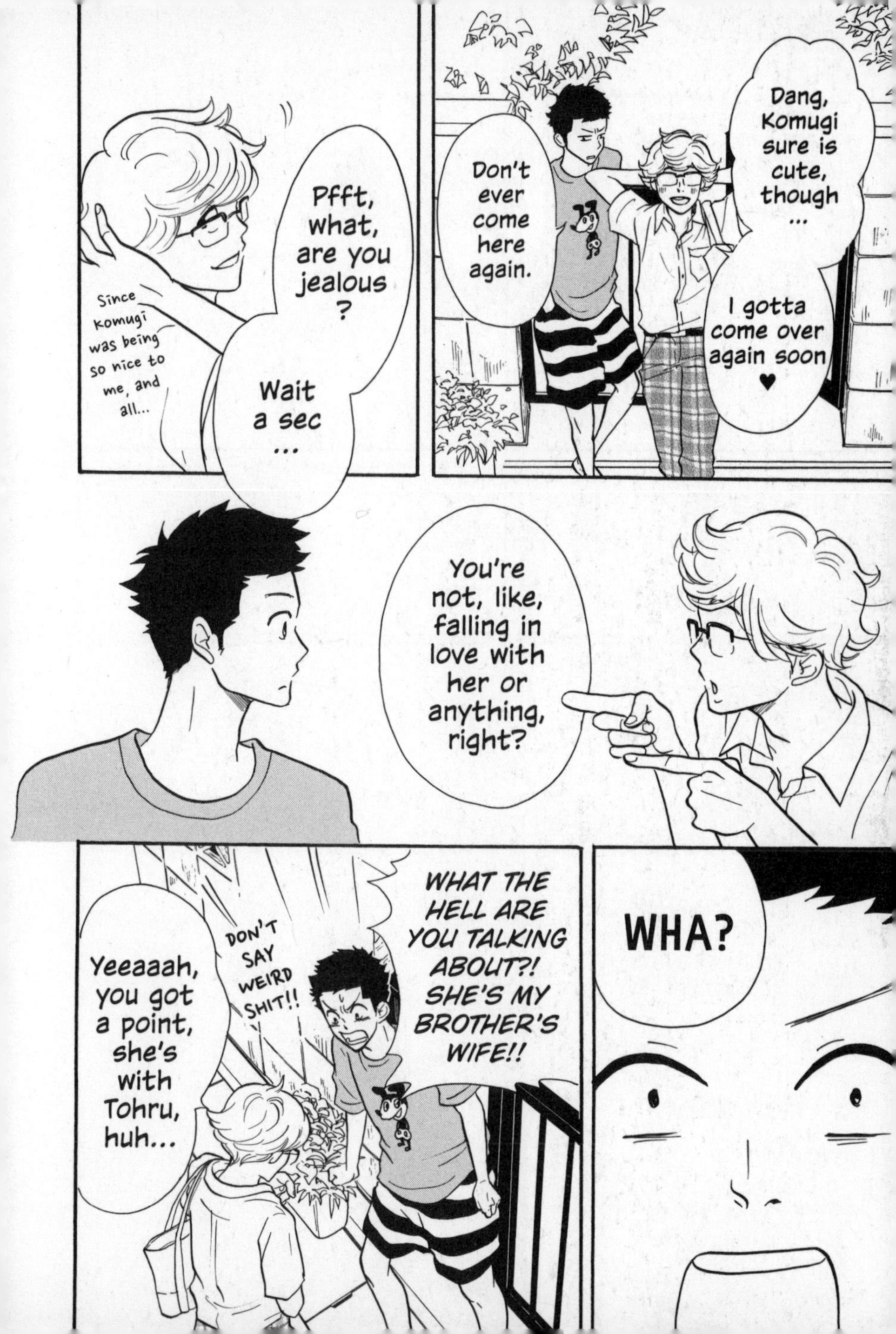
Dang, Komugi sure is cute, though ...
I gotta come over again soon ♥
Don't ever come here again.
Pfft, what, are you jealous ?
Since Komugi was being so nice to me, and all...
Wait a sec ...
You're not, like, falling in love with her or anything, right?
WHA?
WHAT THE HELL ARE YOU TALKING ABOUT?! SHE'S MY BROTHER'S WIFE!!
DON'T SAY WEIRD SHIT!!
Yeeaaah, you got a point, she's with Tohru, huh...

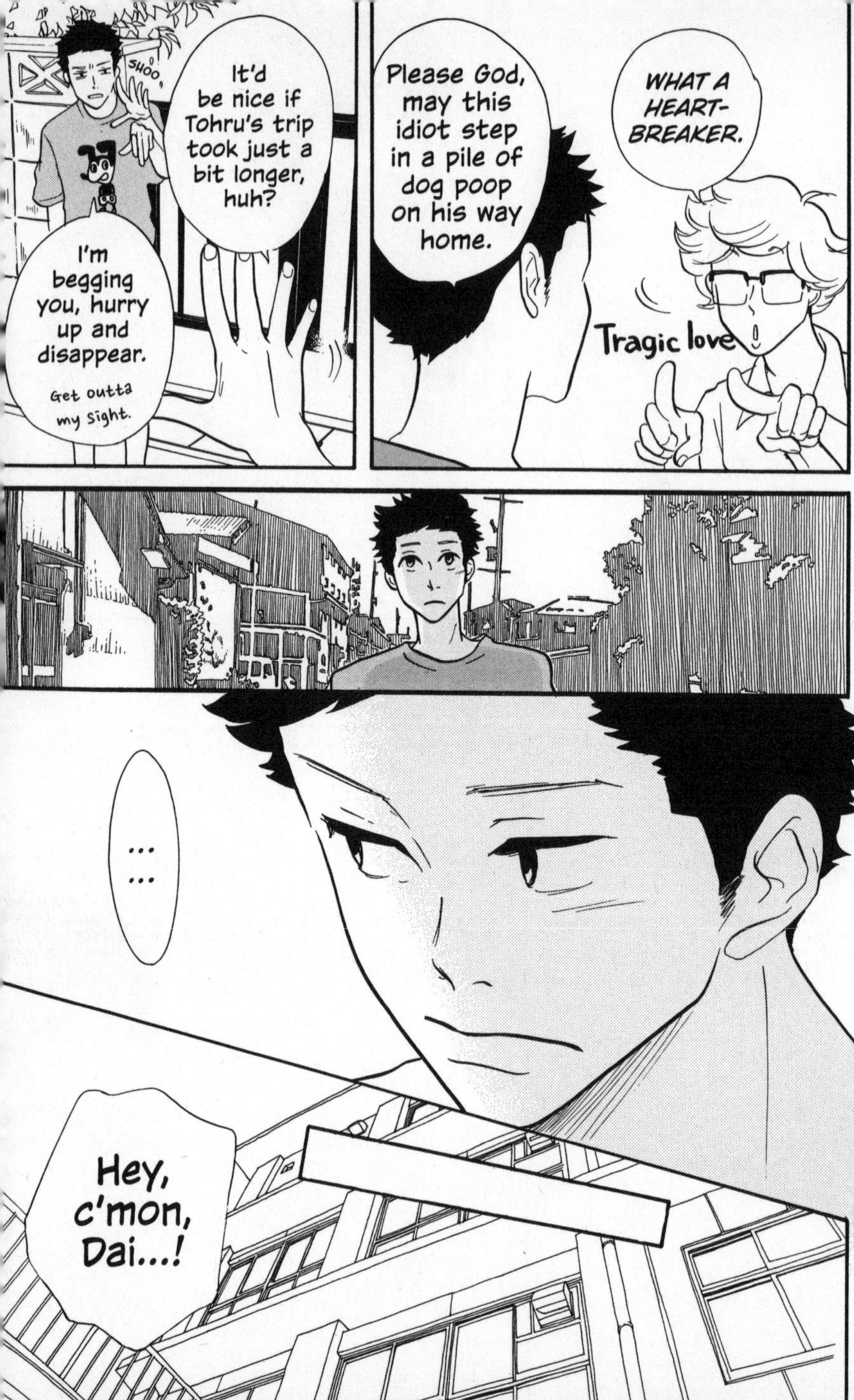
WHAT A HEART-BREAKER.
Tragic love
Please God, may this idiot step in a pile of dog poop on his way home.
It'd be nice if Tohru's trip took just a bit longer, huh?
SHOO,
I'm begging you, hurry up and disappear.
Get outta my sight.
......
Hey, c'mon, Dai...!

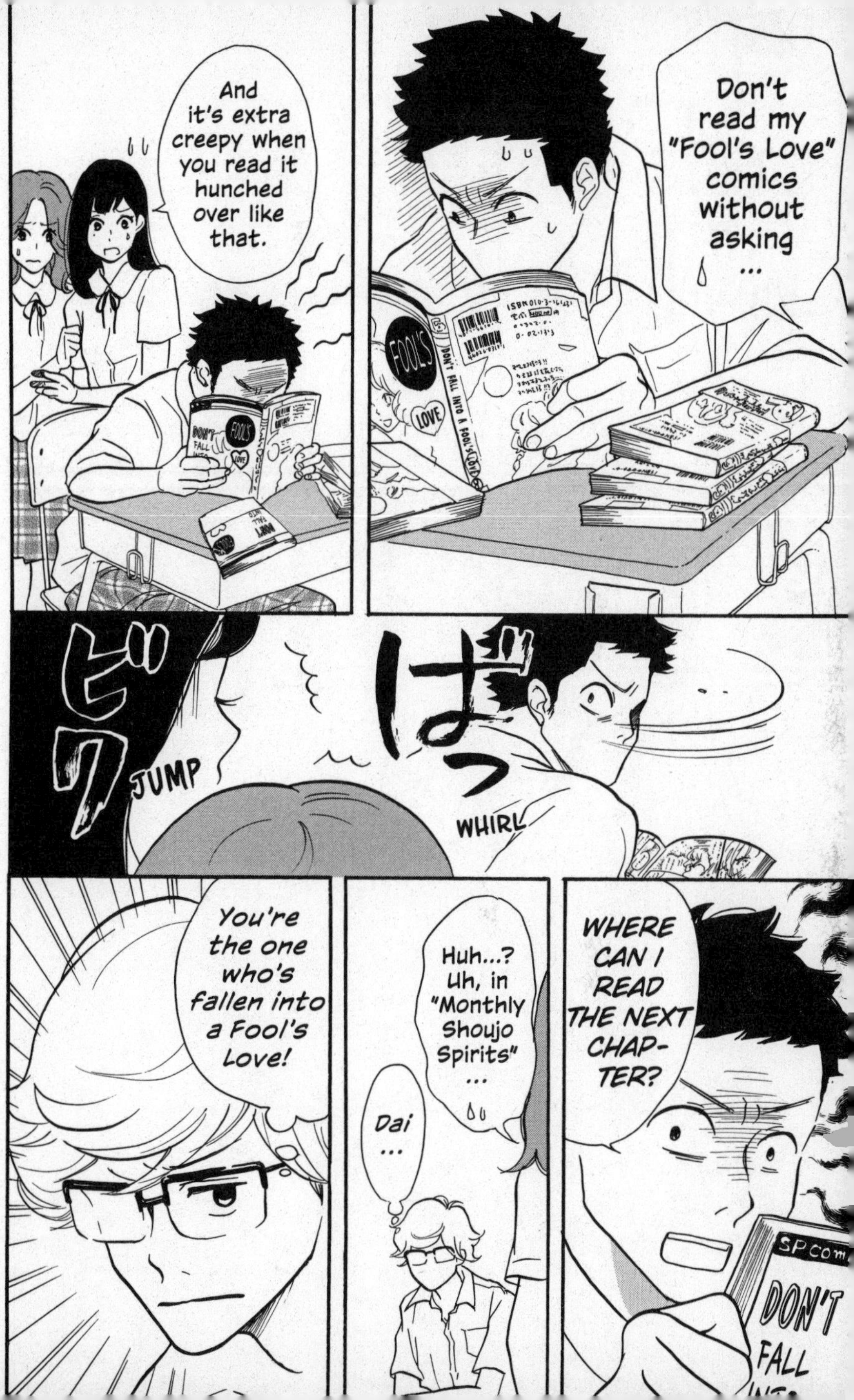
Don't read my "Fool's Love" comics without asking ...
FOOL'S
DON'T FALL INTO A FOOL'S LOVE
LOVE
And it's extra creepy when you read it hunched over like that.
ぱっ
WHIRL
ビク
JUMP
WHERE CAN I READ THE NEXT CHAP-TER?
SP com
DON'T FALL
Huh...? Uh, in "Monthly Shoujo Spirits" ...
Dai ...
You're the one who's fallen into a Fool's Love!

14 FULL OF KOMUGI

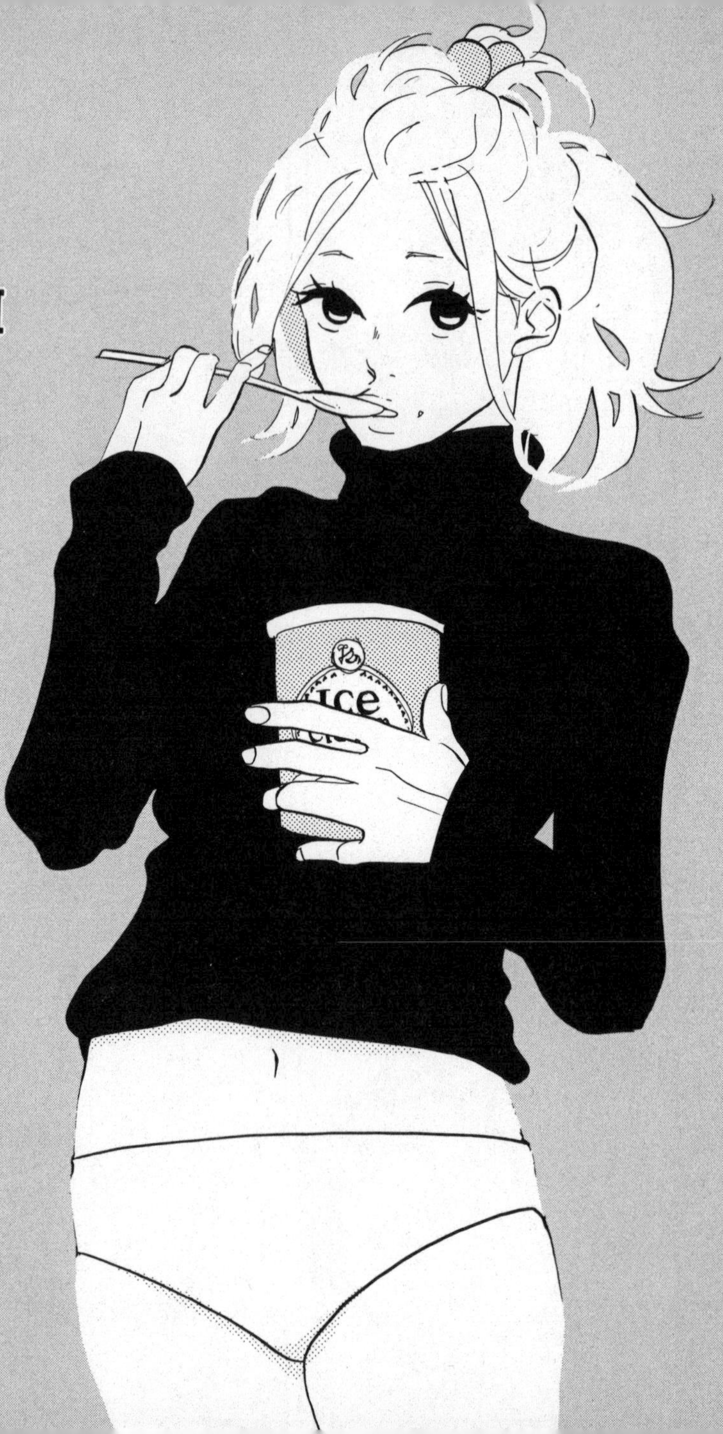
ice

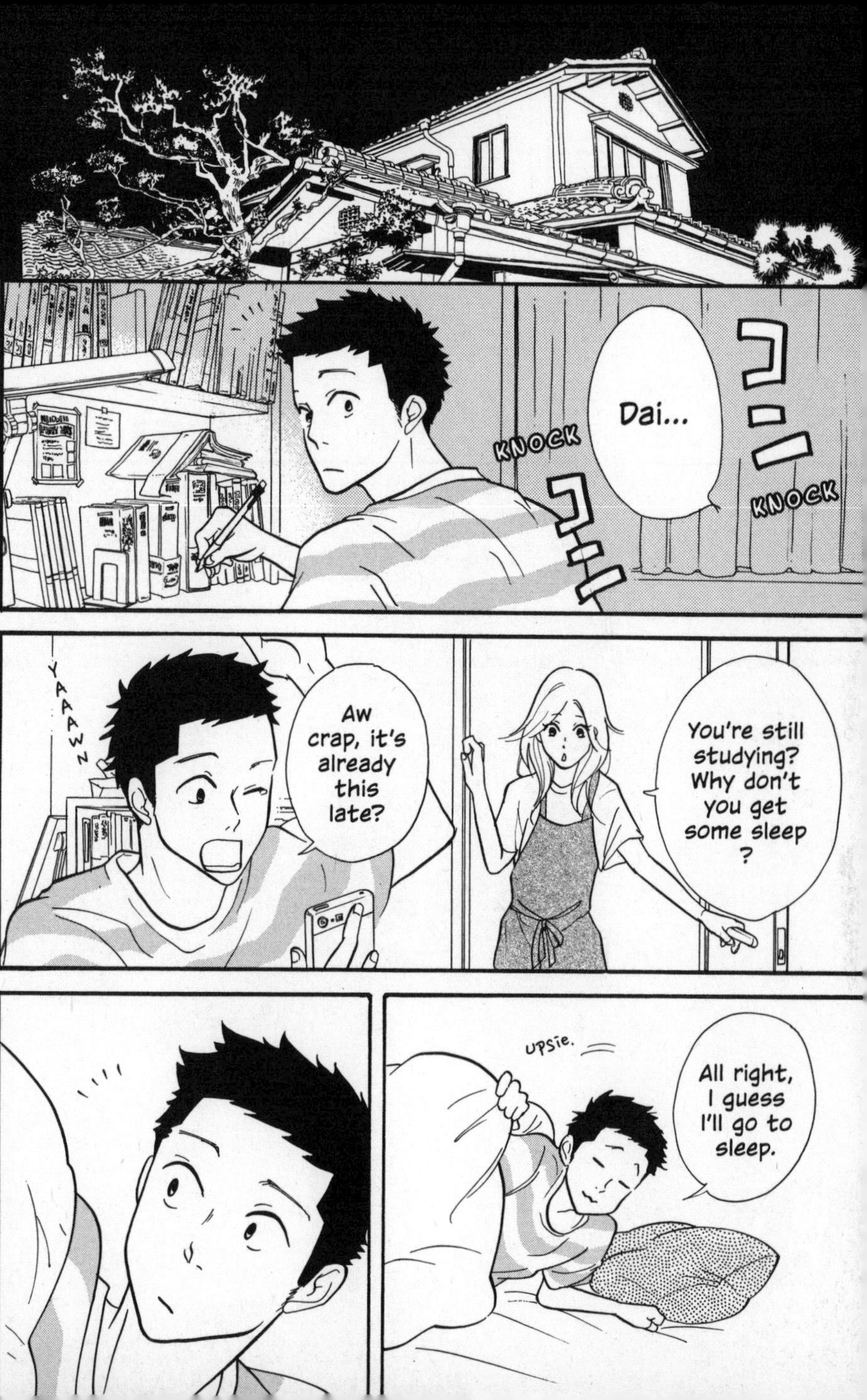
KNOCK
Dai...
KNOCK
You're still studying? Why don't you get some sleep?
Aw crap, it's already this late?
YAAAWN
UPSie.
All right, I guess I'll go to sleep.

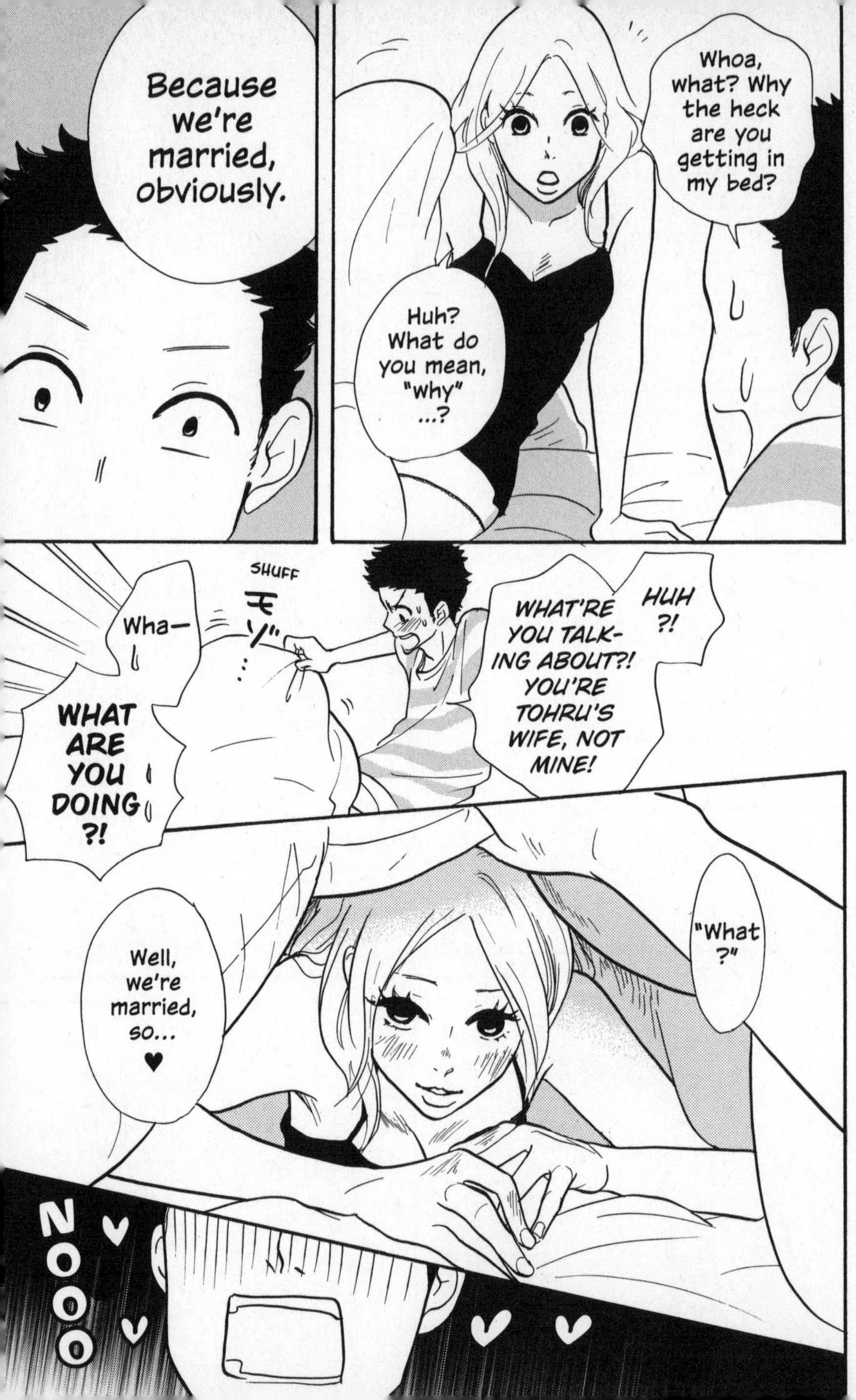
Whoa, what? Why the heck are you getting in my bed?
Huh? What do you mean, "why"...?
Because we're married, obviously.
HUH?!
WHAT'RE YOU TALKING ABOUT?! YOU'RE TOHRU'S WIFE, NOT MINE!
SHUFF
Wha—
WHAT ARE YOU DOING?!
"What?"
Well, we're married, so... ♥
NOOO

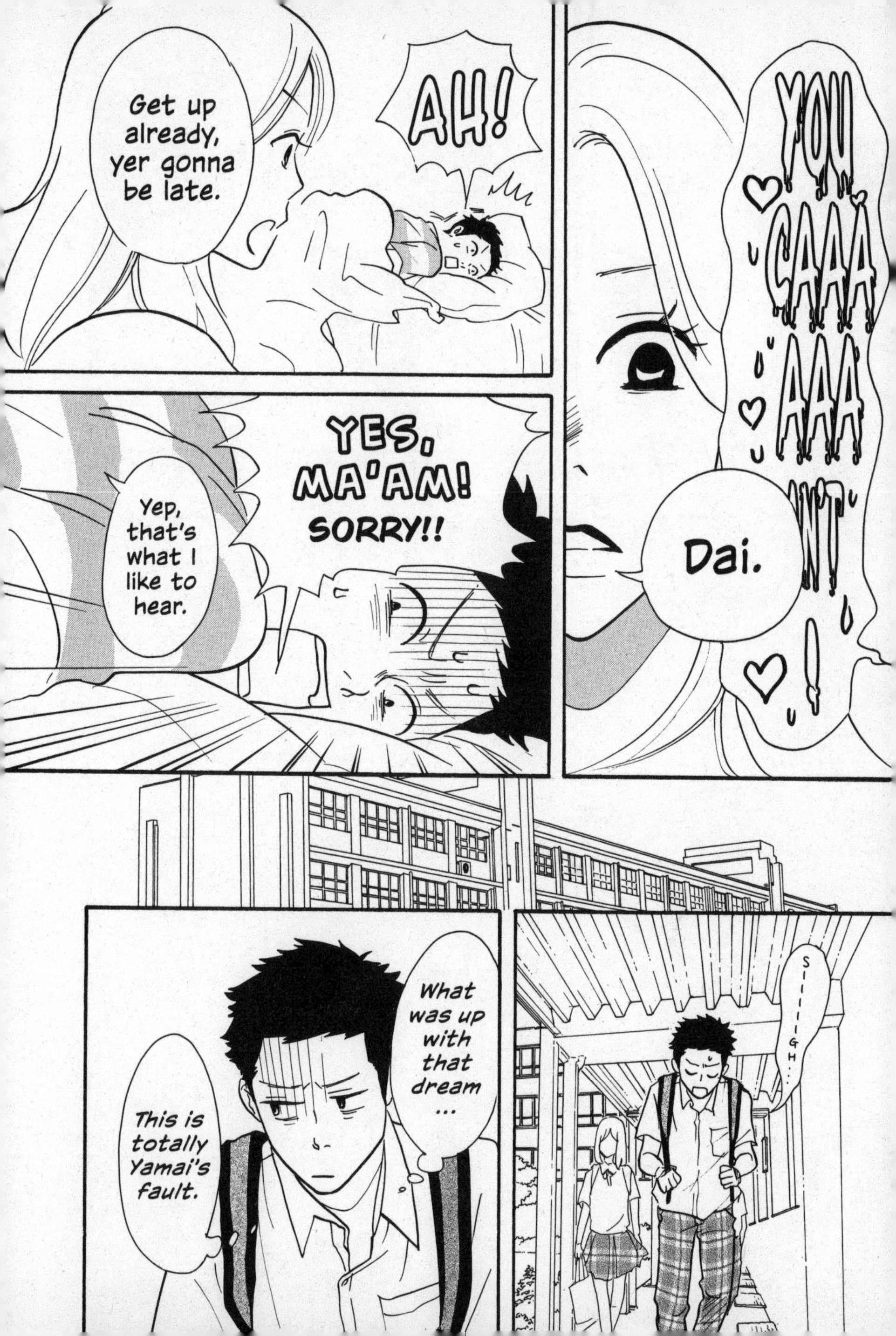

YOU CAAAAAAN'T!
Dai.
AH!
Get up already, yer gonna be late.
YES, MA'AM! SORRY!!
Yep, that's what I like to hear.
S-I-I-I-GH...
What was up with that dream...
This is totally Yamai's fault.

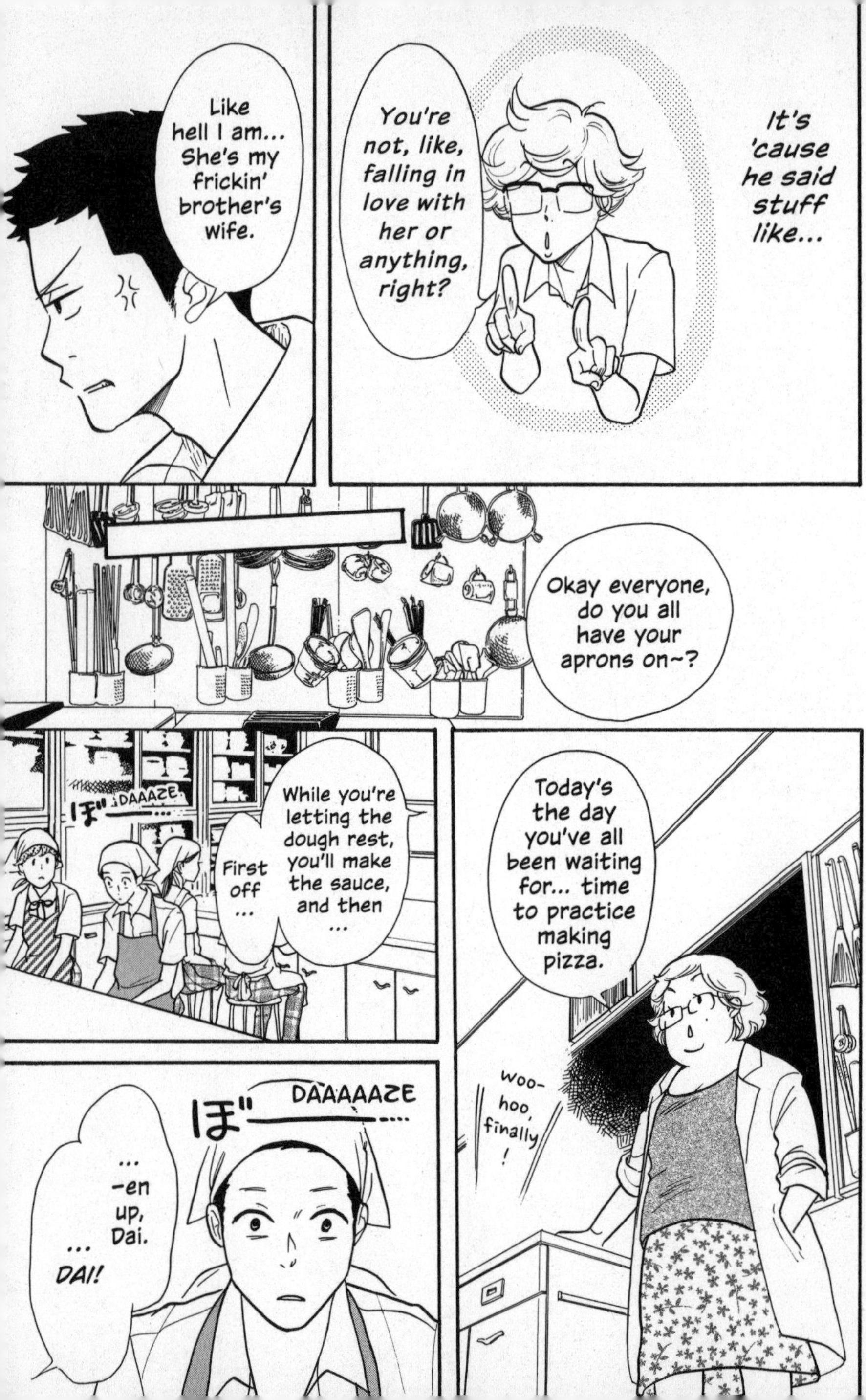
It's 'cause he said stuff like...
You're not, like, falling in love with her or anything, right?
Like hell I am... She's my frickin' brother's wife.
Okay everyone, do you all have your aprons on~?
Today's the day you've all been waiting for... time to practice making pizza.
woo-hoo, finally!
While you're letting the dough rest, you'll make the sauce, and then ...
First off ...
ぼ DAAAZE
ぼ DAAAAAZE
... -en up, Dai. ... DAI!

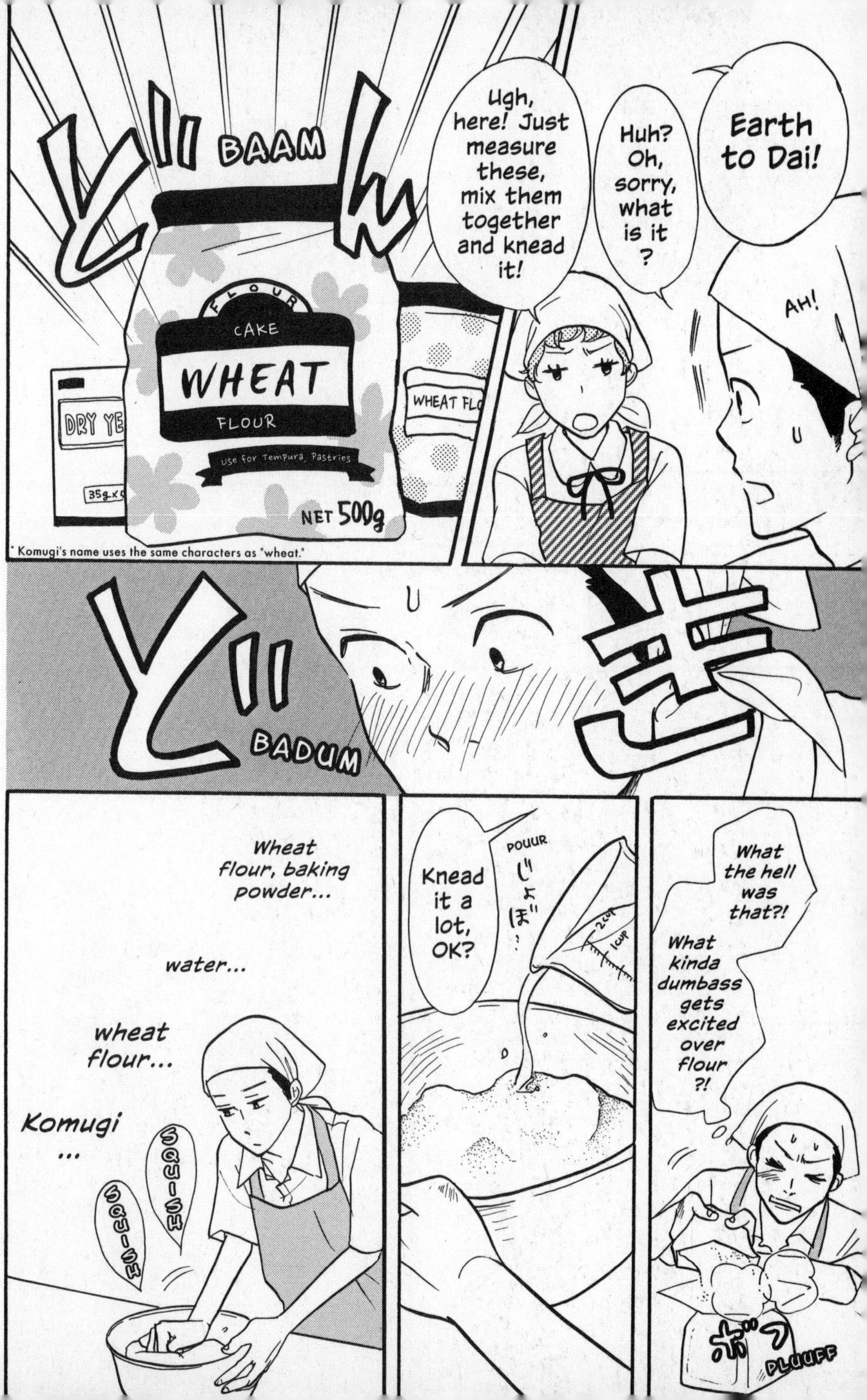
Earth to Dai!
AH!
Huh? Oh, sorry, what is it?
Ugh, here! Just measure these, mix them together and knead it!
BAAM
FLOUR
CAKE
WHEAT
FLOUR
Use for Tempura, Pastries
NET 500g
WHEAT FLO
DRY YE
35g x
* Komugi's name uses the same characters as "wheat."
BADUM
What the hell was that?!
What kinda dumbass gets excited over flour?!
PLUUFF
Knead it a lot, OK?
POUUR
じょぼ
2cup
1cup
Wheat flour, baking powder...
water...
wheat flour...
Komugi...
SQUI-SH
SQUI-SH

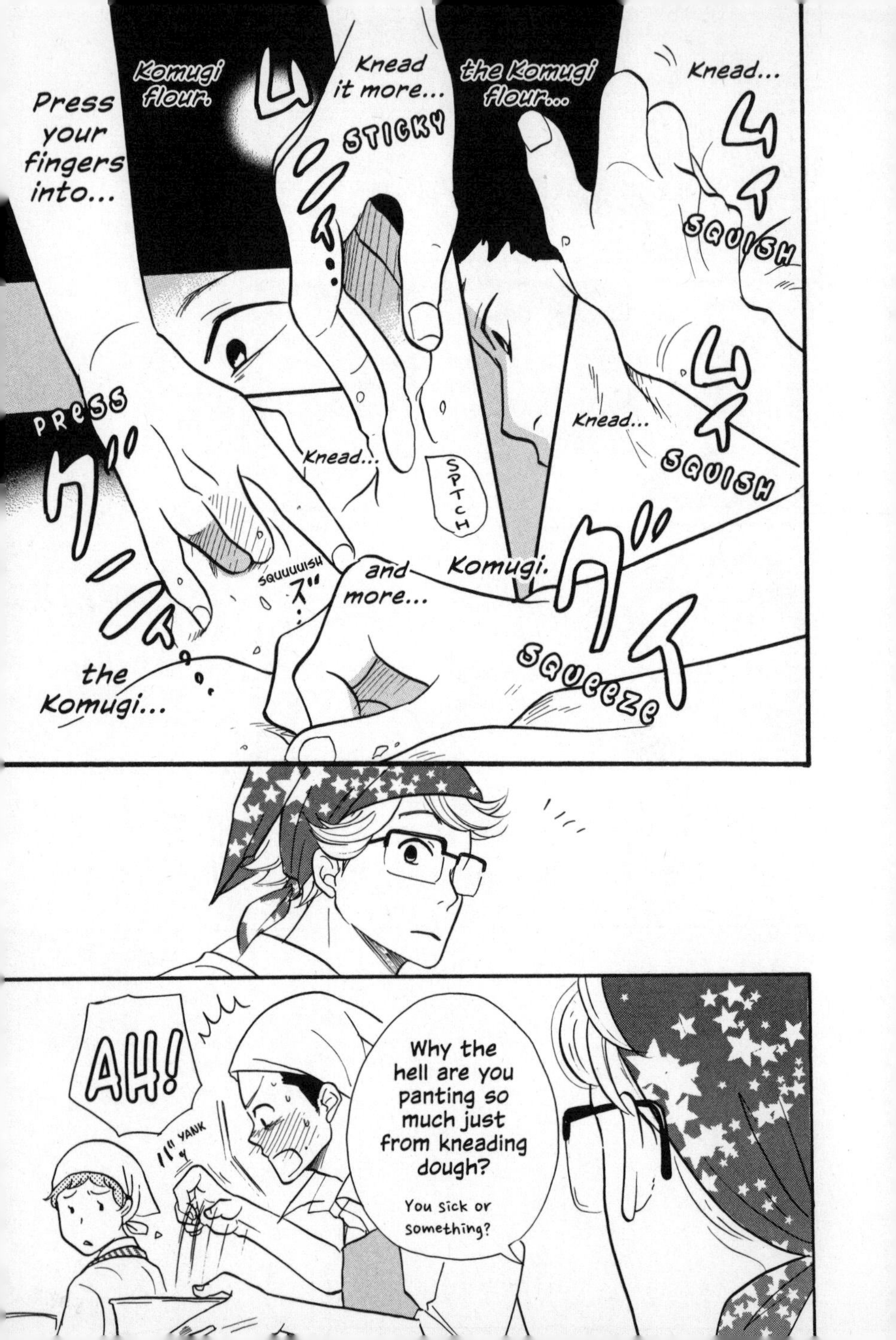

Knead...
SQUISH
the Komugi flour...
Knead it more...
STICKY
Komugi flour.
Press your fingers into...
Knead...
SQUISH
SPTCH
Knead...
Komugi.
SQUEEZE
and more...
SQUUUUISH
PRESS
the Komugi...
Why the hell are you panting so much just from kneading dough?
You sick or something?
AH!
YANK

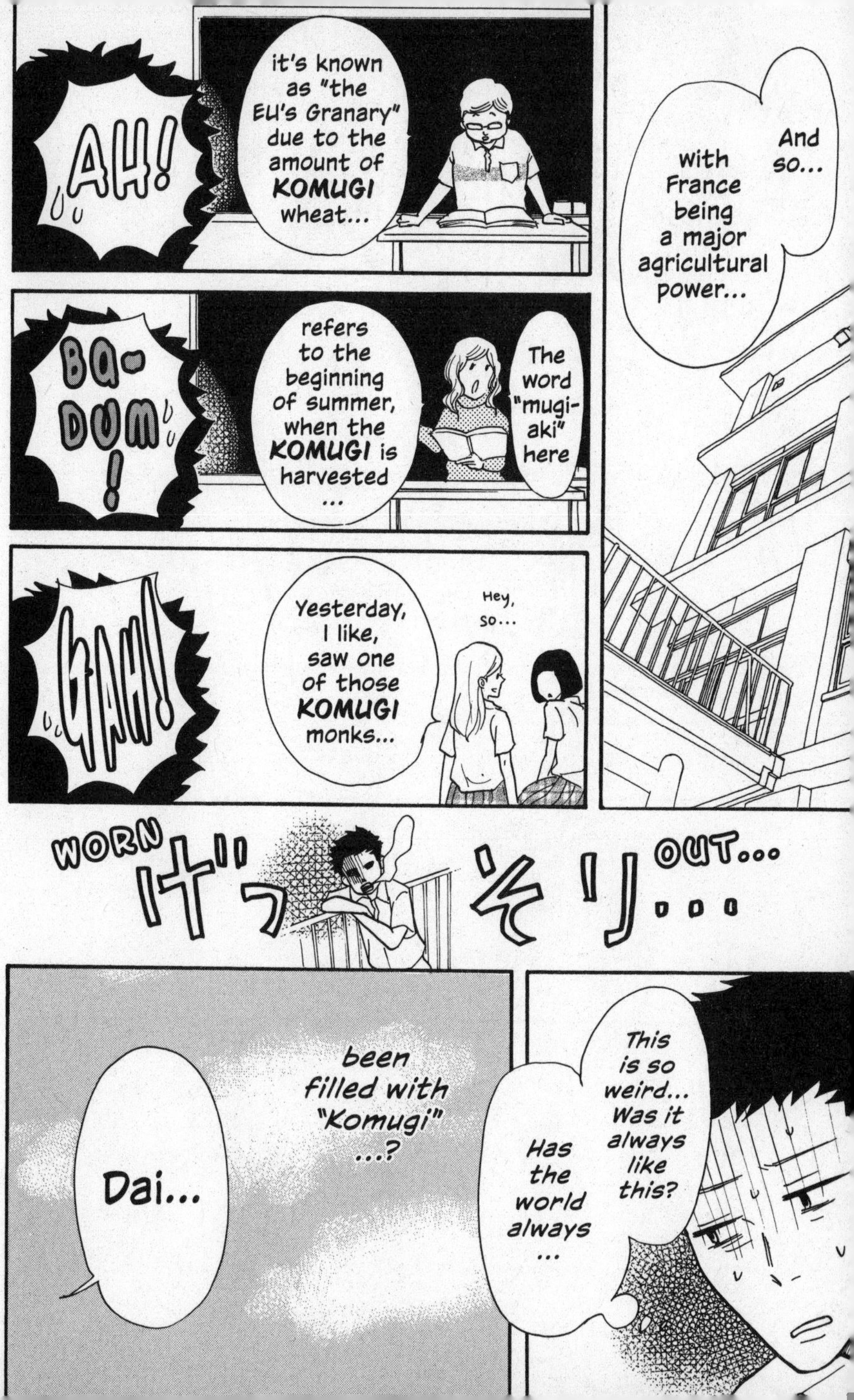
And so... with France being a major agricultural power...
it's known as "the EU's Granary" due to the amount of KOMUGI wheat...
AH!
The word "mugi-aki" here
refers to the beginning of summer, when the KOMUGI is harvested ...
BA-DUM!
Hey, so...
Yesterday, I like, saw one of those KOMUGI monks...
GAH!
WORN げっそり... OUT...
This is so weird... Was it always like this?
Has the world always ...
been filled with "Komugi" ...?
Dai...

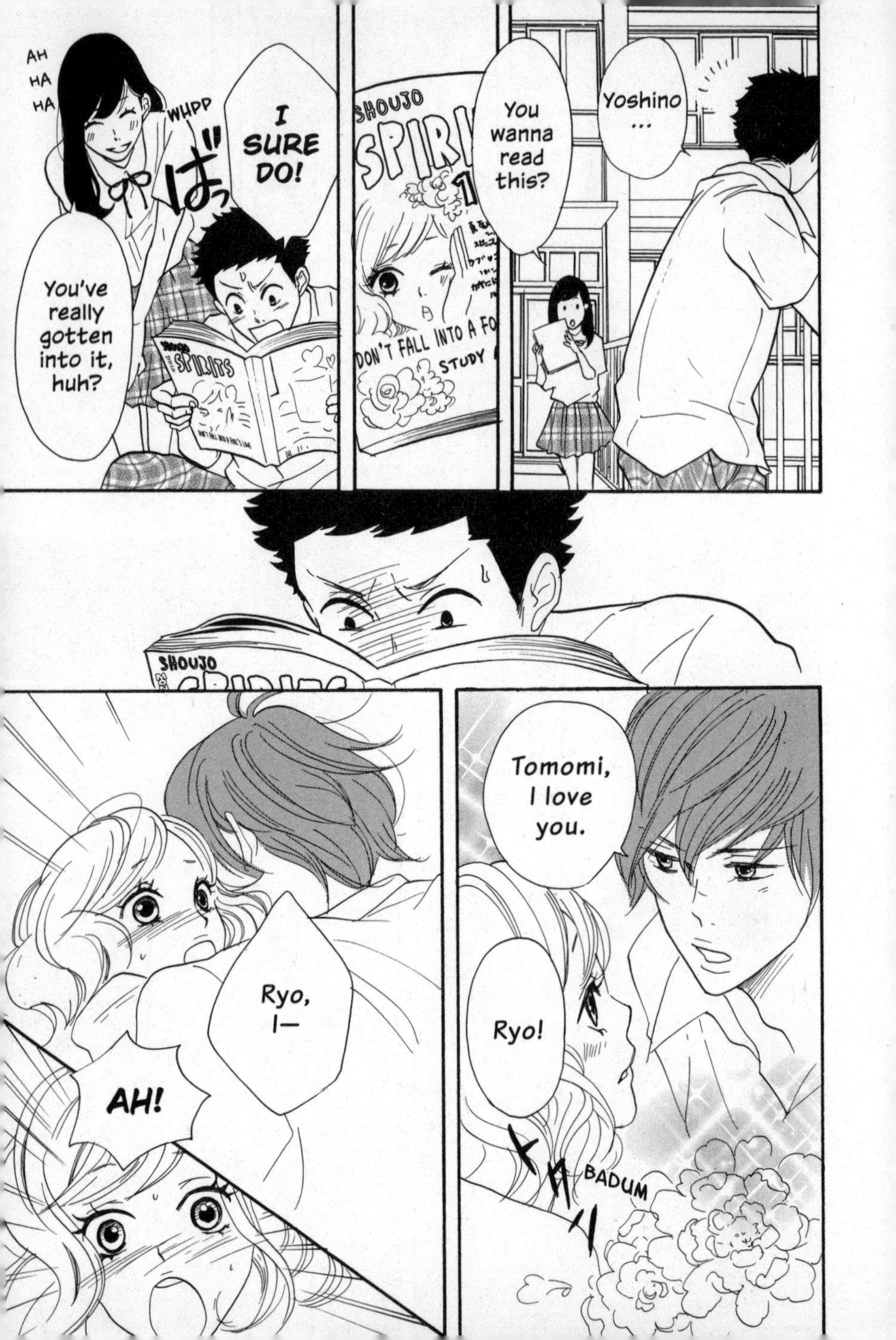
Yoshino...
You wanna read this?
SHOUJO
DON'T FALL INTO A FO
STUDY
I SURE DO!
WHPP
ばっ
AH HA HA
You've really gotten into it, huh?
SHOUJO
SPIRITS
SHOUJO
Tomomi, I love you.
Ryo!
BADUM
Ryo, I—
AH!

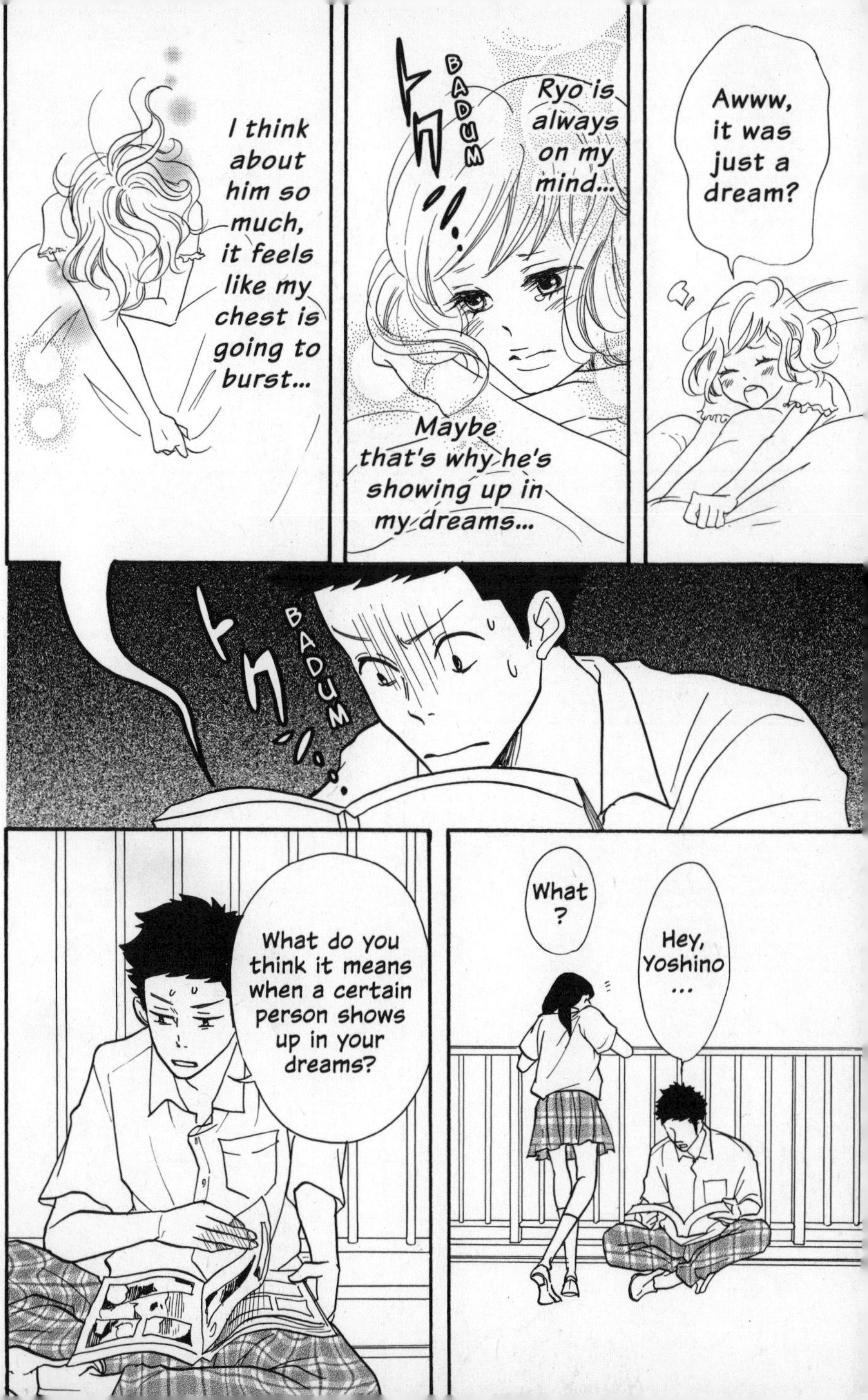
Awww, it was just a dream?
BADUM
Ryo is always on my mind...
Maybe that's why he's showing up in my dreams...
I think about him so much, it feels like my chest is going to burst...
BADUM
Hey, Yoshino...
What?
What do you think it means when a certain person shows up in your dreams?

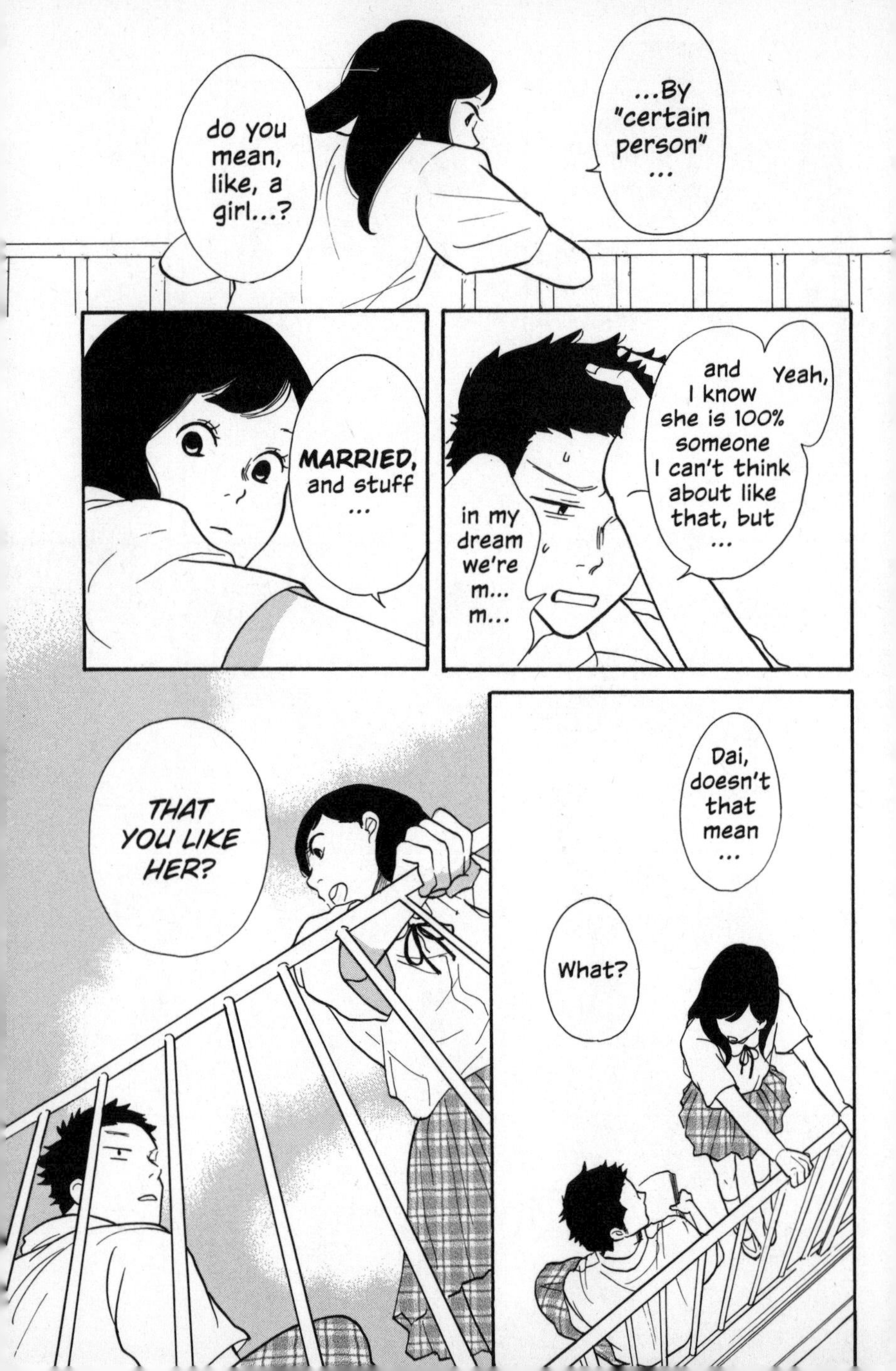
...By "certain person" ...
do you mean, like, a girl...?
Yeah, and I know she is 100% someone I can't think about like that, but ...
in my dream we're m... m...
MARRIED, and stuff ...
Dai, doesn't that mean ...
What?
THAT YOU LIKE HER?

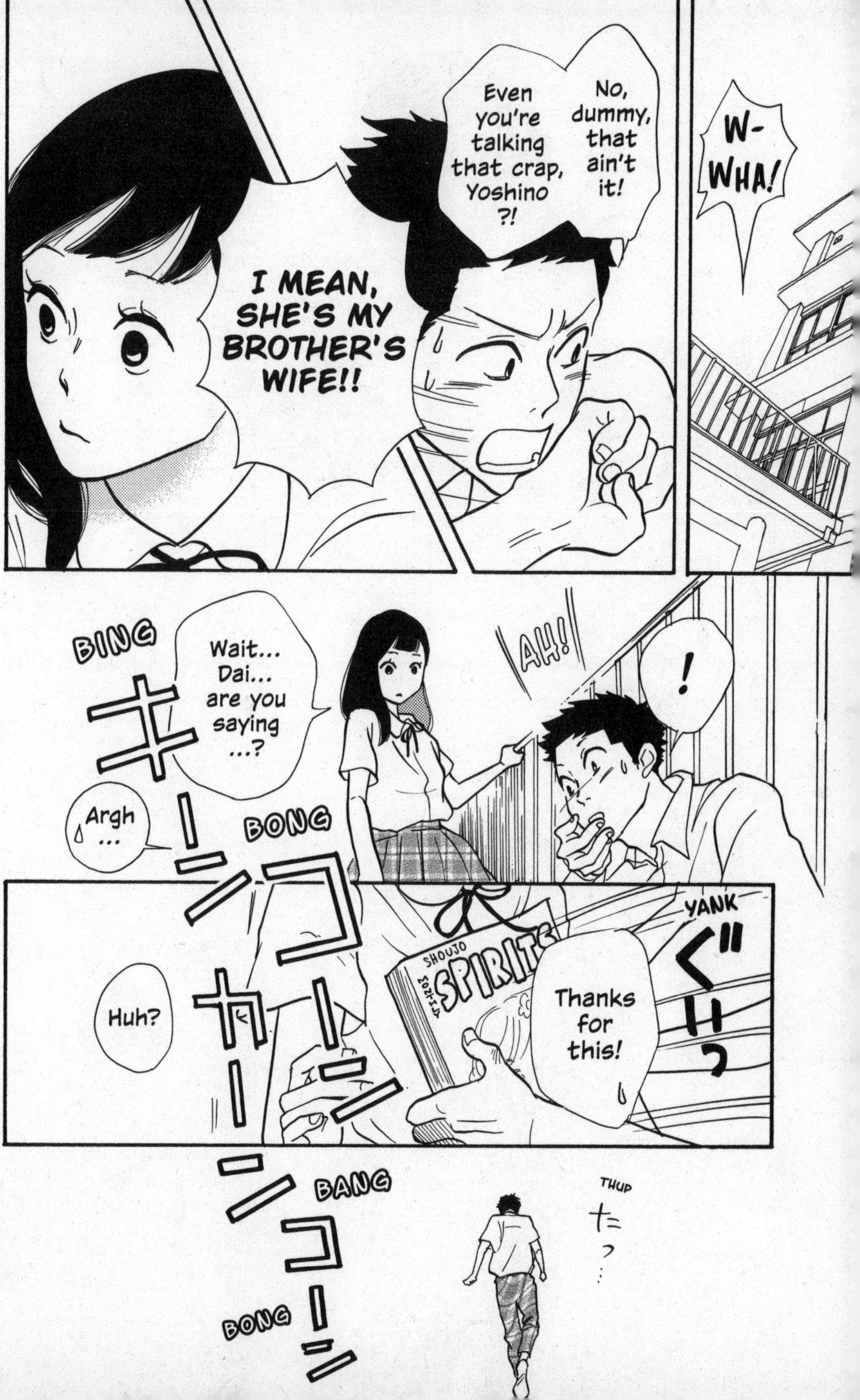
W- WHA!
No, dummy, that ain't it!
Even you're talking that crap, Yoshino?!
I MEAN, SHE'S MY BROTHER'S WIFE!!
!
AH!
Wait... Dai... are you saying...?
BING
キーンコーンカーンコーン
BONG
Argh...
YANK
ぐいっ
Thanks for this!
SHOUJO SPIRITS
Huh?
THUP
たっ
BANG
BONG

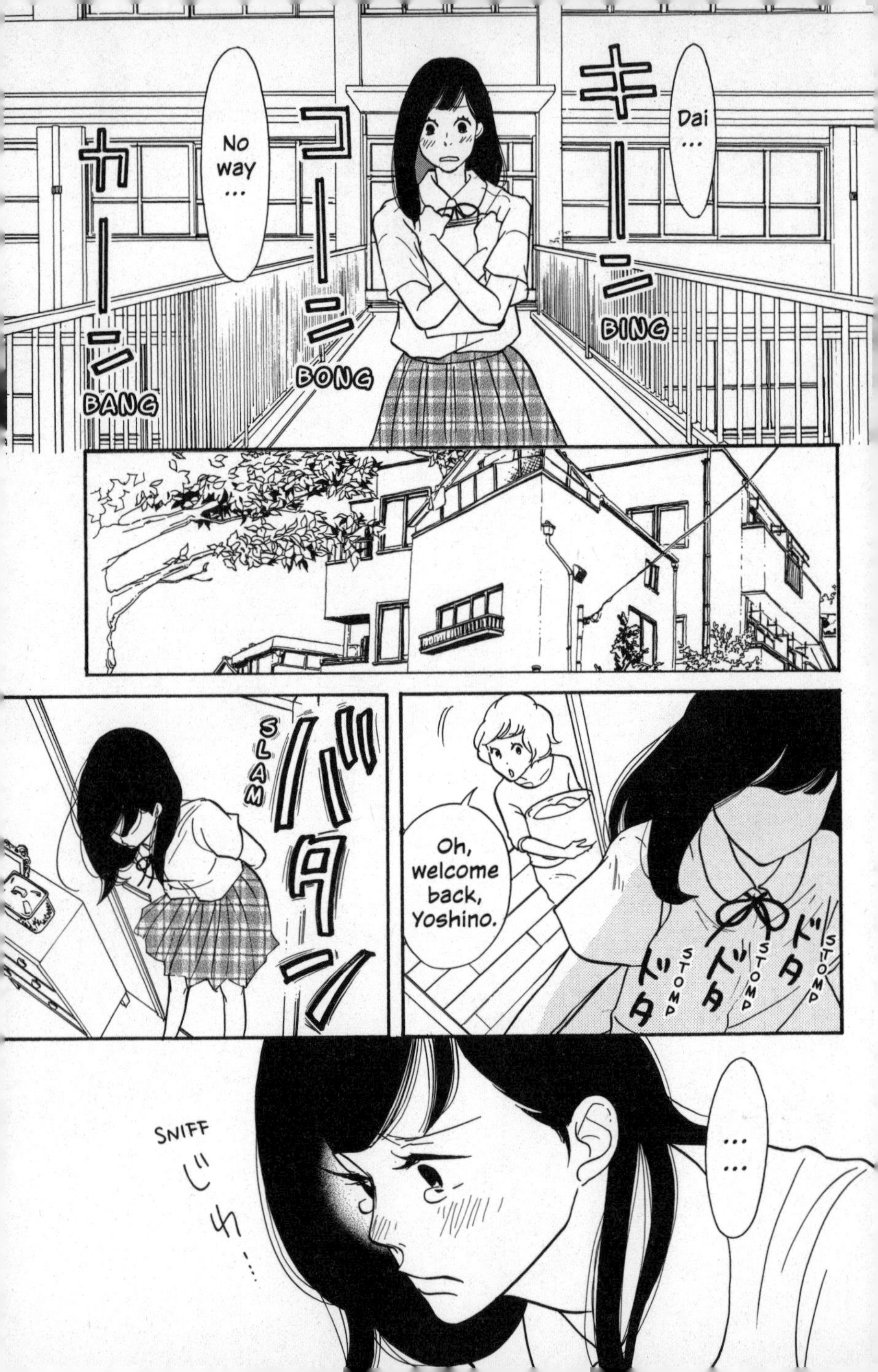
キーン
Dai ...
BING
コーン
No way ...
BONG
カーン
BANG
Oh, welcome back, Yoshino.
ドタドタ
STOMP STOMP STOMP
バタン
SLAM
... ...
SNIFF
じわ…

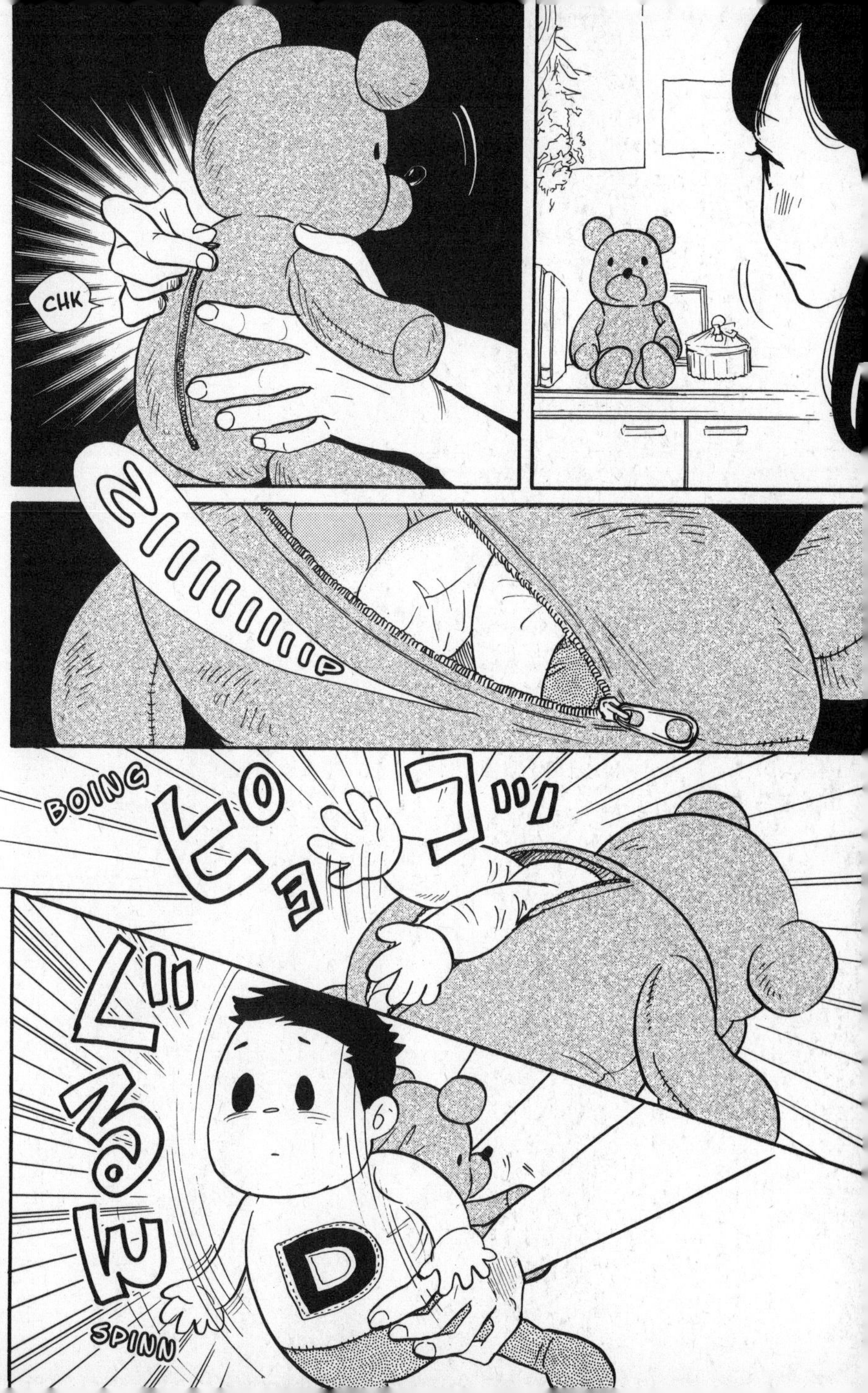
CHK
ZIIIIIIIIIP
BOING
SPINN

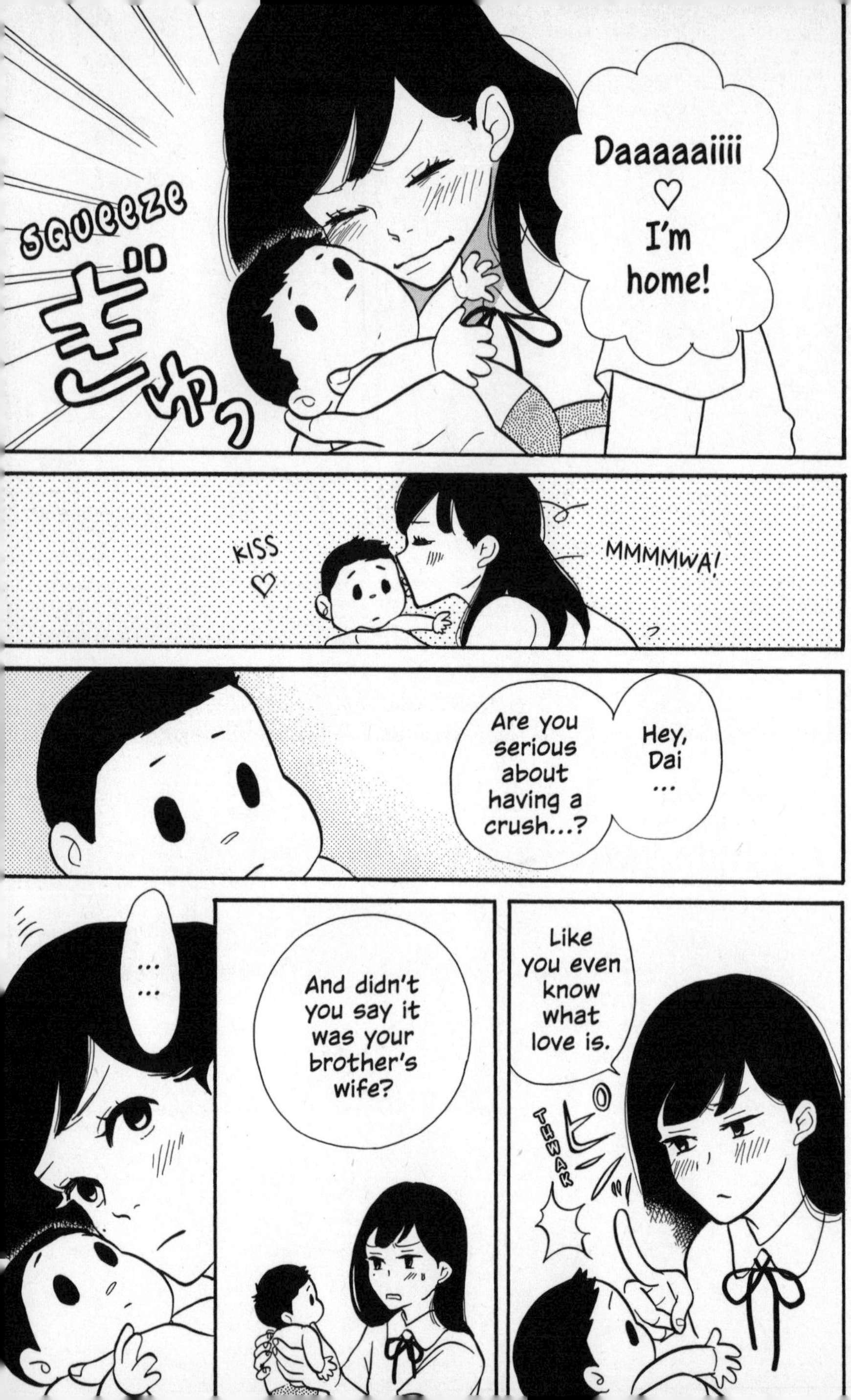
Daaaaaiiii ♡ I'm home!
SQUEEZE
ぎゅっ
MMMMWA!
KISS ♡
Hey, Dai ...
Are you serious about having a crush...?
Like you even know what love is.
THWAK
And didn't you say it was your brother's wife?
......

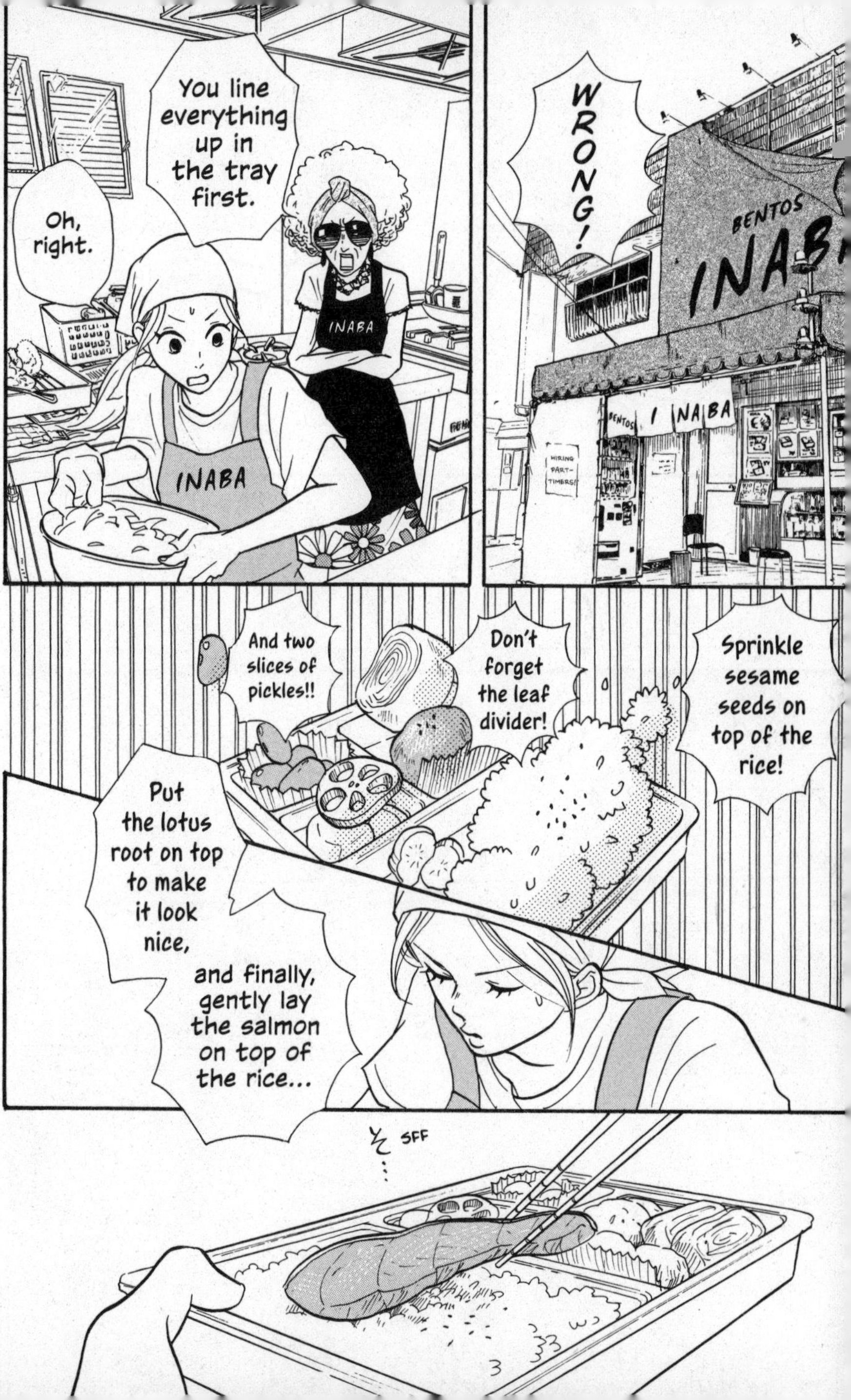
WRONG!
BENTOS
BENTOS I NABA
HIRING PART-TIMERS!
You line everything up in the tray first.
Oh, right.
INABA
INABA
Sprinkle sesame seeds on top of the rice!
Don't forget the leaf divider!
And two slices of pickles!!
Put the lotus root on top to make it look nice,
and finally, gently lay the salmon on top of the rice...
SFF

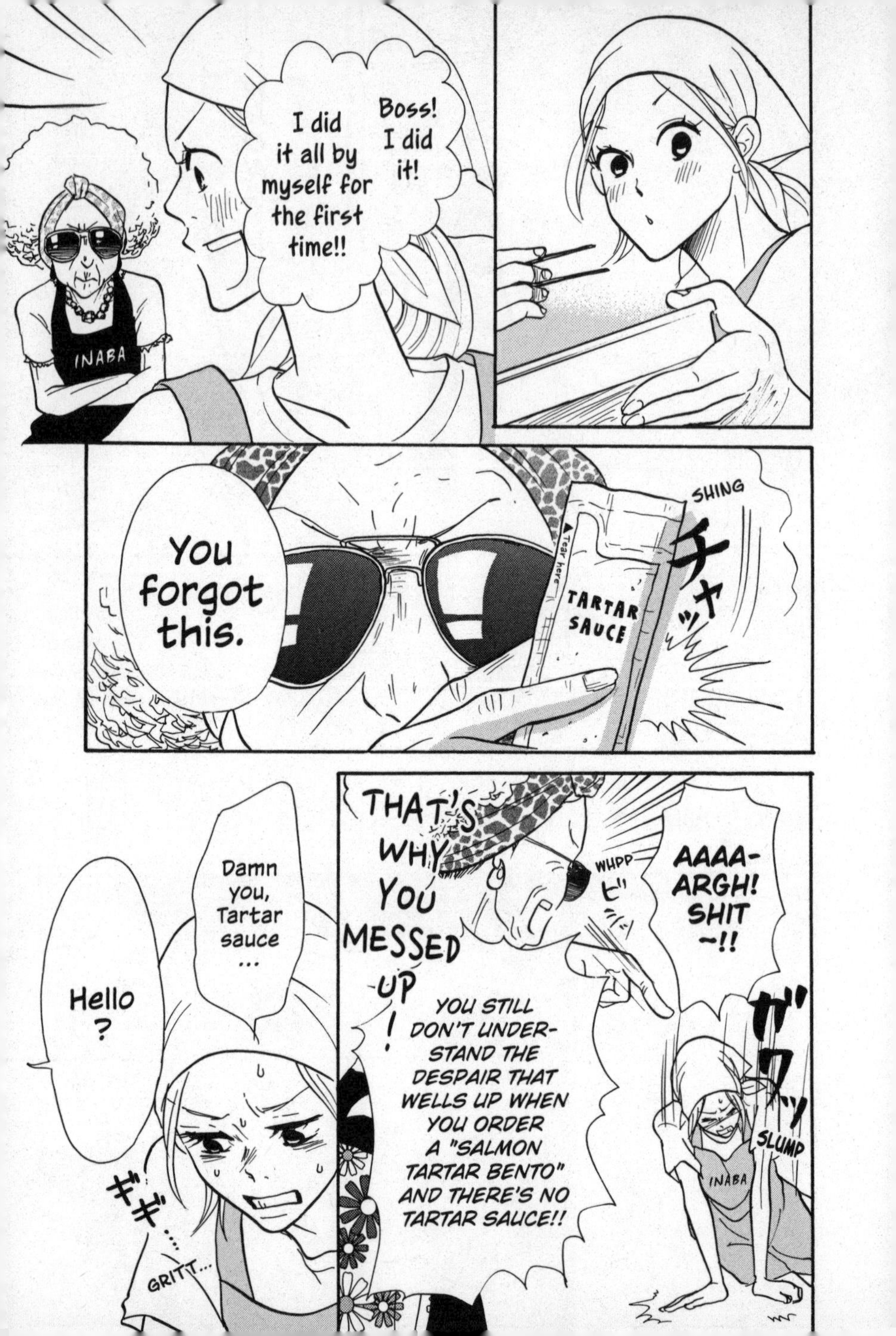
Boss! I did it!
I did it all by myself for the first time!!
INABA
You forgot this.
▲Tear here
TARTAR SAUCE
SHING
チャッ
AAAA-ARGH! SHIT~!!
ザワッ
SLUMP
INABA
WHPP
ビッ
THAT'S WHY YOU MESSED UP!
YOU STILL DON'T UNDER-STAND THE DESPAIR THAT WELLS UP WHEN YOU ORDER A "SALMON TARTAR BENTO" AND THERE'S NO TARTAR SAUCE!!
Damn you, Tartar sauce...
Hello?
ギギ...
GRITT...

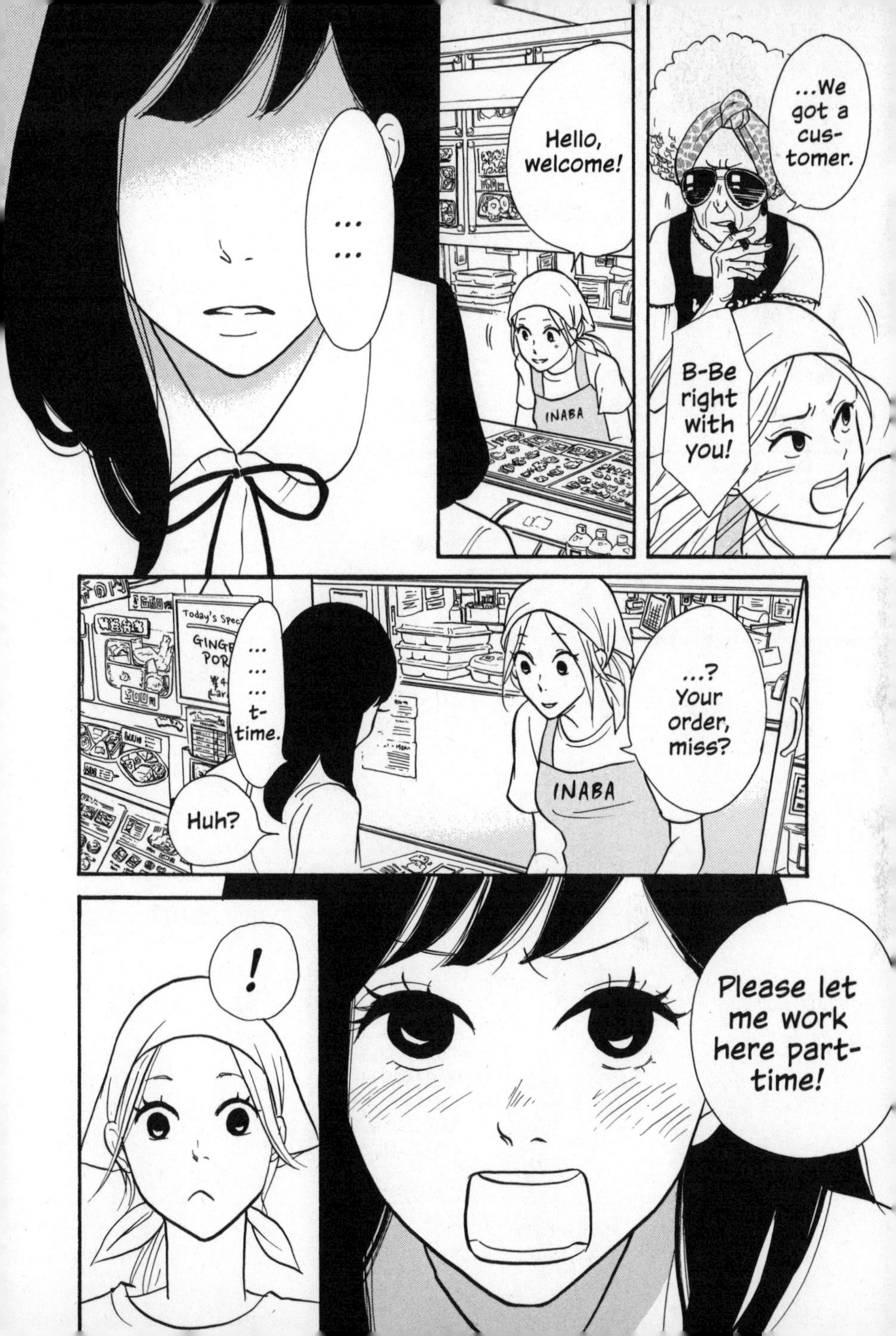
...We got a cus-tomer.
B-Be right with you!
Hello, welcome!
......
...? Your order, miss?
... ... t-time.
Huh?
Please let me work here part-time!
!

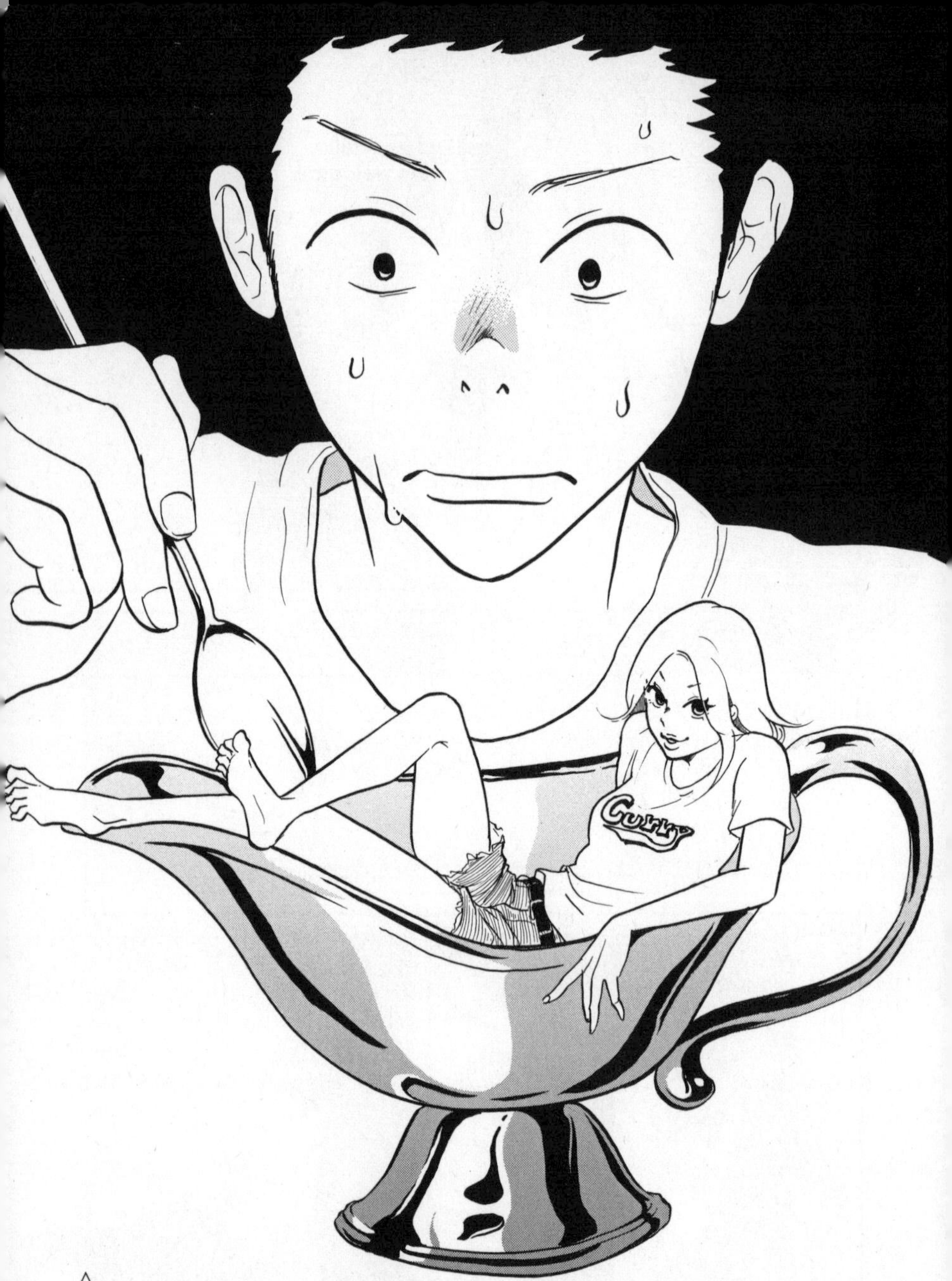
Curry

15 MELTED HEARTS

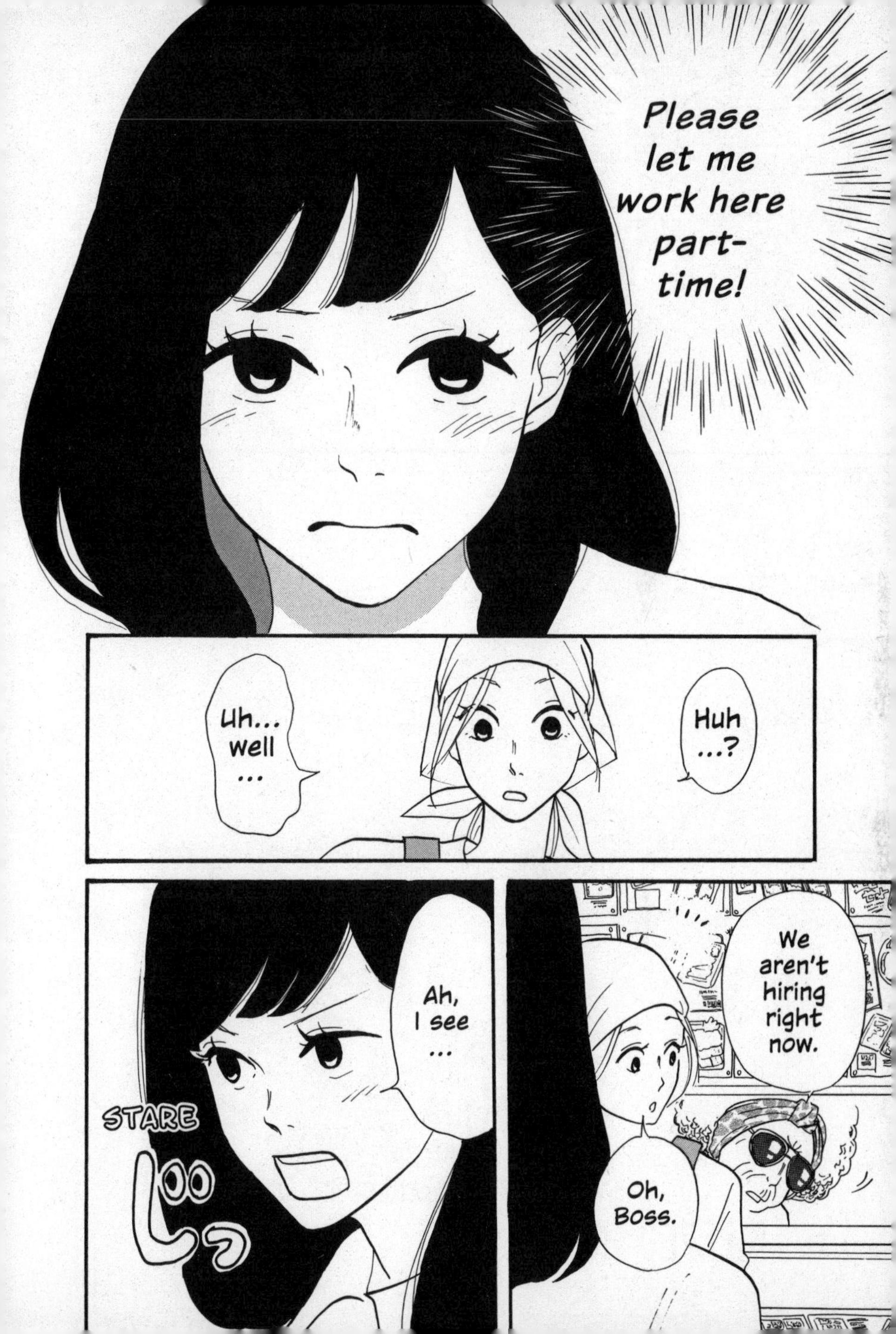
Please let me work here part-time!
Huh ...?
Uh... well ...
We aren't hiring right now.
Oh, Boss.
Ah, I see ...
STARE

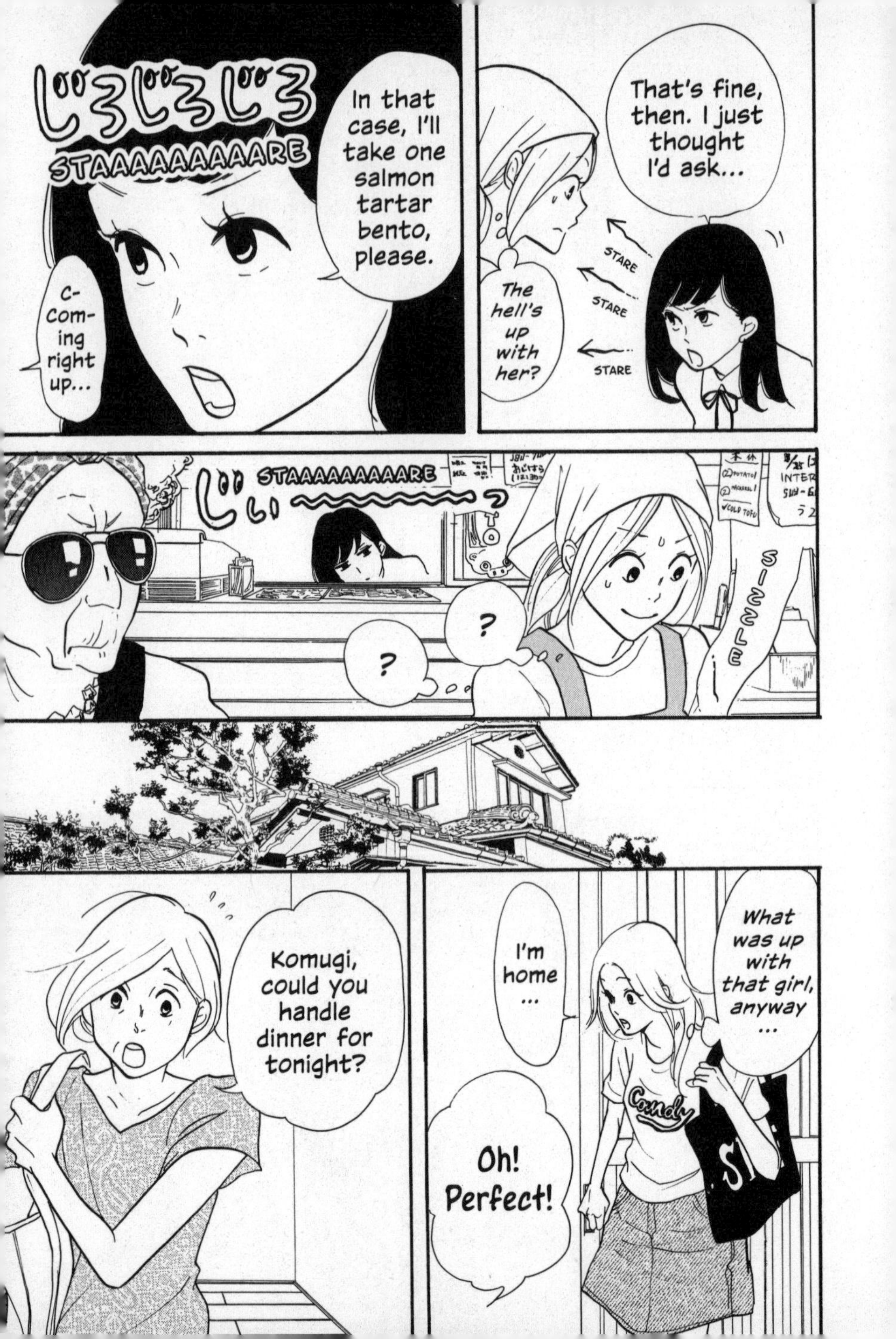
That's fine, then. I just thought I'd ask...
STARE
STARE
STARE
The hell's up with her?
じろじろじろ
STAAAAAAAAARE
In that case, I'll take one salmon tartar bento, please.
C-Coming right up...
じぃ〜〜〜〜〜〜〜?
STAAAAAAAAAARE
SIZZLE
?
?
What was up with that girl, anyway...
I'm home...
Oh! Perfect!
Komugi, could you handle dinner for tonight?

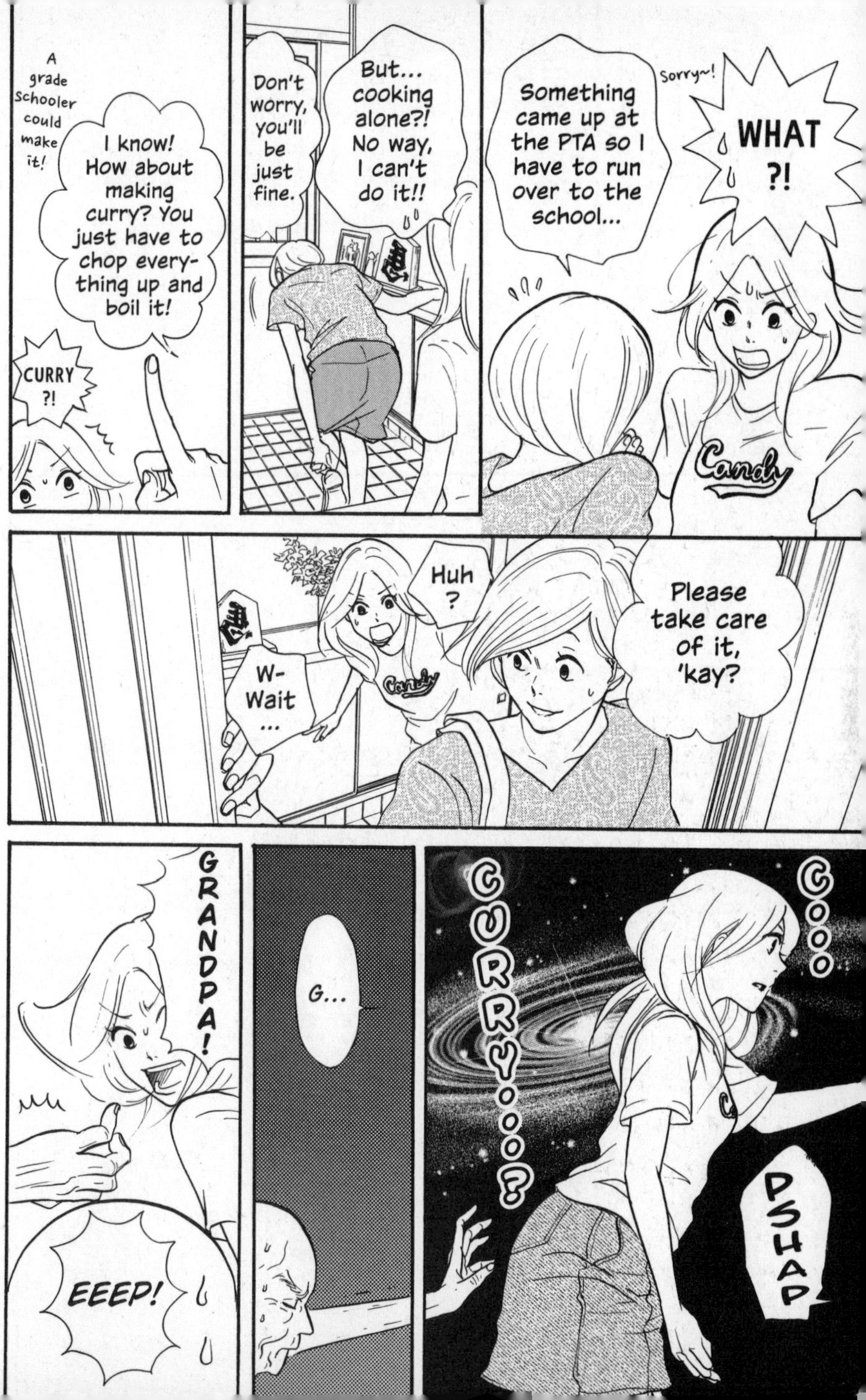

Something came up at the PTA so I have to run over to the school...
Sorry~!
WHAT ?!
But... cooking alone?! No way, I can't do it!!
Don't worry, you'll be just fine.
I know! How about making curry? You just have to chop every-thing up and boil it!
A grade schooler could make it!
CURRY ?!
Please take care of it, 'kay?
Huh ?
W-Wait ...
Cooo
CURRYooo?
PSHAP
G...
GRANDPA!
EEEP!

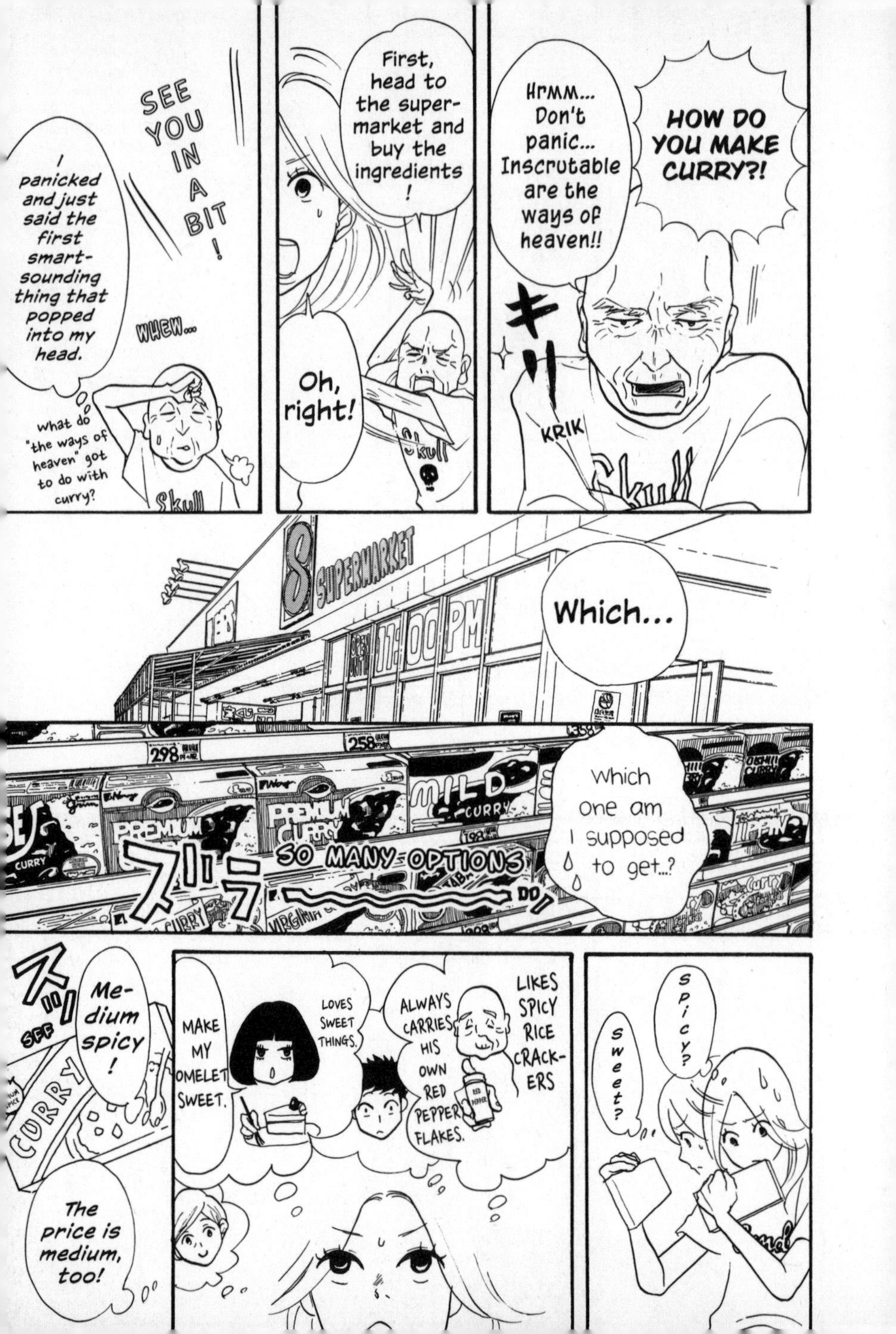
HOW DO YOU MAKE CURRY?!
Hrmm... Don't panic... Inscrutable are the ways of heaven!!
KRIK
Skull
First, head to the super-market and buy the ingredients!
Oh, right!
Skull
SEE YOU IN A BIT!
I panicked and just said the first smart-sounding thing that popped into my head.
WHEW...
What do "the ways of heaven" got to do with curry?
Skull
SUPERMARKET
11:00 PM
Which...
Which one am I supposed to get...?
SO MANY OPTIONS
DOI
MILD CURRY
PREMIUM CURRY
CURRY
Spicy?
Sweet?
LIKES SPICY RICE CRACK-ERS
ALWAYS CARRIES HIS OWN RED PEPPER FLAKES.
RED PEPPER
LOVES SWEET THINGS.
MAKE MY OMELET SWEET.
Me-dium spicy!
SFF
CURRY
The price is medium, too!

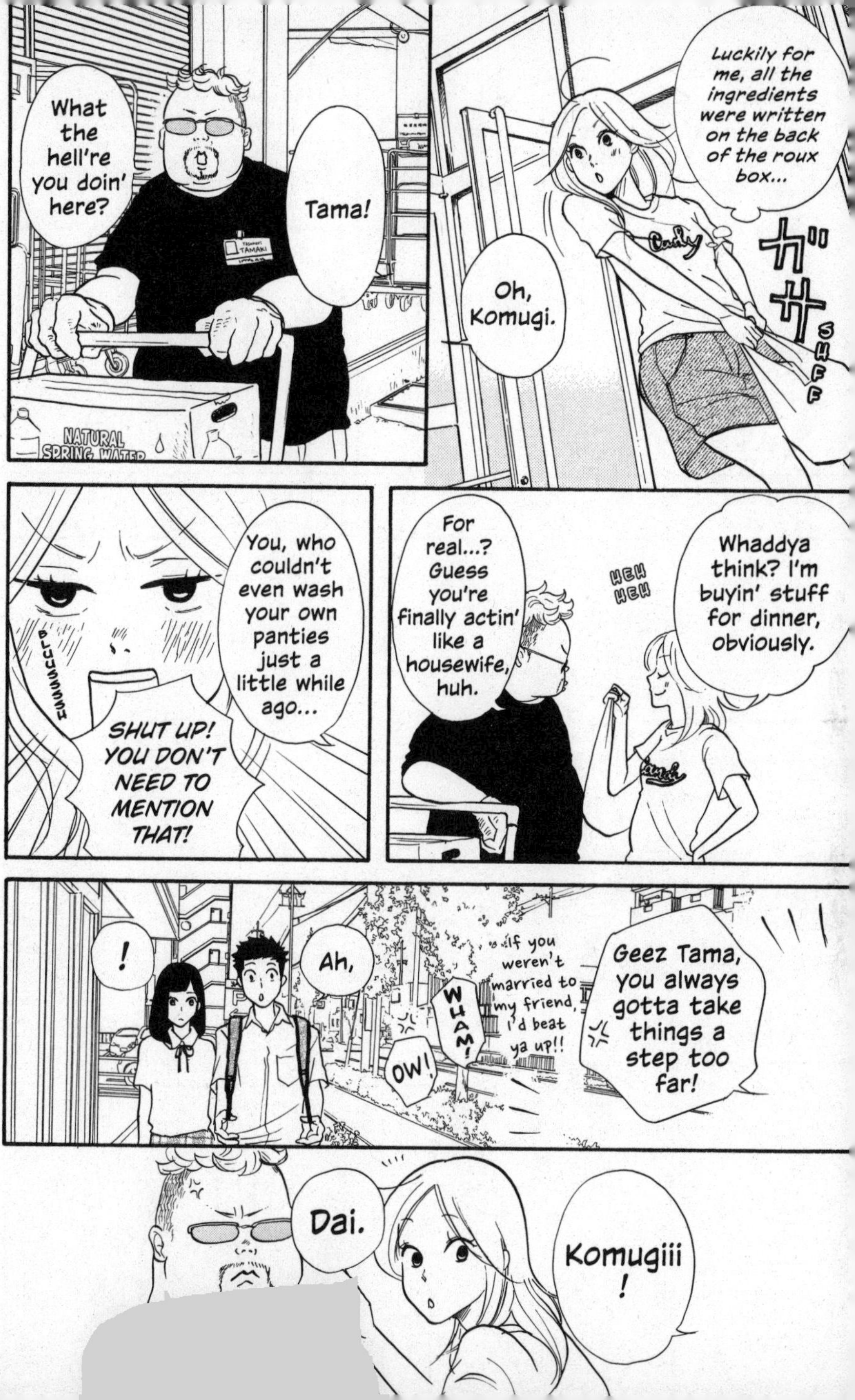
Luckily for me, all the ingredients were written on the back of the roux box...
ガサ
SHUFF
Oh, Komugi.
Tama!
What the hell're you doin' here?
TAMAKI
NATURAL SPRING WATER
Whaddya think? I'm buyin' stuff for dinner, obviously.
HEH HEH
For real...? Guess you're finally actin' like a housewife, huh.
You, who couldn't even wash your own panties just a little while ago...
BLUSSSSH
SHUT UP! YOU DON'T NEED TO MENTION THAT!
Geez Tama, you always gotta take things a step too far!
...If you weren't married to my friend, I'd beat ya up!!
WHAM!
OW!
Ah,
!
Komugiii!
Dai.

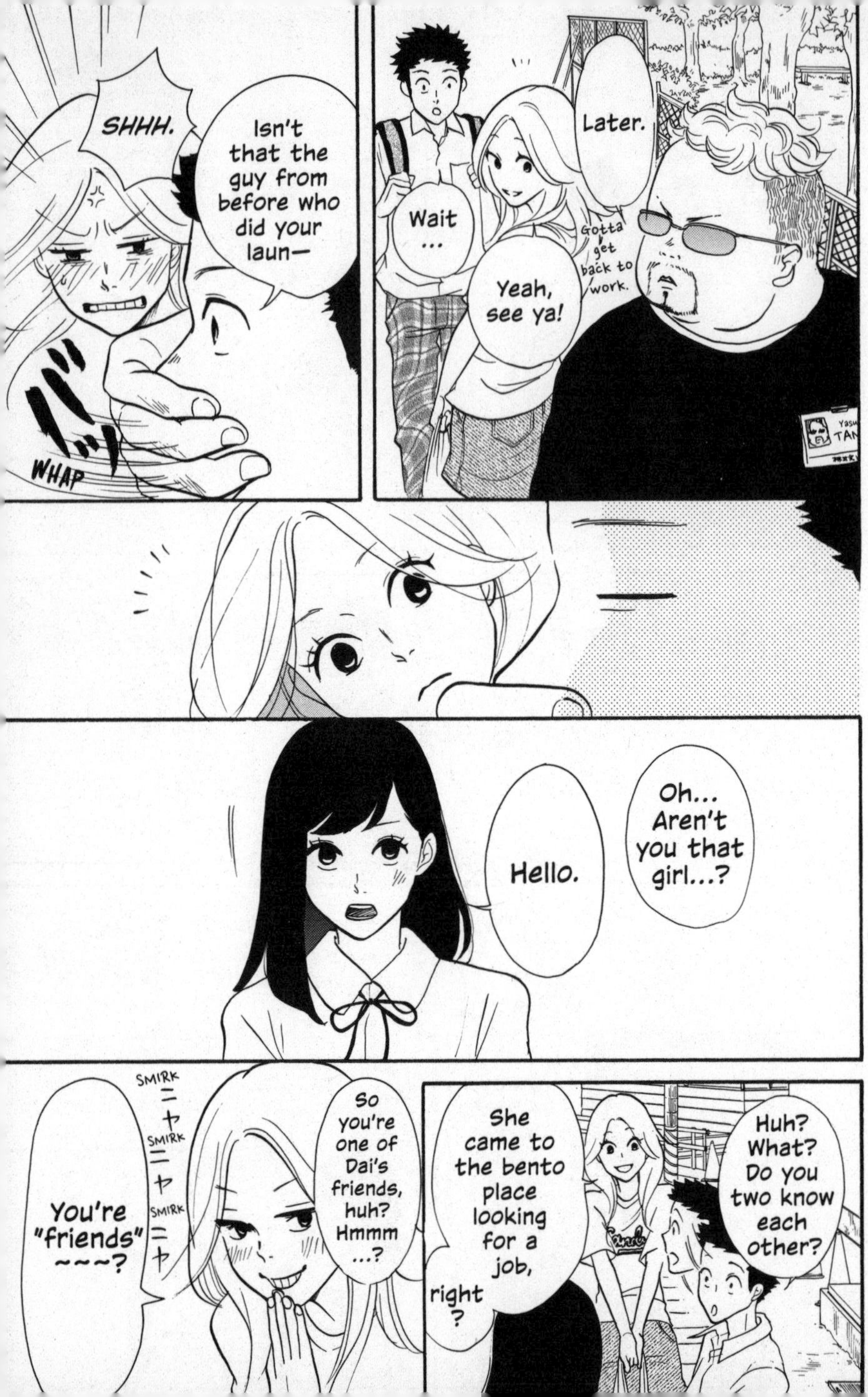
Later.
Gotta get back to work.
Wait ...
Yeah, see ya!
Isn't that the guy from before who did your laun—
SHHH.
WHAP
Oh... Aren't you that girl...?
Hello.
Huh? What? Do you two know each other?
She came to the bento place looking for a job, right?
So you're one of Dai's friends, huh? Hmmm ...?
SMIRK ニヤ
SMIRK ニヤ
SMIRK ニヤ
You're "friends" ~~~?

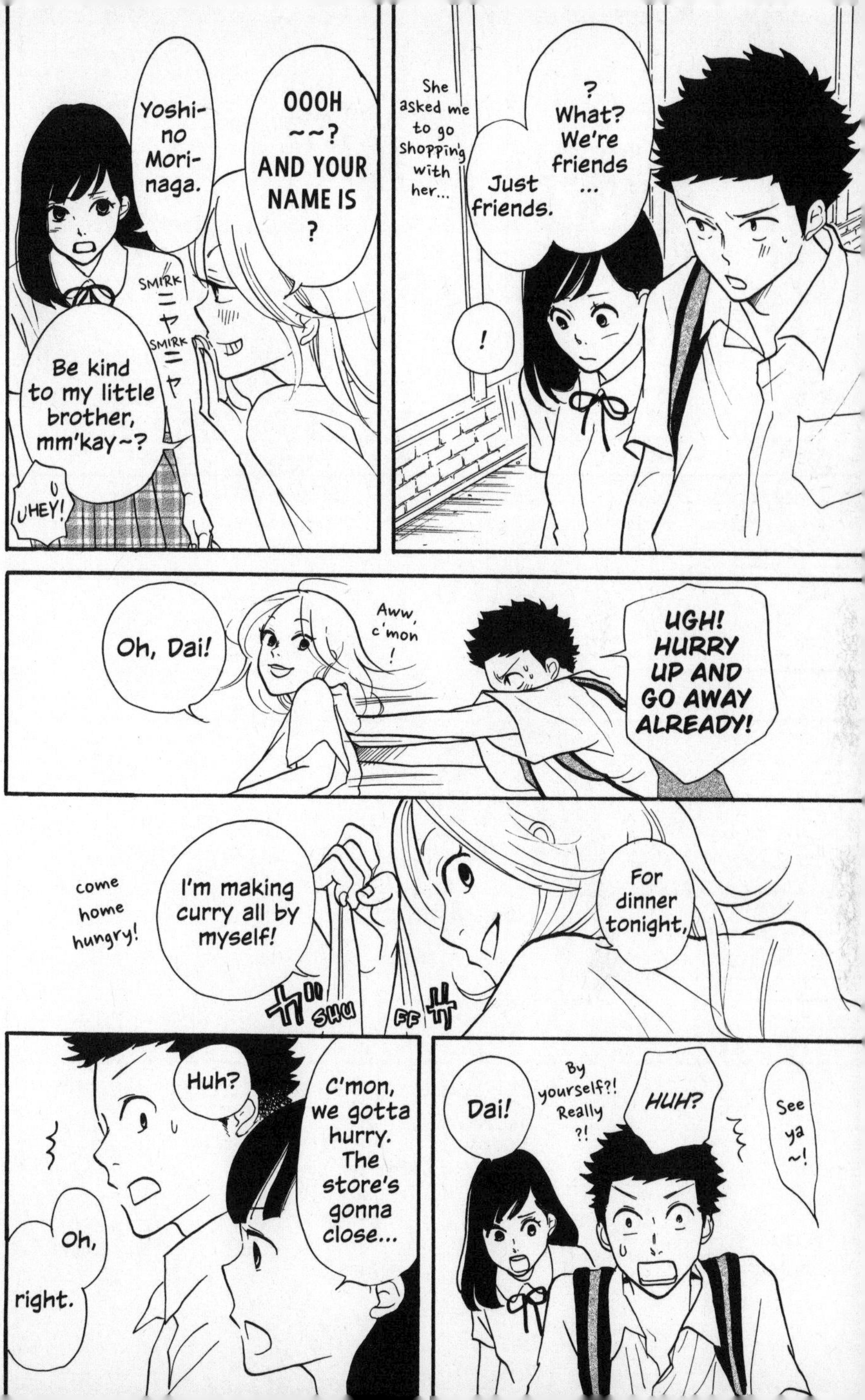

? What? We're friends ...
Just friends.
She asked me to go shopping with her...
!
OOOH ~~? AND YOUR NAME IS ?
Yoshino Morinaga.
SMIRK ニヤ
SMIRK ニヤ
Be kind to my little brother, mm'kay~?
HEY!
UGH! HURRY UP AND GO AWAY ALREADY!
Aww, c'mon!
Oh, Dai!
For dinner tonight,
I'm making curry all by myself!
come home hungry!
SHUFF
See ya~!
HUH?
By yourself?! Really?!
Dai!
C'mon, we gotta hurry. The store's gonna close...
Huh?
Oh, right.

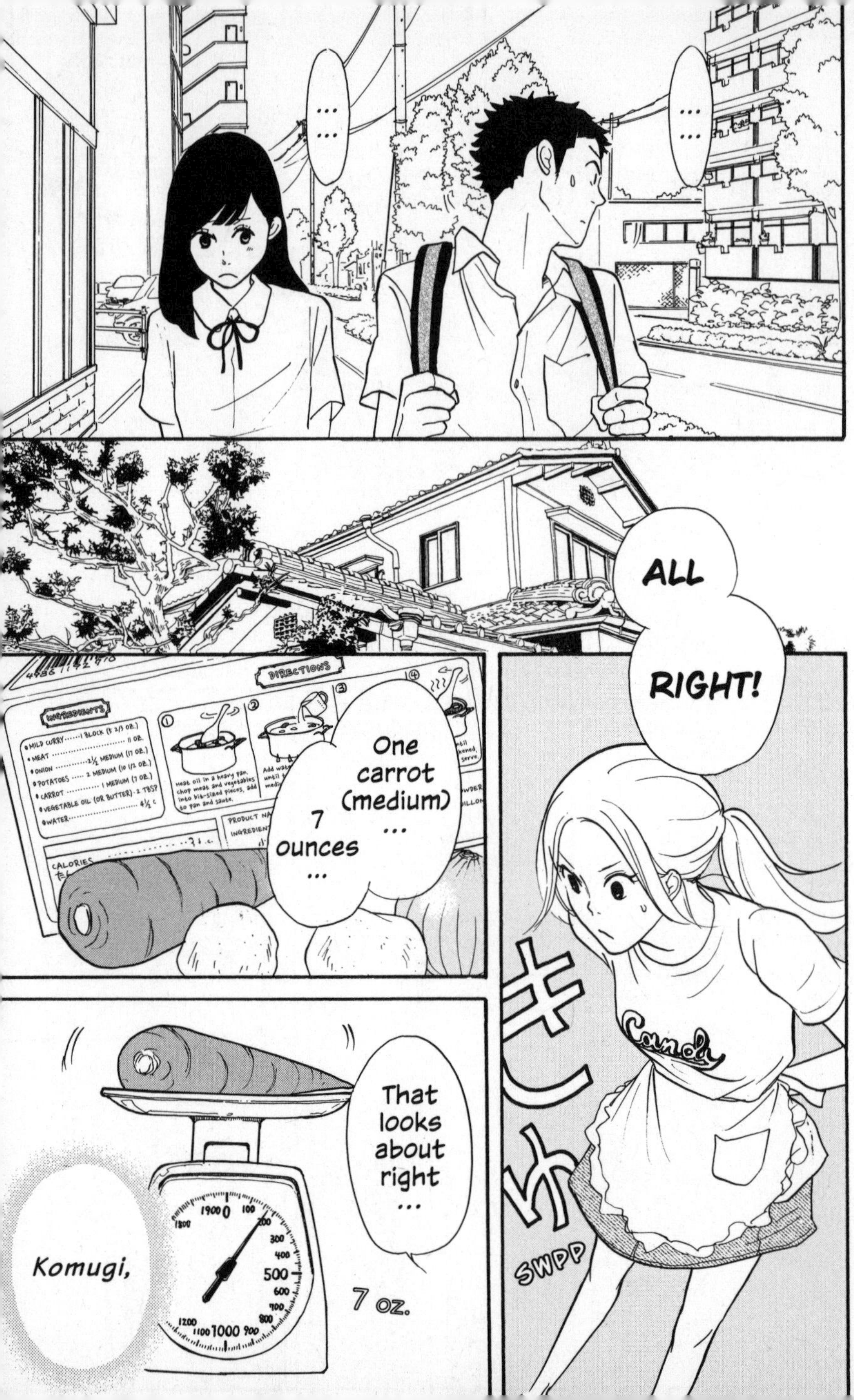

... ...
... ...
ALL RIGHT!
INGREDIENTS
MILD CURRY .... 1 BLOCK (5 2/3 OZ.)
MEAT .... 11 OZ.
ONION .... 2 1/2 MEDIUM (17 OZ.)
POTATOES .... 2 MEDIUM (10 1/2 OZ.)
CARROT .... 1 MEDIUM (7 OZ.)
VEGETABLE OIL (OR BUTTER) · 2 TBSP
WATER .... 4 1/2 C
DIRECTIONS
CALORIES
One carrot (medium) ...
7 ounces ...
SWPP
That looks about right ...
7 oz.
Komugi,

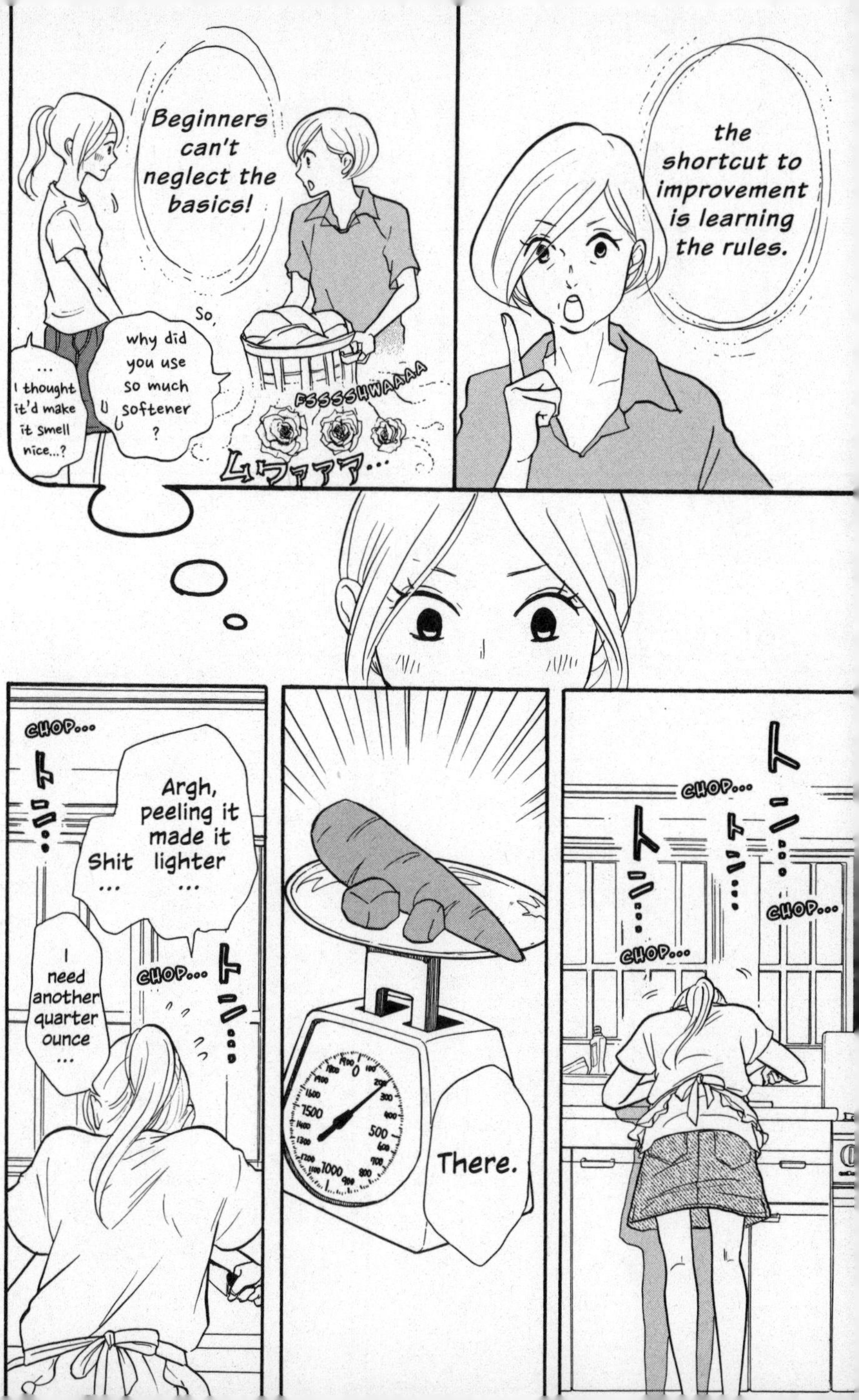

the shortcut to improvement is learning the rules.
Beginners can't neglect the basics!
So,
why did you use so much softener?
... I thought it'd make it smell nice...?
FSSSSHWAAAA
ムファァァ…
トン… CHOP…
トン… CHOP…
トン… CHOP…
There.
Argh, peeling it made it lighter...
Shit...
I need another quarter ounce...
トン… CHOP…
トン… CHOP…

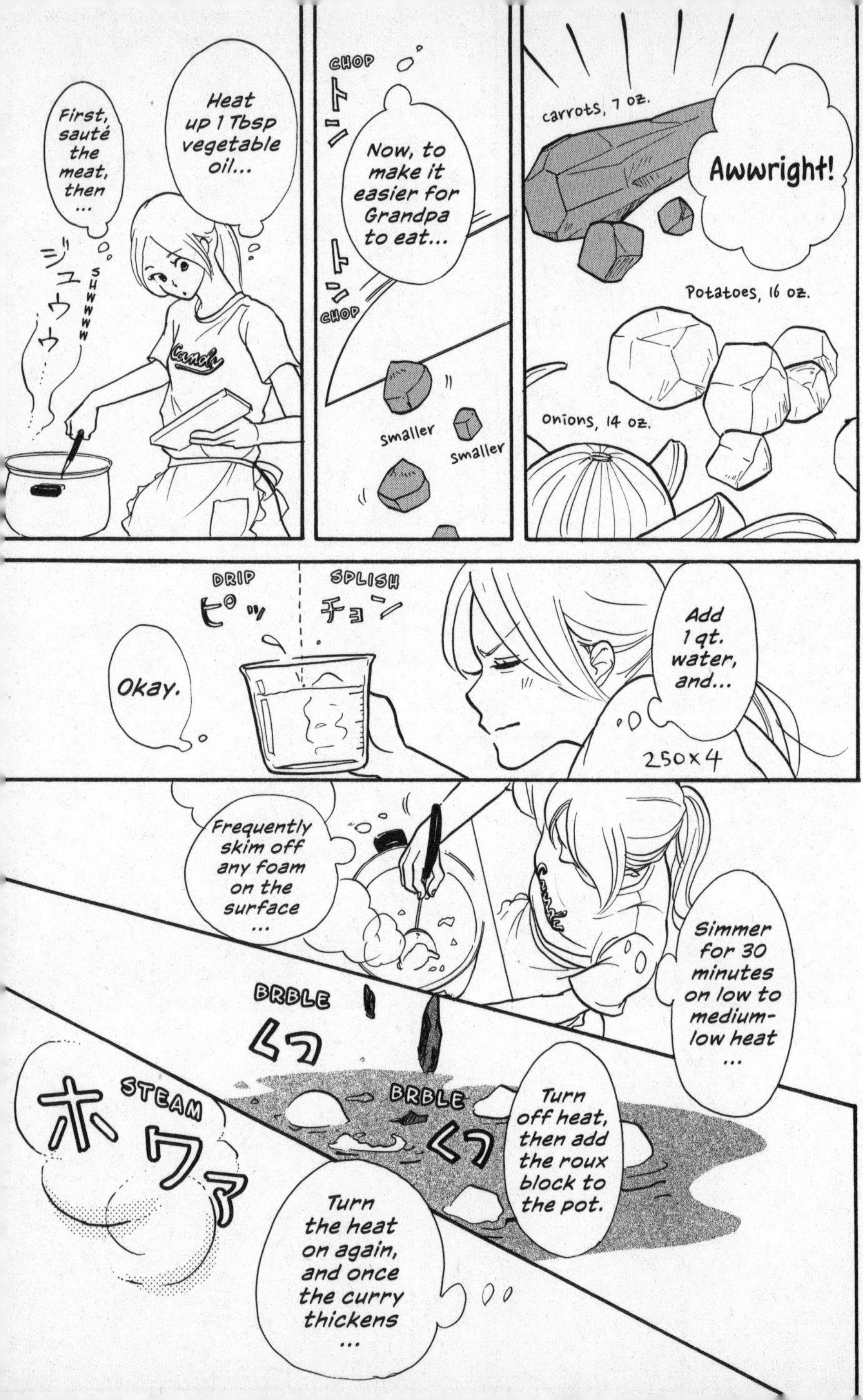

Awwright!
carrots, 7 oz.
Potatoes, 16 oz.
Onions, 14 oz.
CHOP
Now, to make it easier for Grandpa to eat...
CHOP
smaller
smaller
Heat up 1 Tbsp vegetable oil...
First, sauté the meat, then ...
SHWWWW
Add 1 qt. water, and...
250x4
SPLISH
DRIP
Okay.
Simmer for 30 minutes on low to medium-low heat ...
Frequently skim off any foam on the surface ...
BRBLE
BRBLE
Turn off heat, then add the roux block to the pot.
Turn the heat on again, and once the curry thickens ...
STEAM

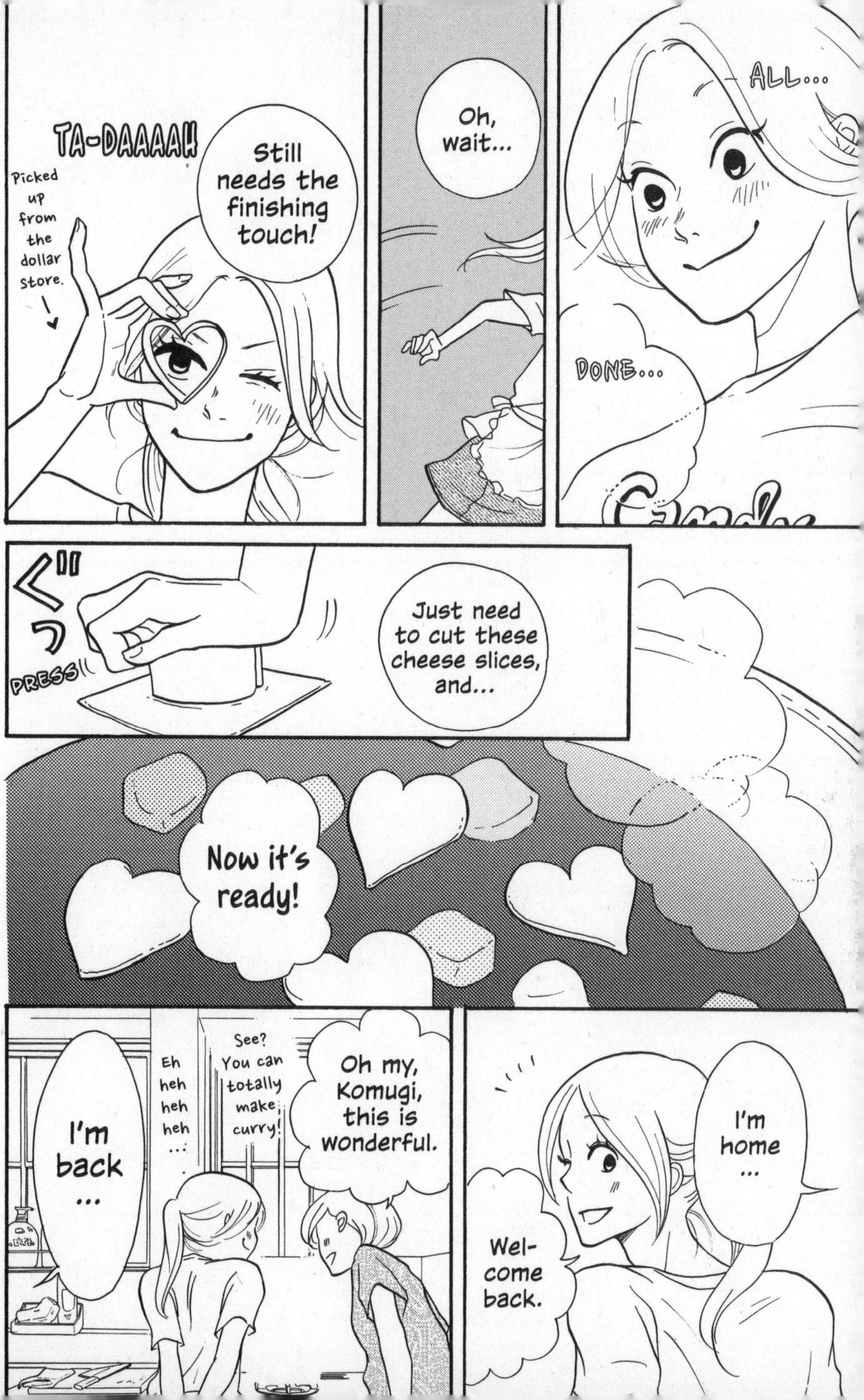
ALL...
DONE...
Oh, wait...
Still needs the finishing touch!
TA-DAAAAH
Picked up from the dollar store.
Just need to cut these cheese slices, and...
ぐっ
PRESS
Now it's ready!
I'm home...
Wel-come back.
Oh my, Komugi, this is wonderful.
See? You can totally make curry!
Eh heh heh heh...
I'm back...

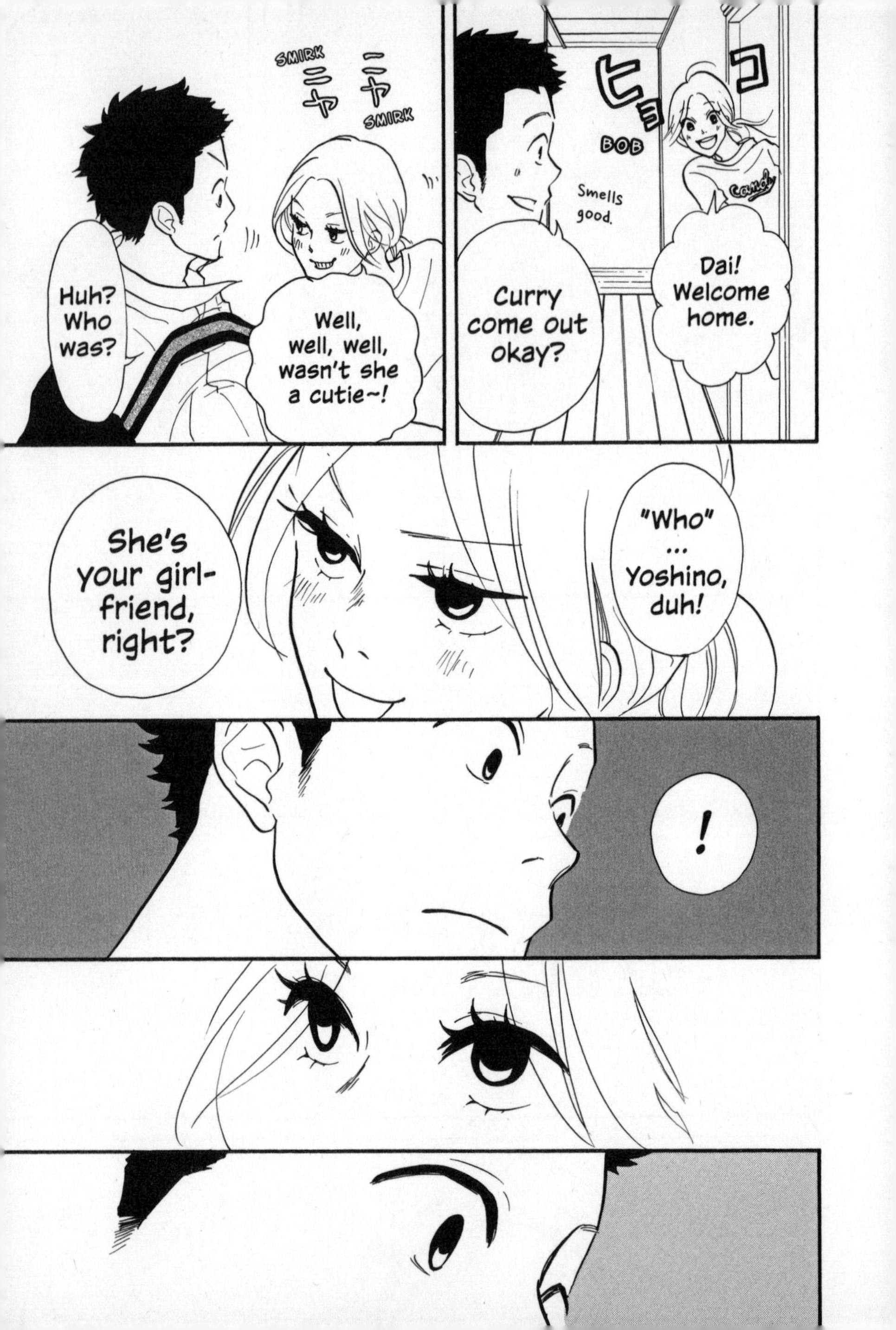
ヒョコ
BOB
Smells good.
Dai! Welcome home.
Curry come out okay?
SMIRK
ニヤニヤ
SMIRK
Well, well, well, wasn't she a cutie~!
Huh? Who was?
"Who" ... Yoshino, duh!
She's your girl-friend, right?
!

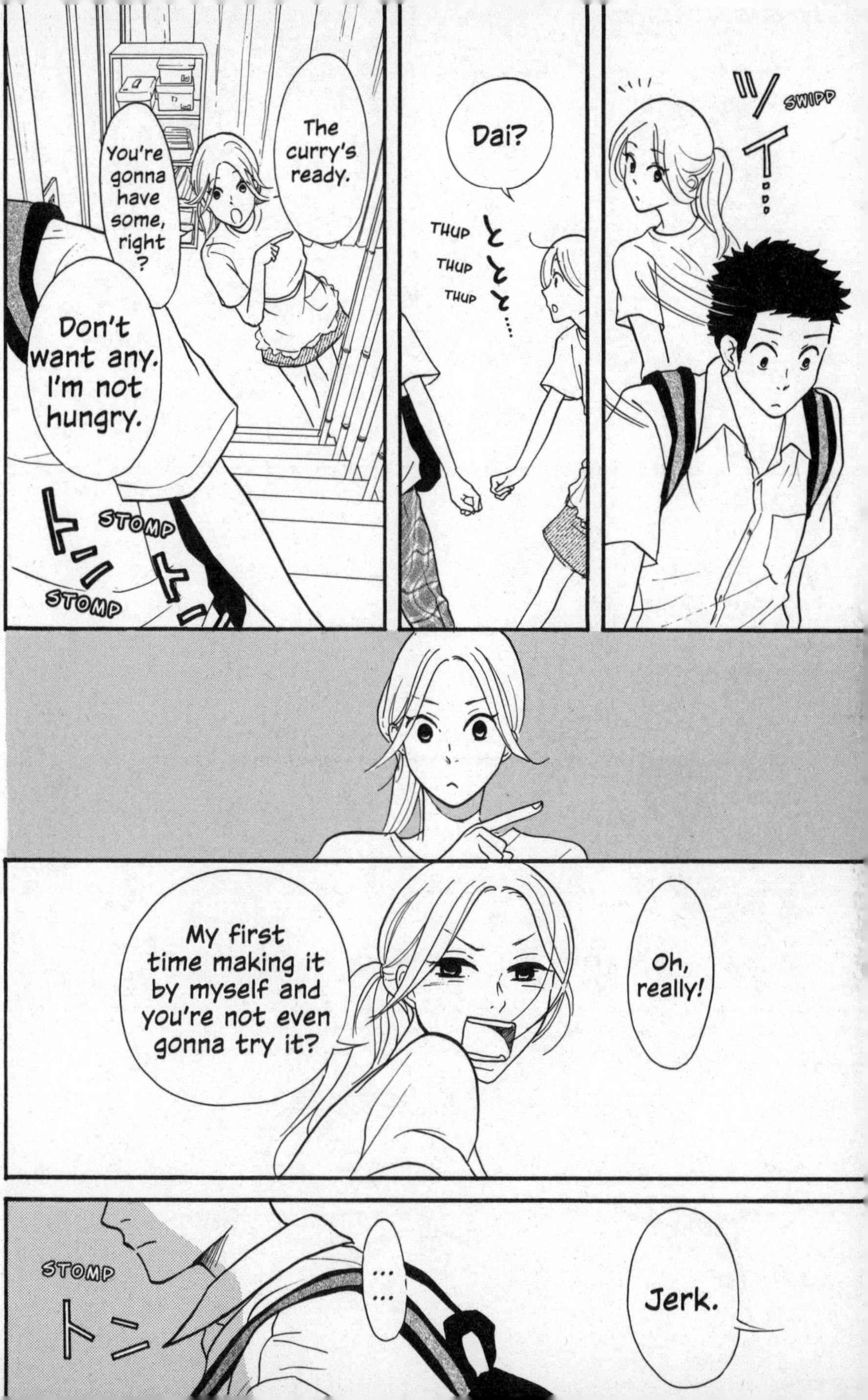
SWIPP
Dai?
THUP
THUP
THUP
The curry's ready.
You're gonna have some, right?
Don't want any. I'm not hungry.
STOMP
STOMP
Oh, really!
My first time making it by myself and you're not even gonna try it?
Jerk.
……
……
STOMP

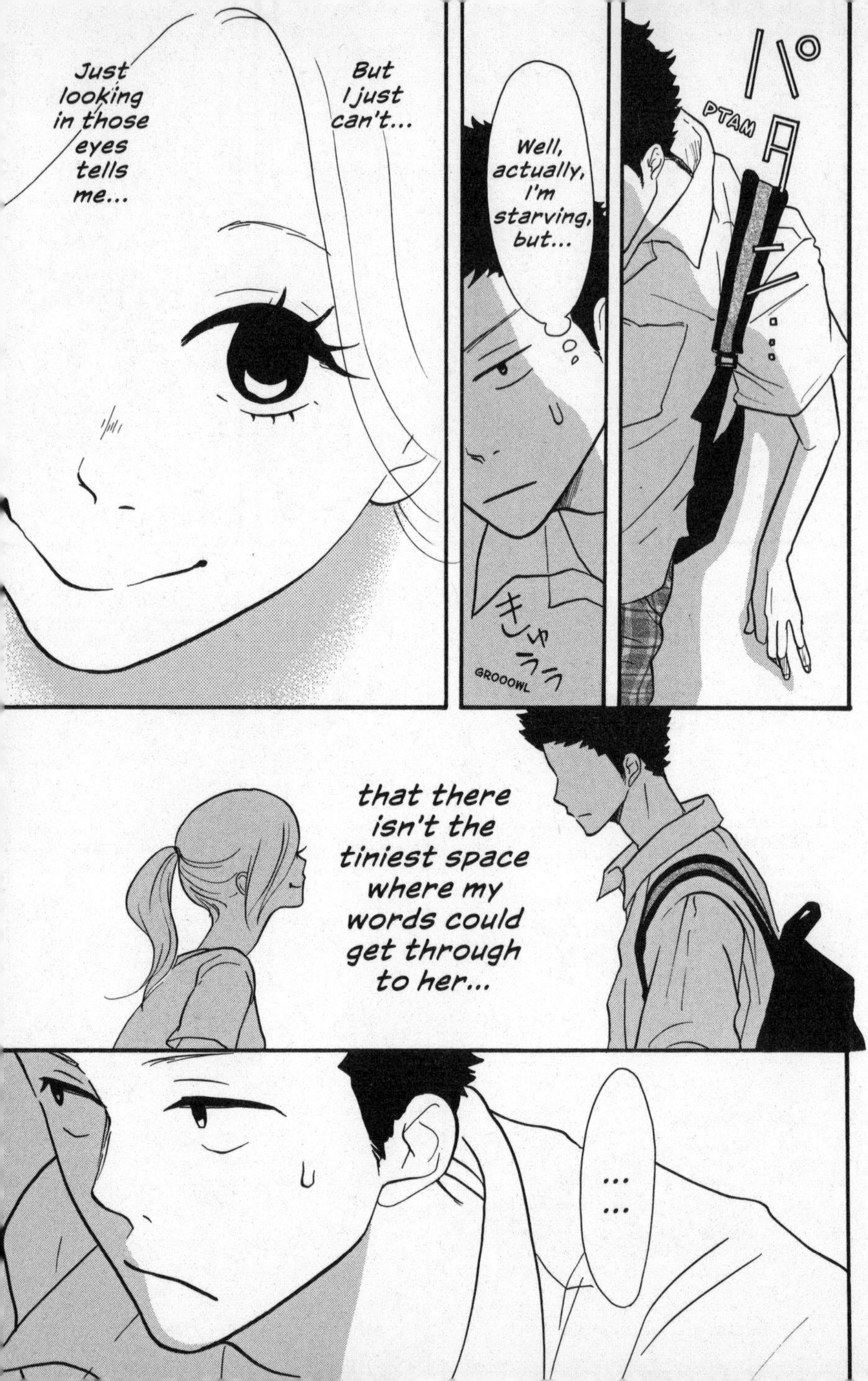

PTAM
Well, actually, I'm starving, but...
GROOOWL
But I just can't...
Just looking in those eyes tells me...
that there isn't the tiniest space where my words could get through to her...
... ...

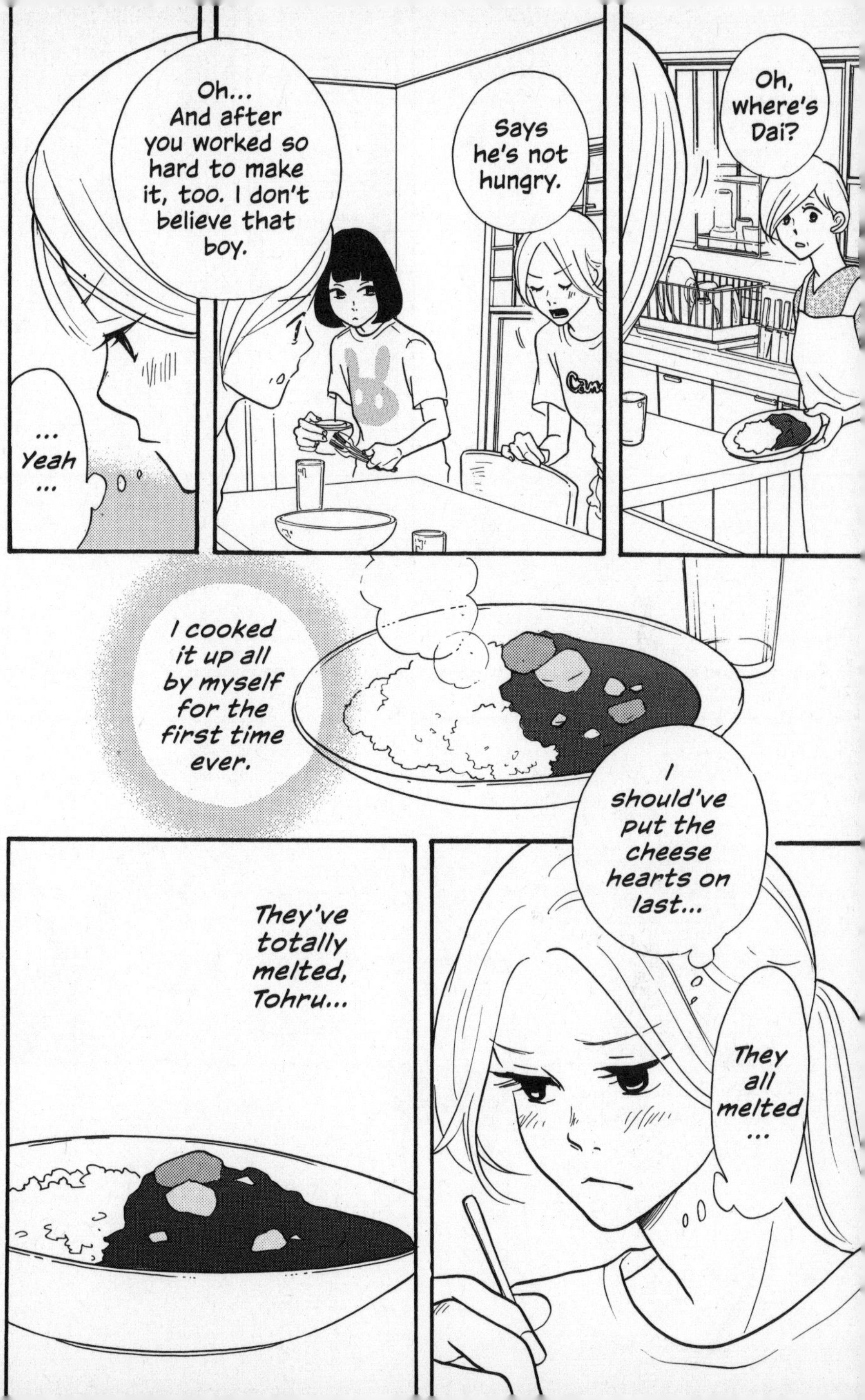
Oh, where's Dai?
Says he's not hungry.
Oh... And after you worked so hard to make it, too. I don't believe that boy.
...Yeah...
I cooked it up all by myself for the first time ever.
I should've put the cheese hearts on last...
They all melted...
They've totally melted, Tohru...

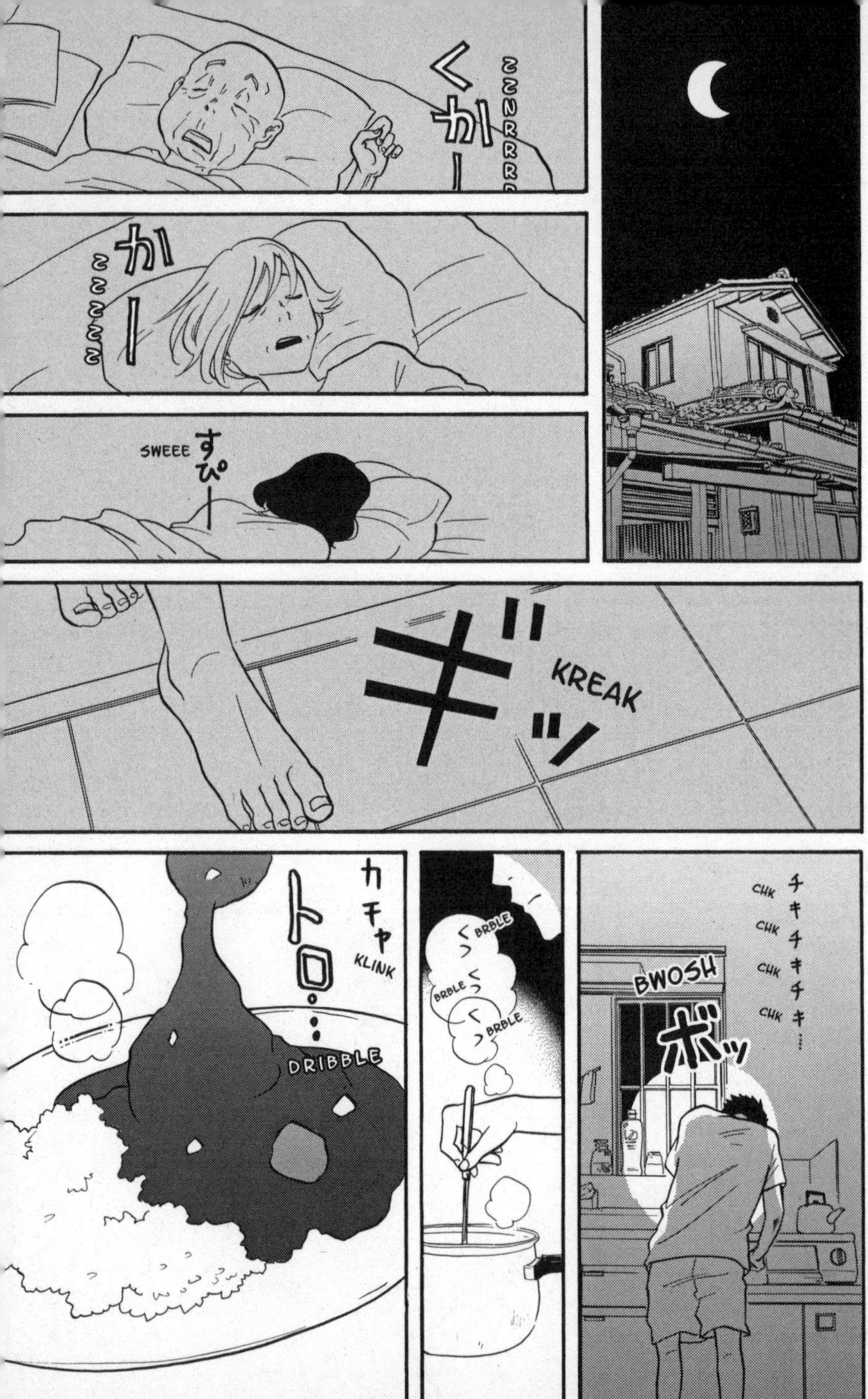

くかー
ZZZNRRRR
かー
zzzzz
すぴー
SWEEE
ギッ
KREAK
チキチキチキ…
CHK CHK CHK CHK
ボッ
BWOSH
くつくつくつ
BRBLE BRBLE BRBLE
カチャ
KLINK
トロ…
DRIBBLE

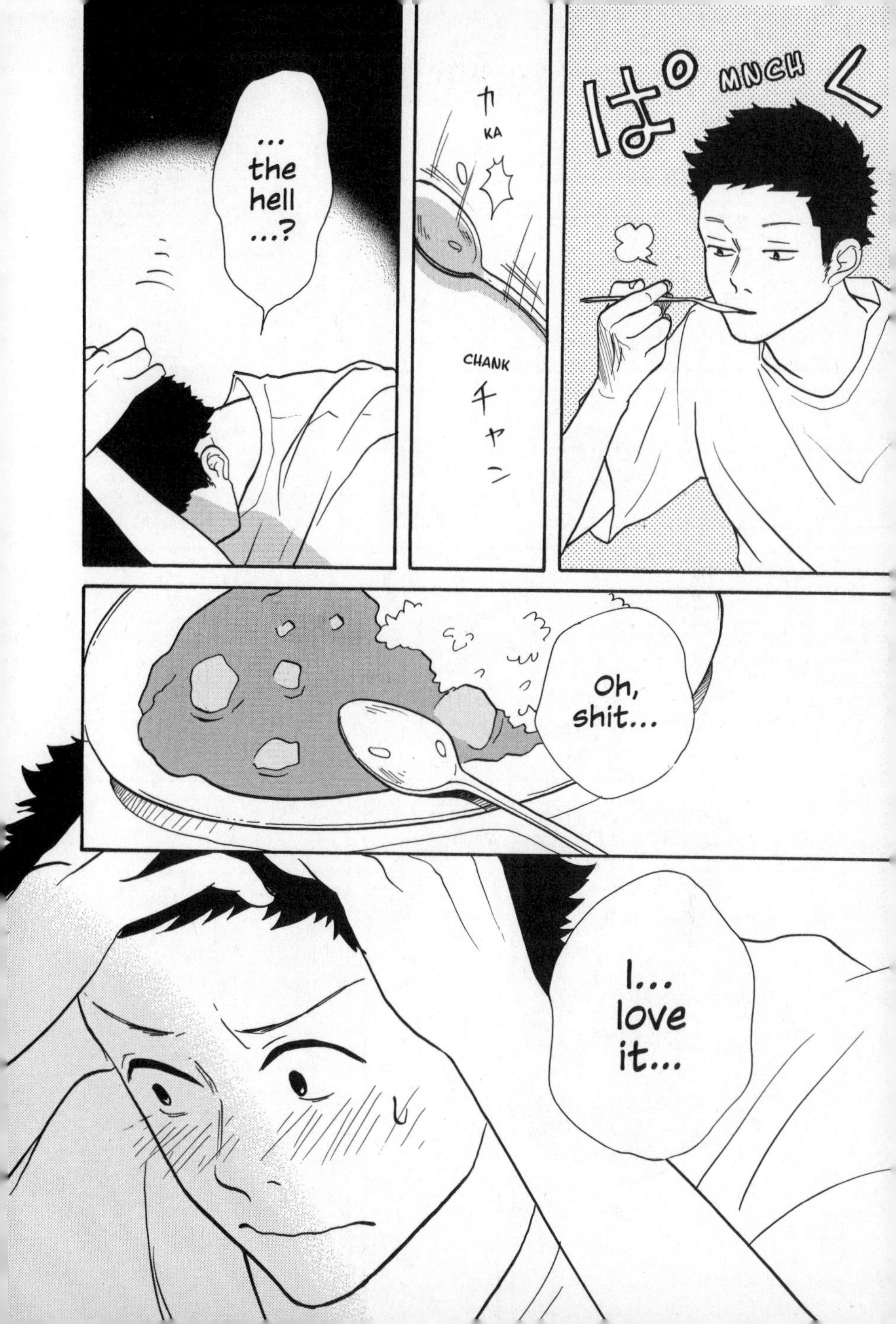

MNCH
カ
KA
CHANK
チャン
... the hell ...?
Oh, shit...
I... love it...

16 I WANT TO HOLD HANDS

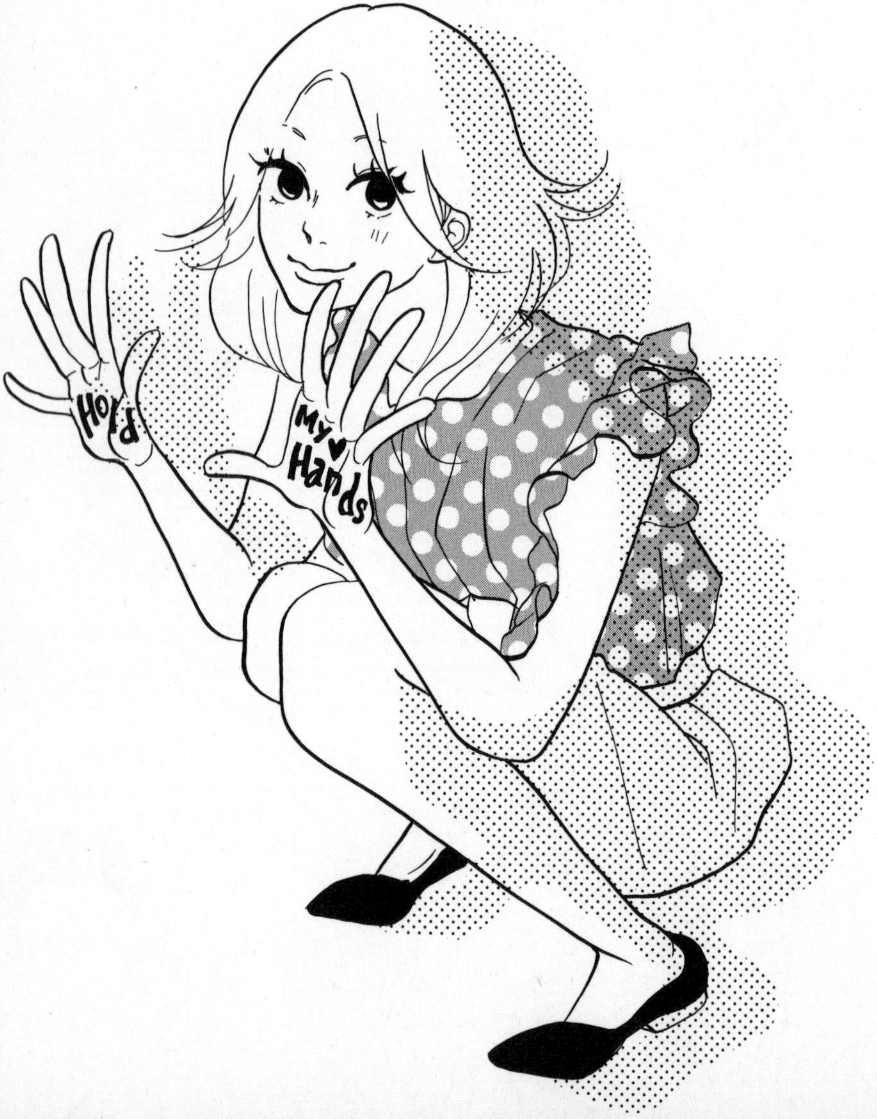
Hold
My♥ Hands

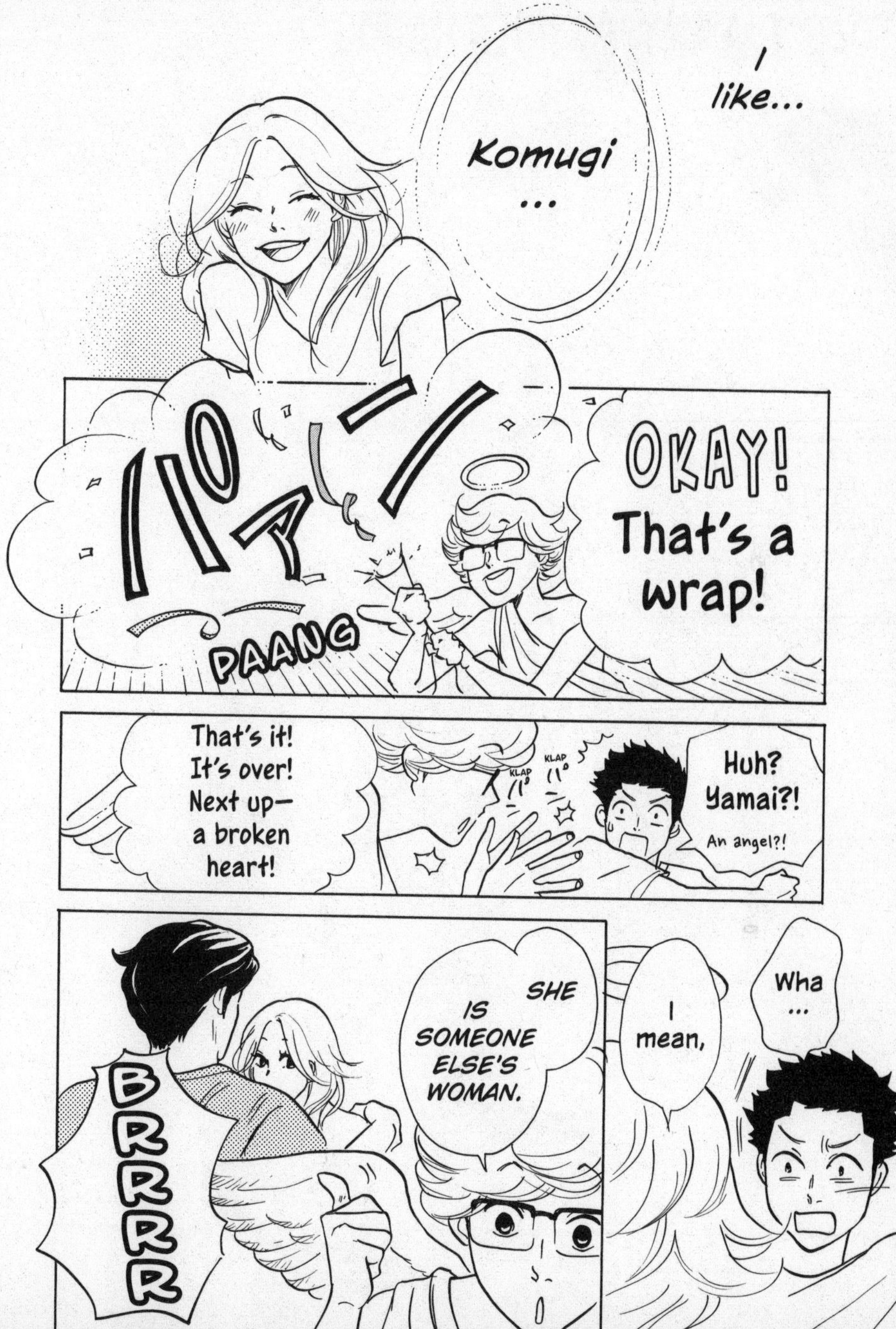
I like...
Komugi ...
OKAY! That's a wrap!
PAANG
Huh? Yamai?!
An angel?!
KLAP
KLAP
That's it! It's over! Next up—a broken heart!
Wha ...
I mean,
SHE IS SOMEONE ELSE'S WOMAN.
BRRRR

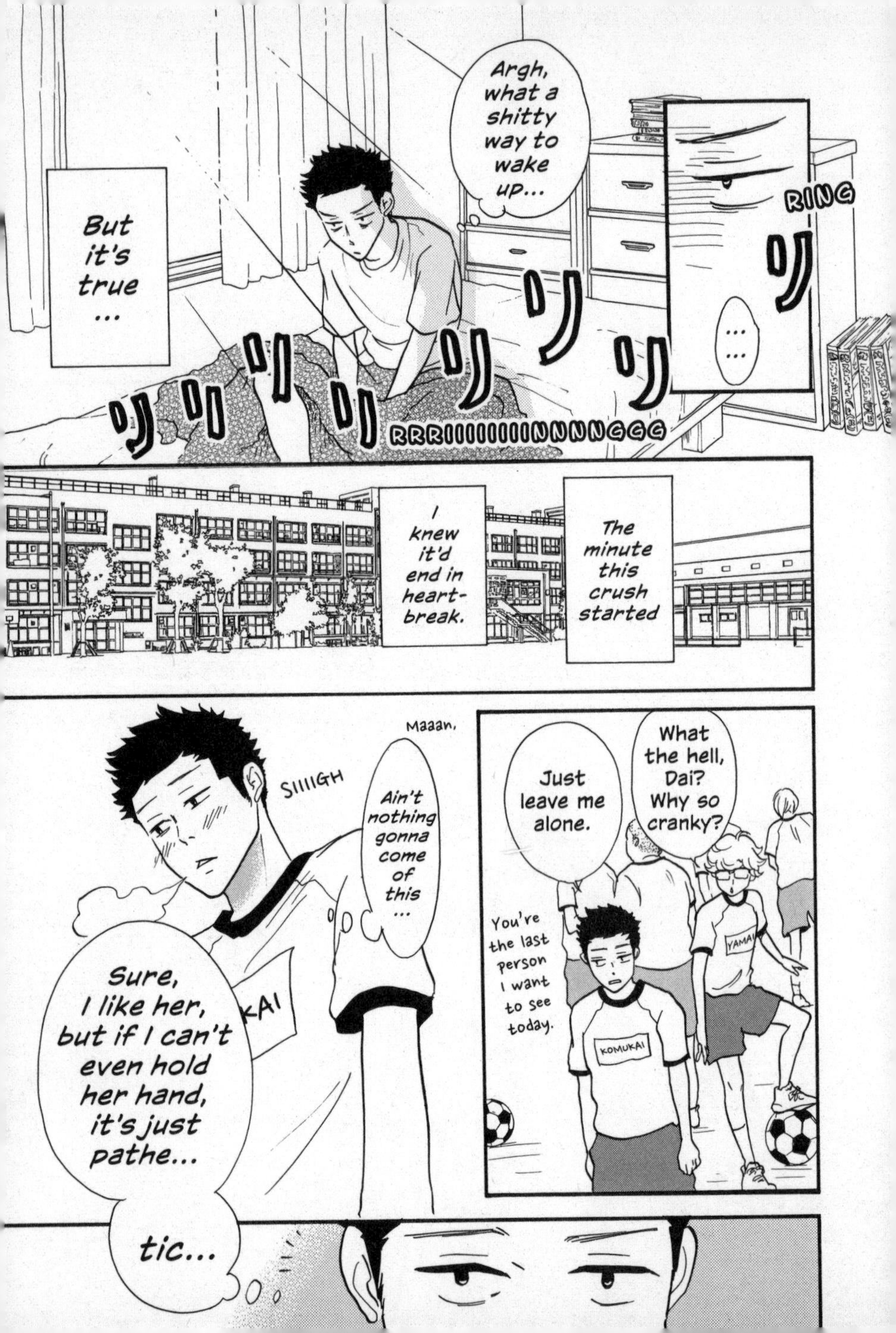
RING
...
...
Argh, what a shitty way to wake up...
RRRIIIIIIIIINNNNGGG
But it's true...
The minute this crush started
I knew it'd end in heart-break.
What the hell, Dai? Why so cranky?
Just leave me alone.
You're the last person I want to see today.
YAMAI
KOMUKAI
Maaan,
Ain't nothing gonna come of this...
SIIIIGH
KAI
Sure, I like her, but if I can't even hold her hand, it's just pathe...
tic...

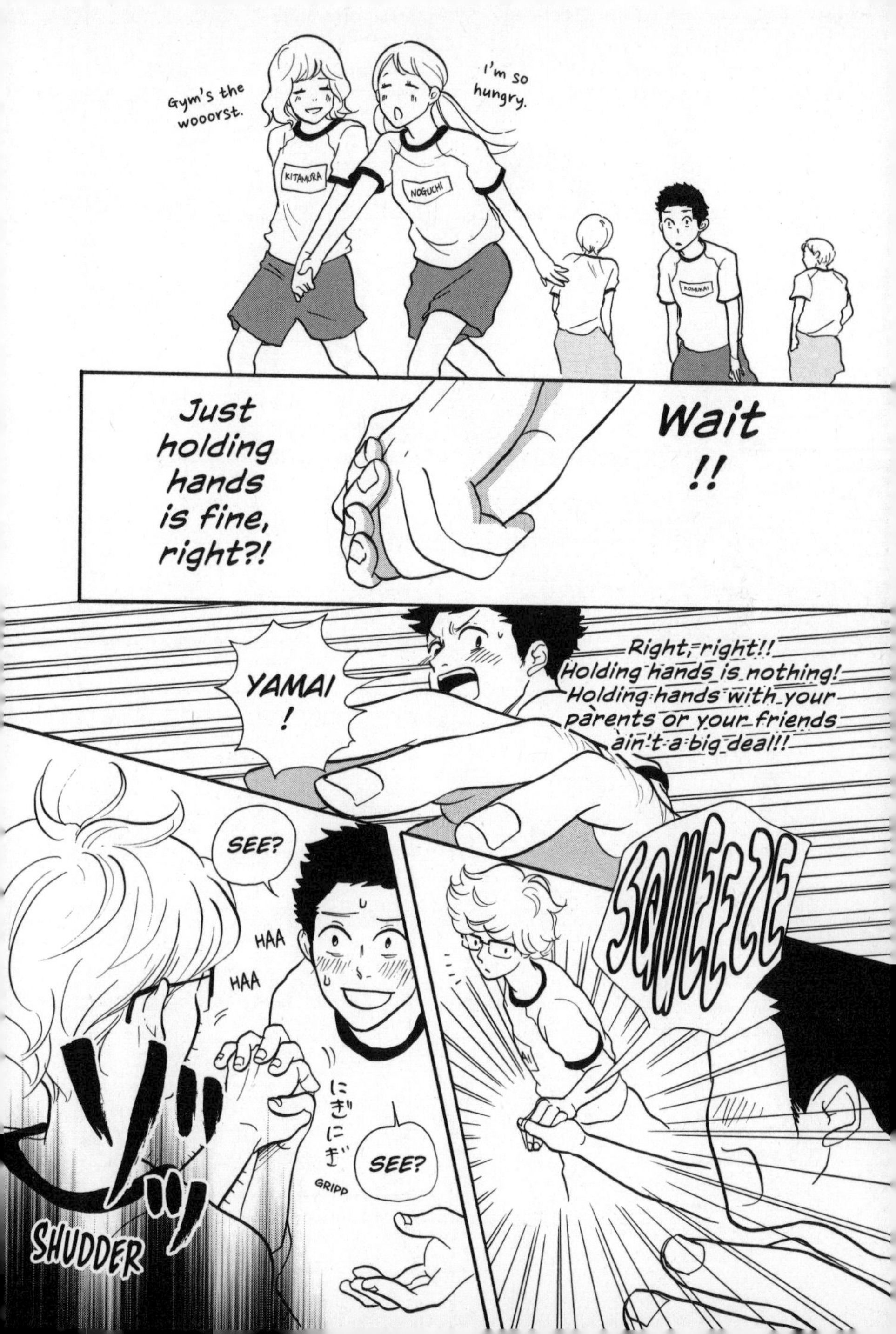
I'm so hungry.
Gym's the wooorst.
KITAMURA
NOGUCHI
KOMUKAI
Wait !!
Just holding hands is fine, right?!
Right, right!! Holding hands is nothing! Holding hands with your parents or your friends ain't a big deal!!
YAMAI !
SQUEEZE
SEE?
HAA
HAA
にぎにぎ
GRIPP
SEE?
SHUDDER

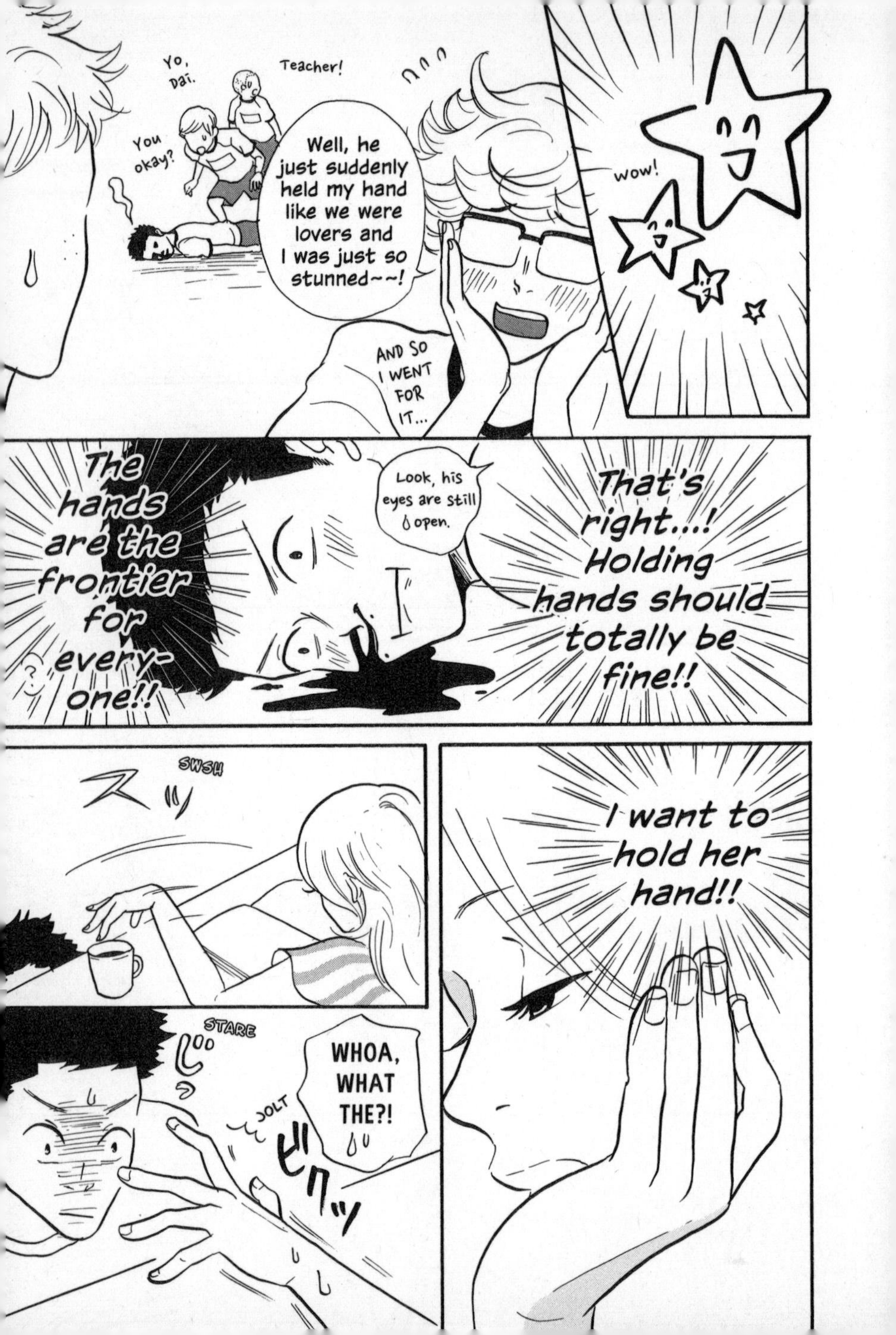
WOW!
Well, he just suddenly held my hand like we were lovers and I was just so stunned~~!
AND SO I WENT FOR IT...
Teacher!
Yo, Dai.
You okay?
That's right...! Holding hands should totally be fine!!
Look, his eyes are still open.
The hands are the frontier for every-one!!
I want to hold her hand!!
SWSH
STARE
WHOA, WHAT THE?!
JOLT

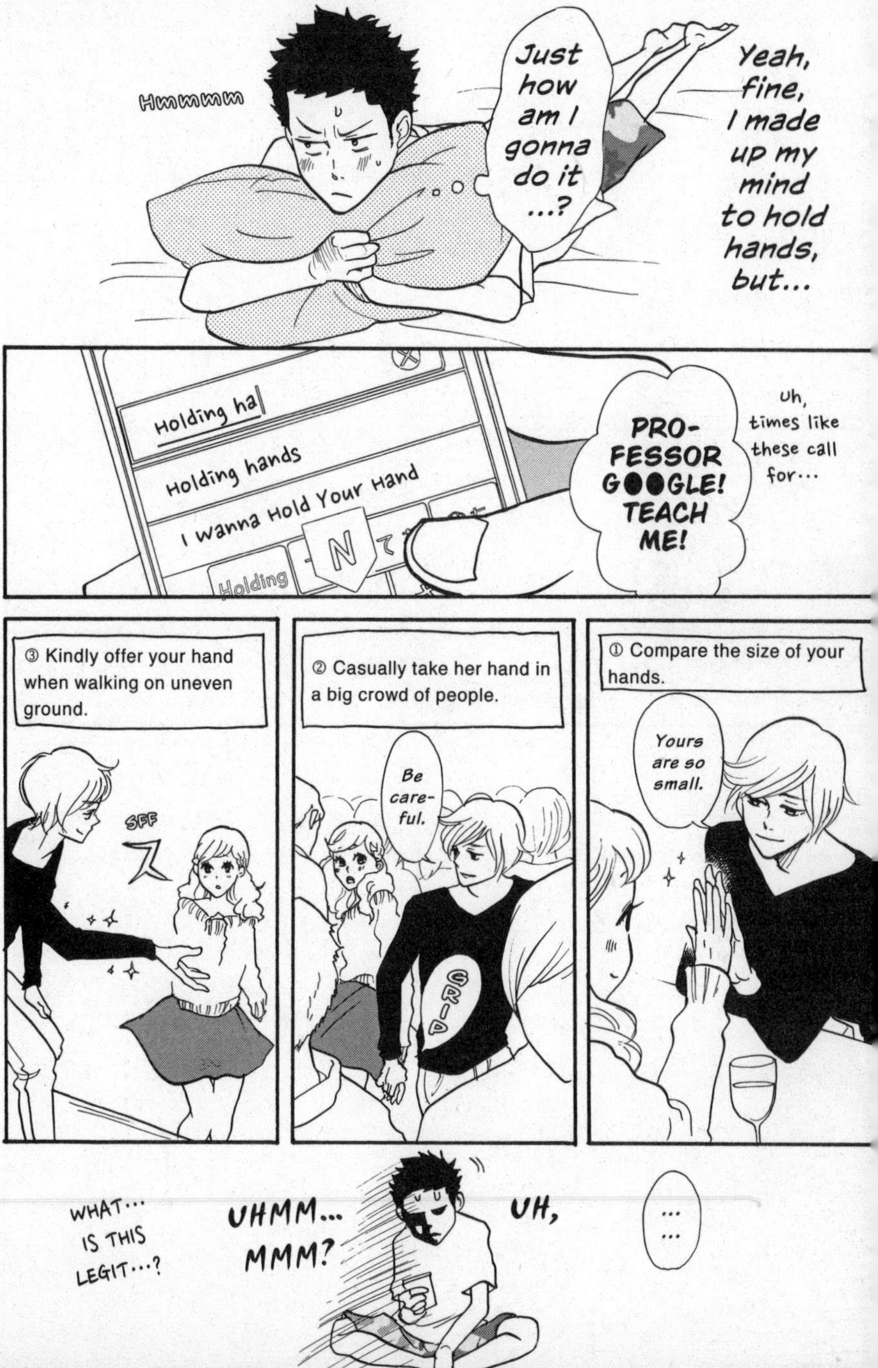
Yeah, fine, I made up my mind to hold hands, but...
Just how am I gonna do it ...?
Hmmmm
Uh, times like these call for...
PRO-FESSOR GOOGLE! TEACH ME!
Holding ha
Holding hands
I wanna Hold Your Hand
N
Holding
① Compare the size of your hands.
Yours are so small.
② Casually take her hand in a big crowd of people.
Be care-ful.
GRIP
③ Kindly offer your hand when walking on uneven ground.
SFF
ス
……
UH,
UHMM... MMM?
WHAT... IS THIS LEGIT...?

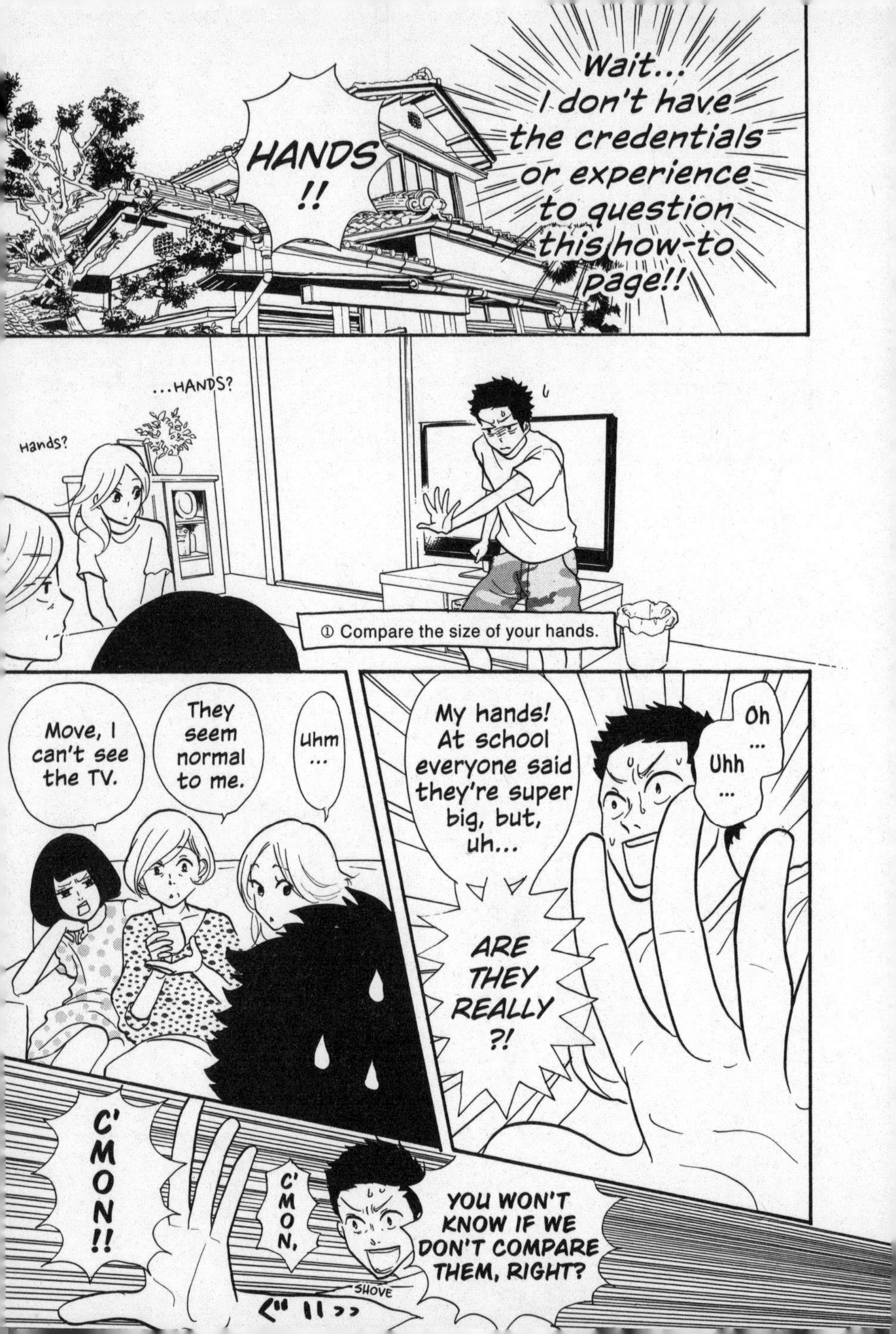
Wait... I don't have the credentials or experience to question this how-to page!!
HANDS !!
...HANDS?
Hands?
① Compare the size of your hands.
Oh ... Uhh ...
My hands! At school everyone said they're super big, but, uh...
ARE THEY REALLY ?!
Uhm ...
They seem normal to me.
Move, I can't see the TV.
YOU WON'T KNOW IF WE DON'T COMPARE THEM, RIGHT?
C'MON,
C'MON!!
SHOVE

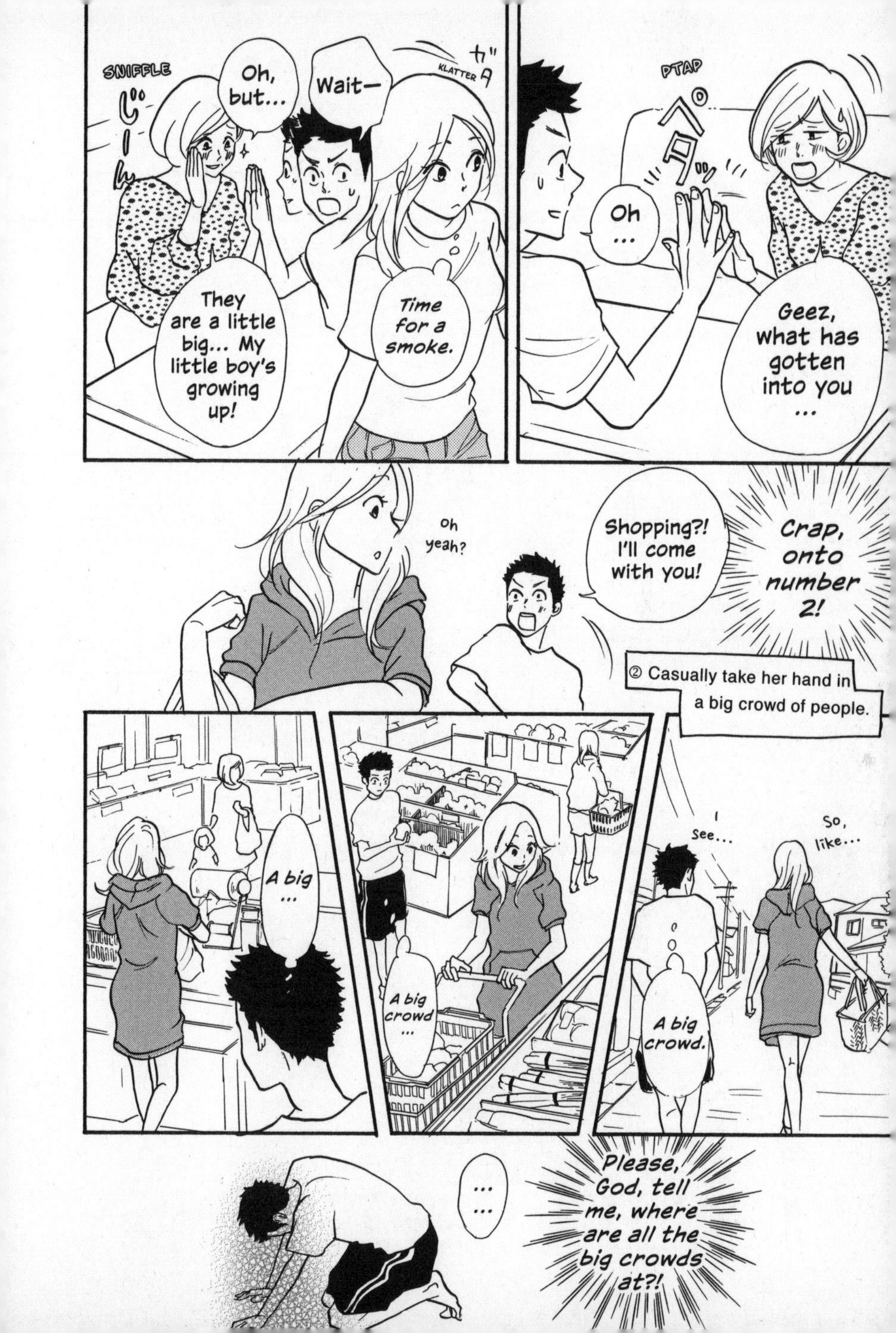
PTAP
Oh ...
Geez, what has gotten into you ...
KLATTER
Wait—
Oh, but...
SNIFFLE
Time for a smoke.
They are a little big... My little boy's growing up!
Crap, onto number 2!
② Casually take her hand in a big crowd of people.
Shopping?! I'll come with you!
Oh yeah?
So, like...
I see...
A big crowd.
A big crowd ...
A big ...
Please, God, tell me, where are all the big crowds at?!
... ...

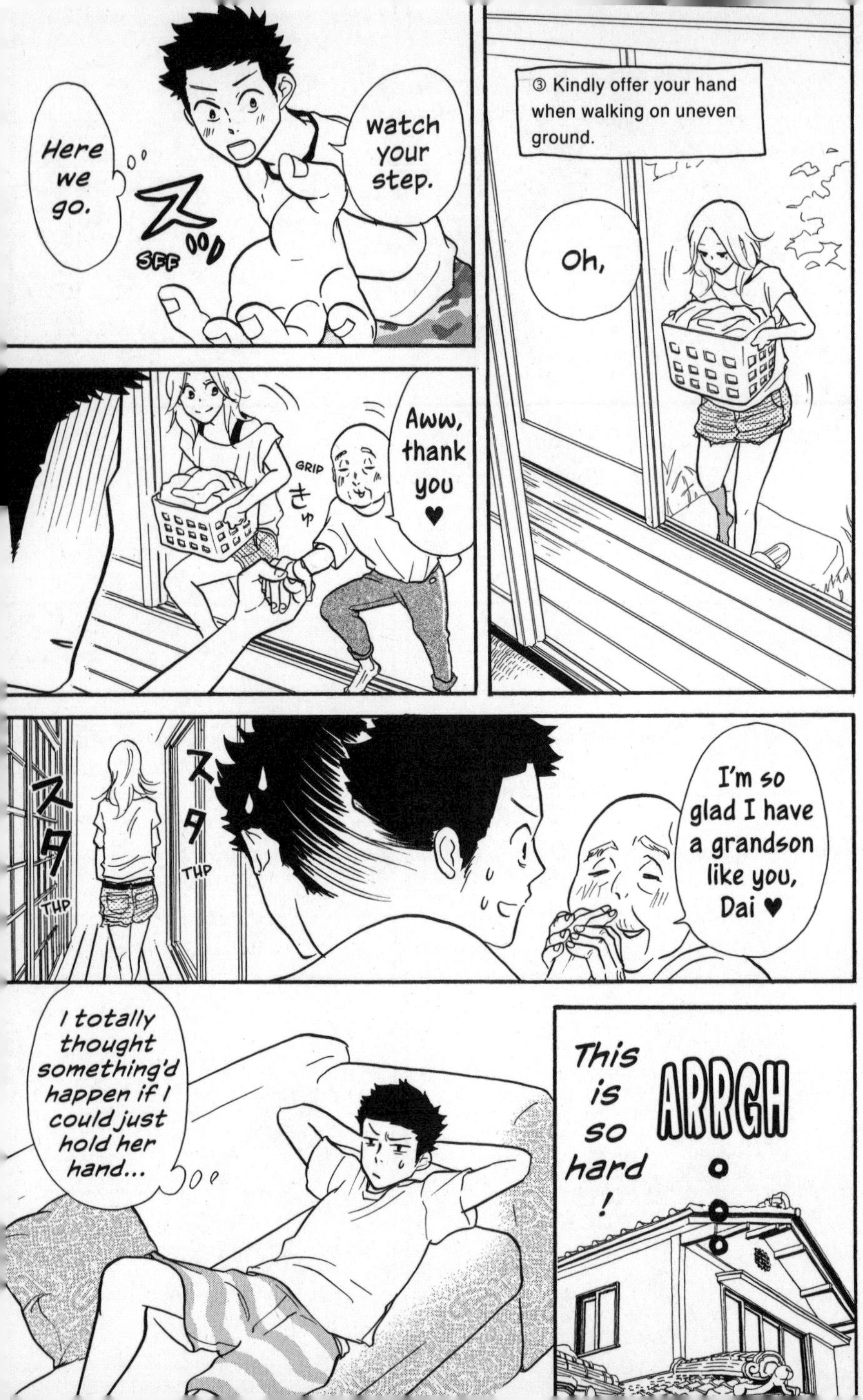
③ Kindly offer your hand when walking on uneven ground.
Oh,
watch your step.
Here we go.
ス
SFF
Aww, thank you ♥
GRIP
きゅ
I'm so glad I have a grandson like you, Dai ♥
スタ
THP
スタ
THP
This is so hard!
ARRGH
I totally thought something'd happen if I could just hold her hand...

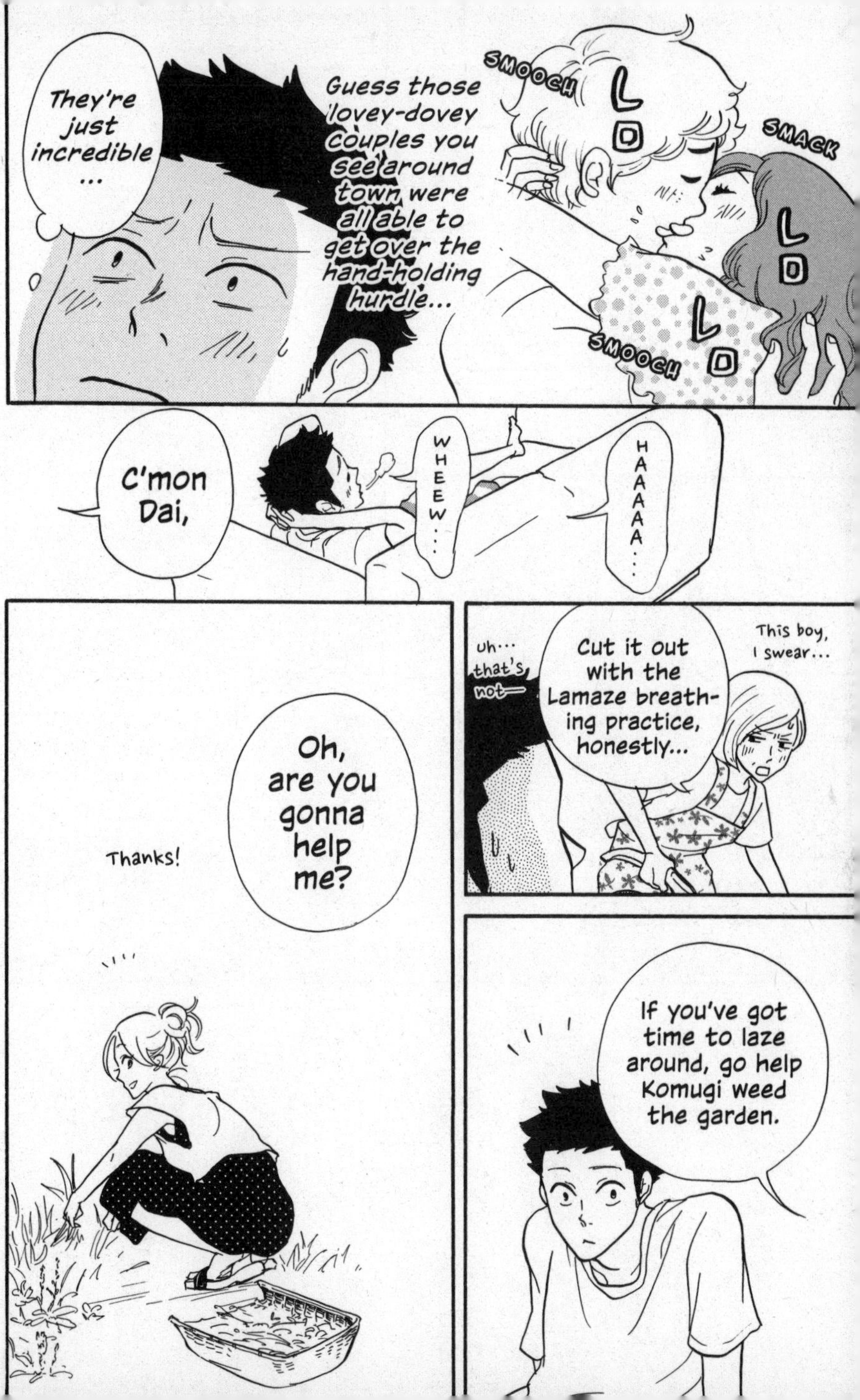

SMACK
LD
LD
SMOOCH
LD
LD
SMOOCH
LD
Guess those lovey-dovey couples you see around town were all able to get over the hand-holding hurdle...
They're just incredible...
HAAAAA...
WHEEEW...
C'mon Dai,
This boy, I swear...
Cut it out with the Lamaze breathing practice, honestly...
uh... that's not—
If you've got time to laze around, go help Komugi weed the garden.
Oh, are you gonna help me?
Thanks!

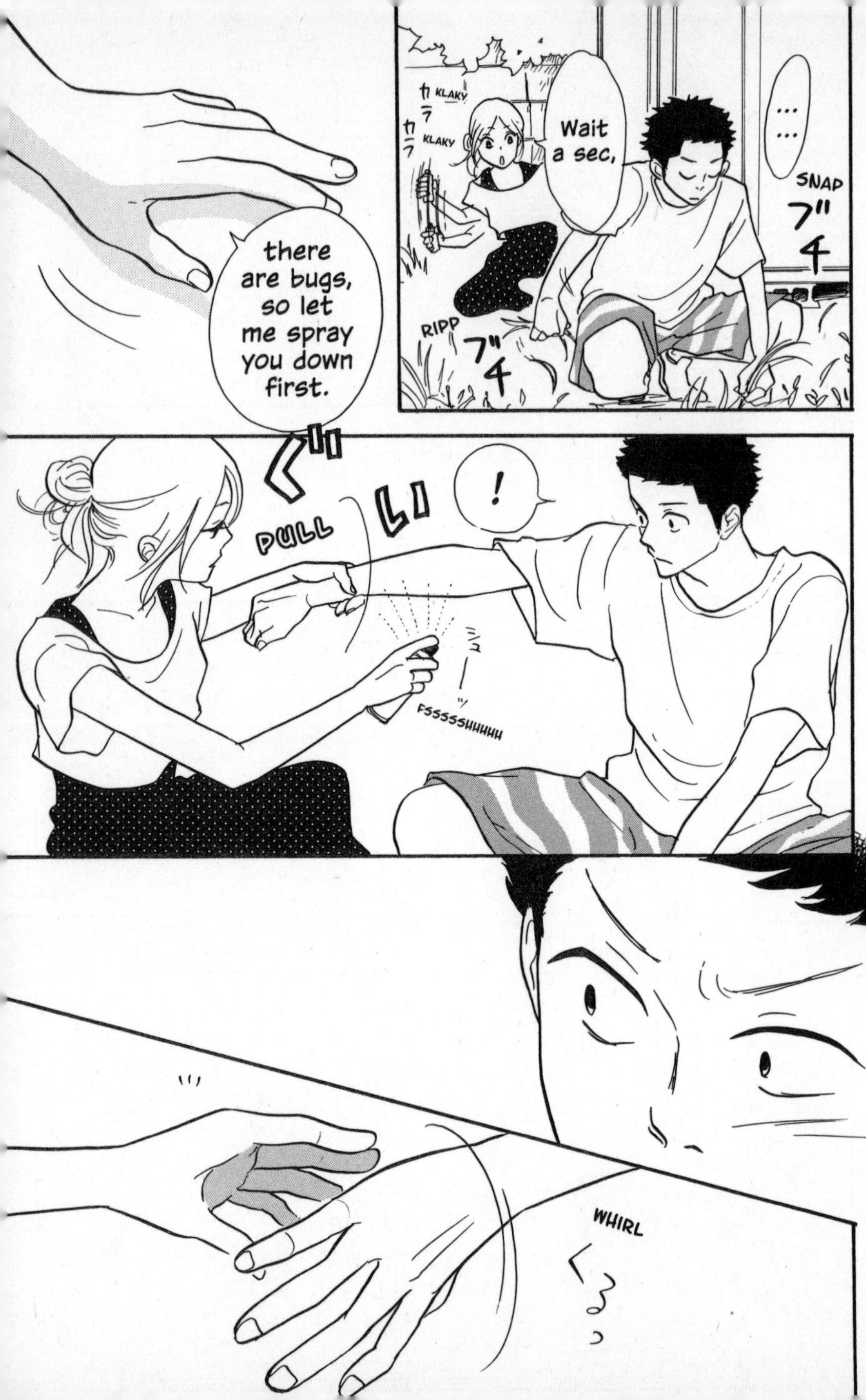
......
......
SNAP
Wait a sec,
KLAKY
KLAKY
RIPP
there are bugs, so let me spray you down first.
!
PULL
FSSSSSHHHHH
WHIRL

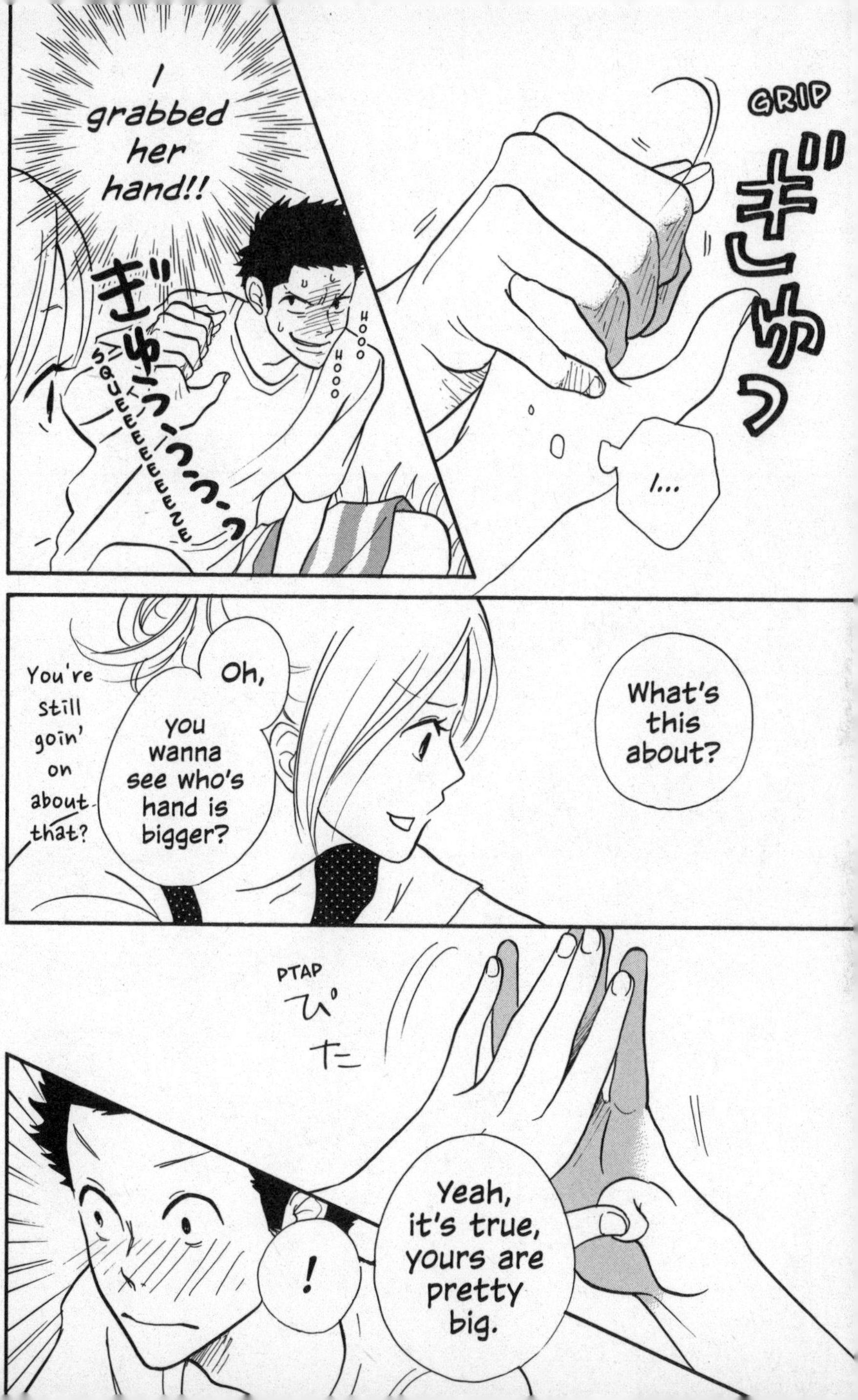
GRIP
ぎしゅっ
I...
I grabbed her hand!!
ぎゅーっ
SQUEEEEEEEEEZE
HOOO
HOOO
What's this about?
Oh, you wanna see who's hand is bigger?
You're still goin' on about that?
PTAP
ぴた
Yeah, it's true, yours are pretty big.
!

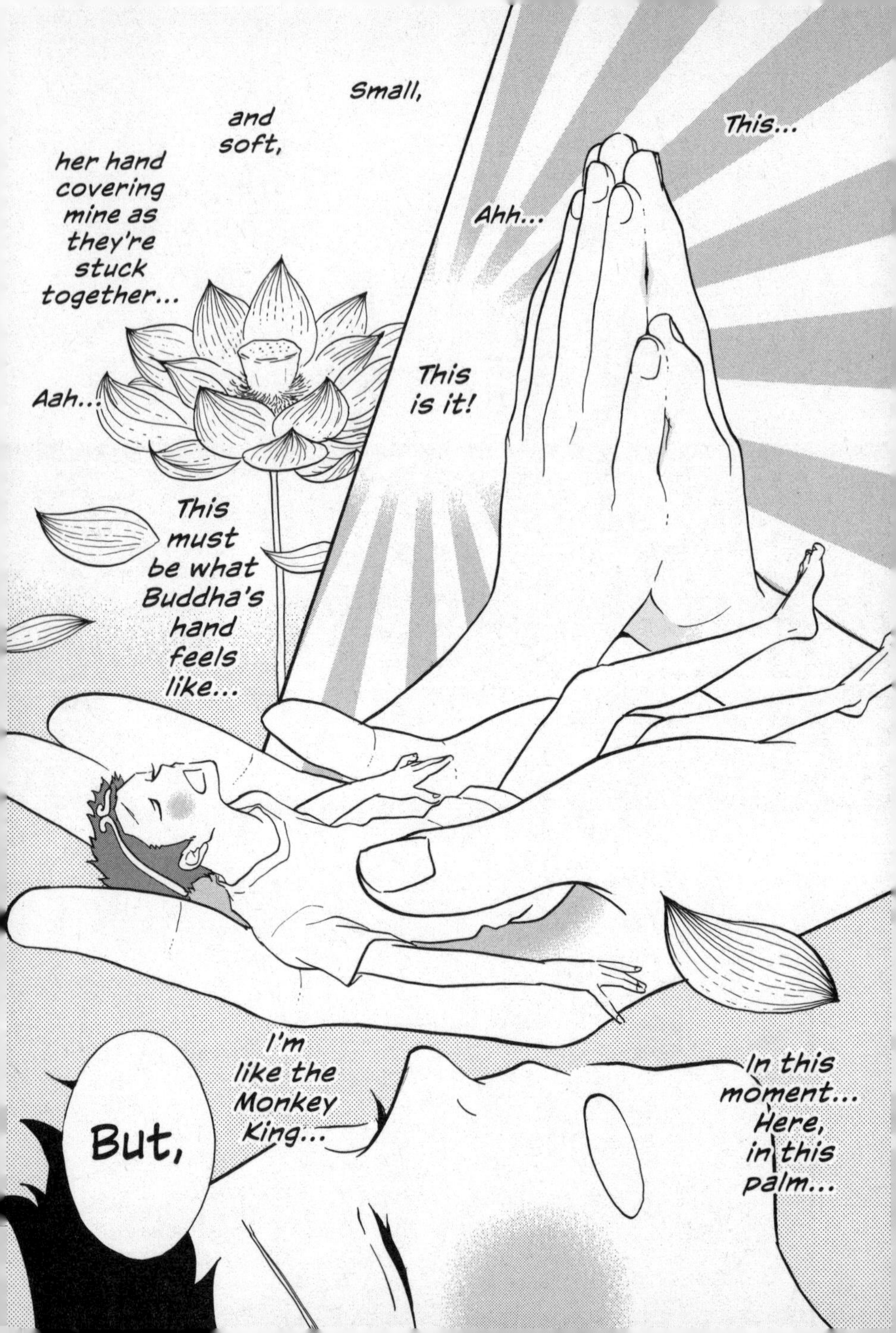
This...
Ahh...
Small,
and soft,
her hand covering mine as they're stuck together...
This is it!
Aah...
This must be what Buddha's hand feels like...
In this moment... Here, in this palm...
I'm like the Monkey King...
But,

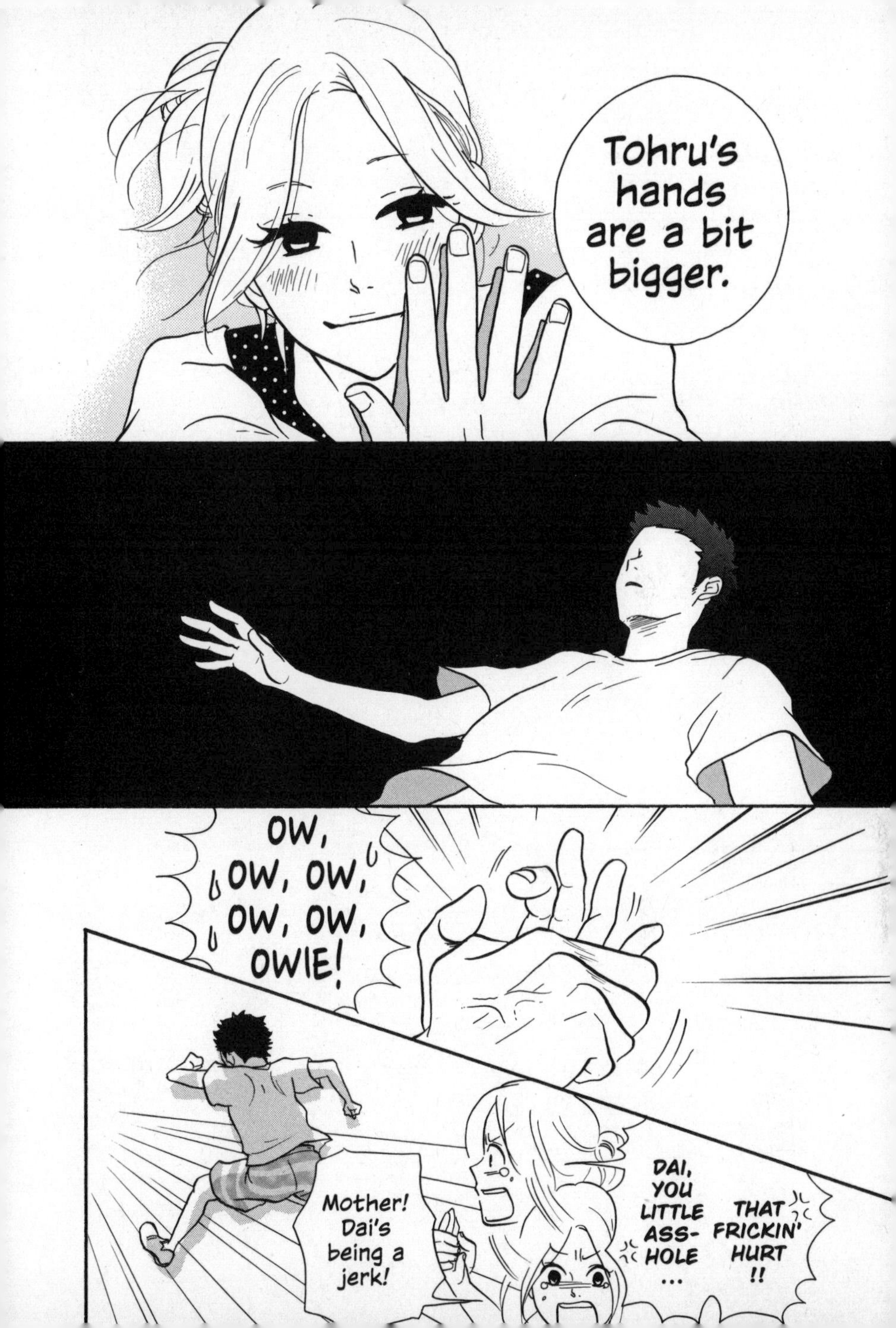
Tohru's hands are a bit bigger.
OW, OW, OW, OW, OW, OWIE!
THAT FRICKIN' HURT !!
DAI, YOU LITTLE ASS-HOLE ...
Mother! Dai's being a jerk!

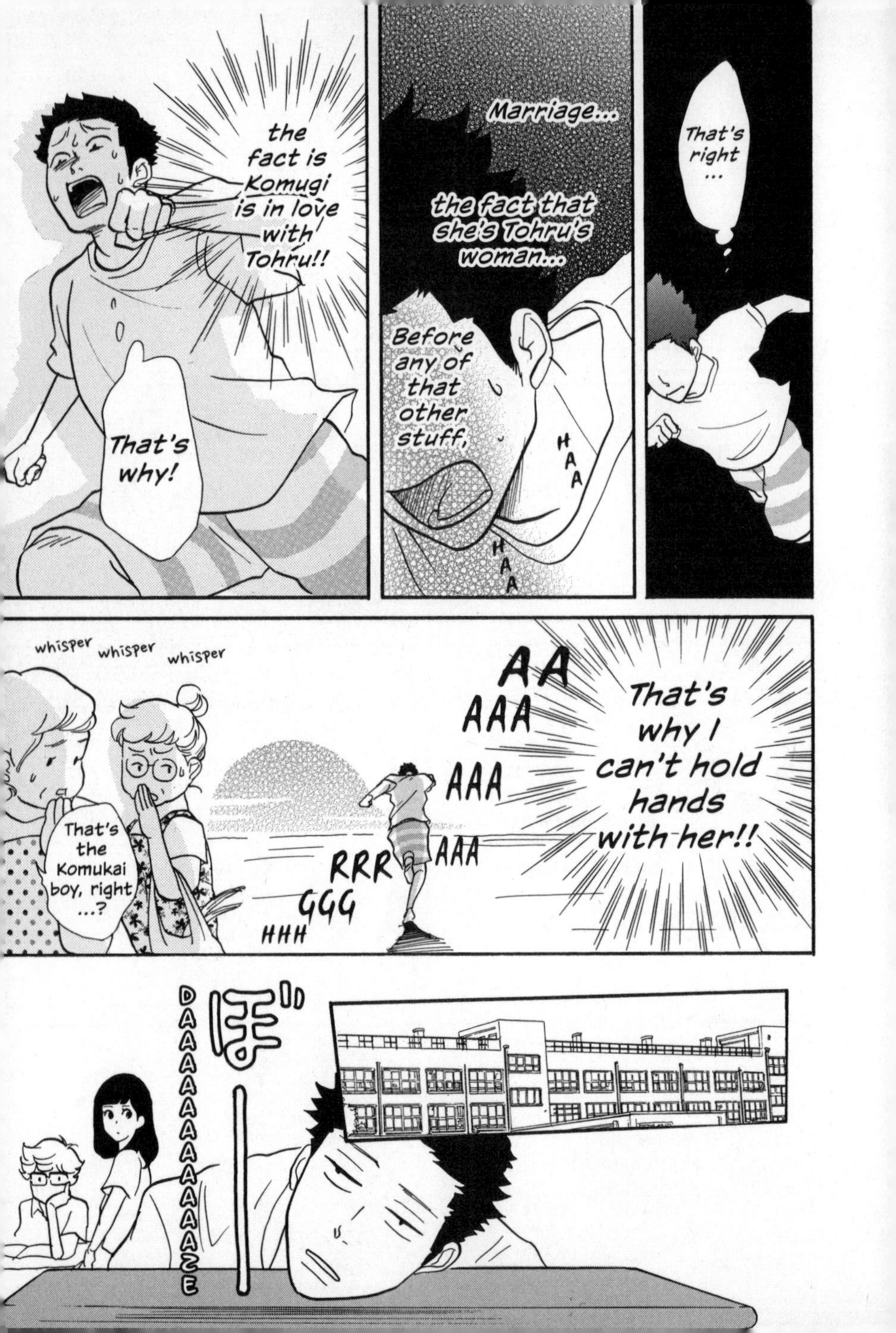
That's right...
Marriage...
the fact that she's Tohru's woman...
Before any of that other stuff,
HAA
HAA
the fact is Komugi is in love with Tohru!!
That's why!
That's why I can't hold hands with her!!
AA AAA AAA AAA
RRR GGG HHH
whisper whisper whisper
That's the Komukai boy, right...?
DAAAAAAAAAAAAAAZE

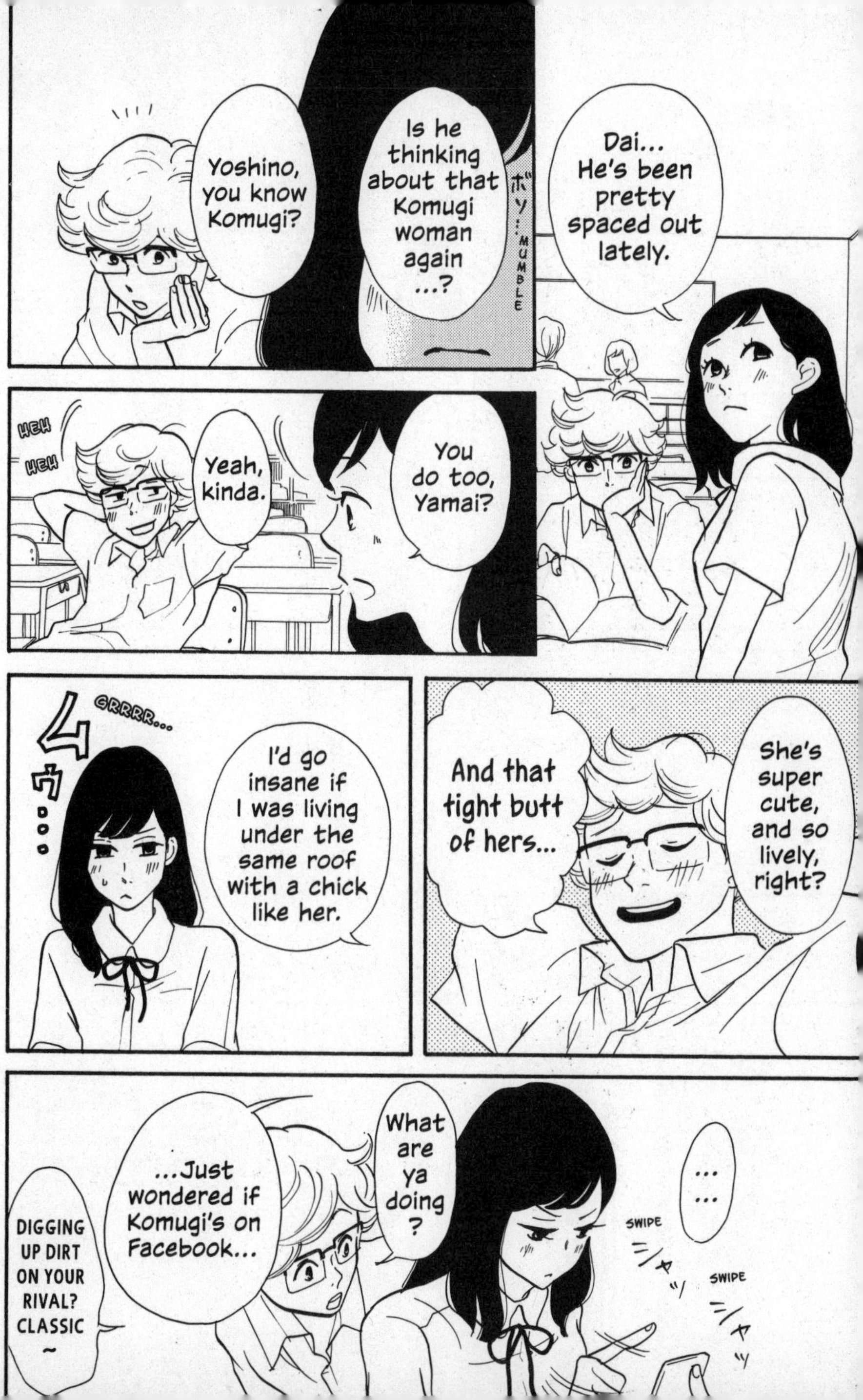
Dai... He's been pretty spaced out lately.
Is he thinking about that Komugi woman again ...?
ボソ… MUMBLE
Yoshino, you know Komugi?
You do too, Yamai?
Yeah, kinda.
HEH HEH
She's super cute, and so lively, right?
And that tight butt of hers...
I'd go insane if I was living under the same roof with a chick like her.
ムウ… GRRRR...
……
SWIPE シャッ
SWIPE シャッ
What are ya doing?
...Just wondered if Komugi's on Facebook...
DIGGING UP DIRT ON YOUR RIVAL? CLASSIC ~

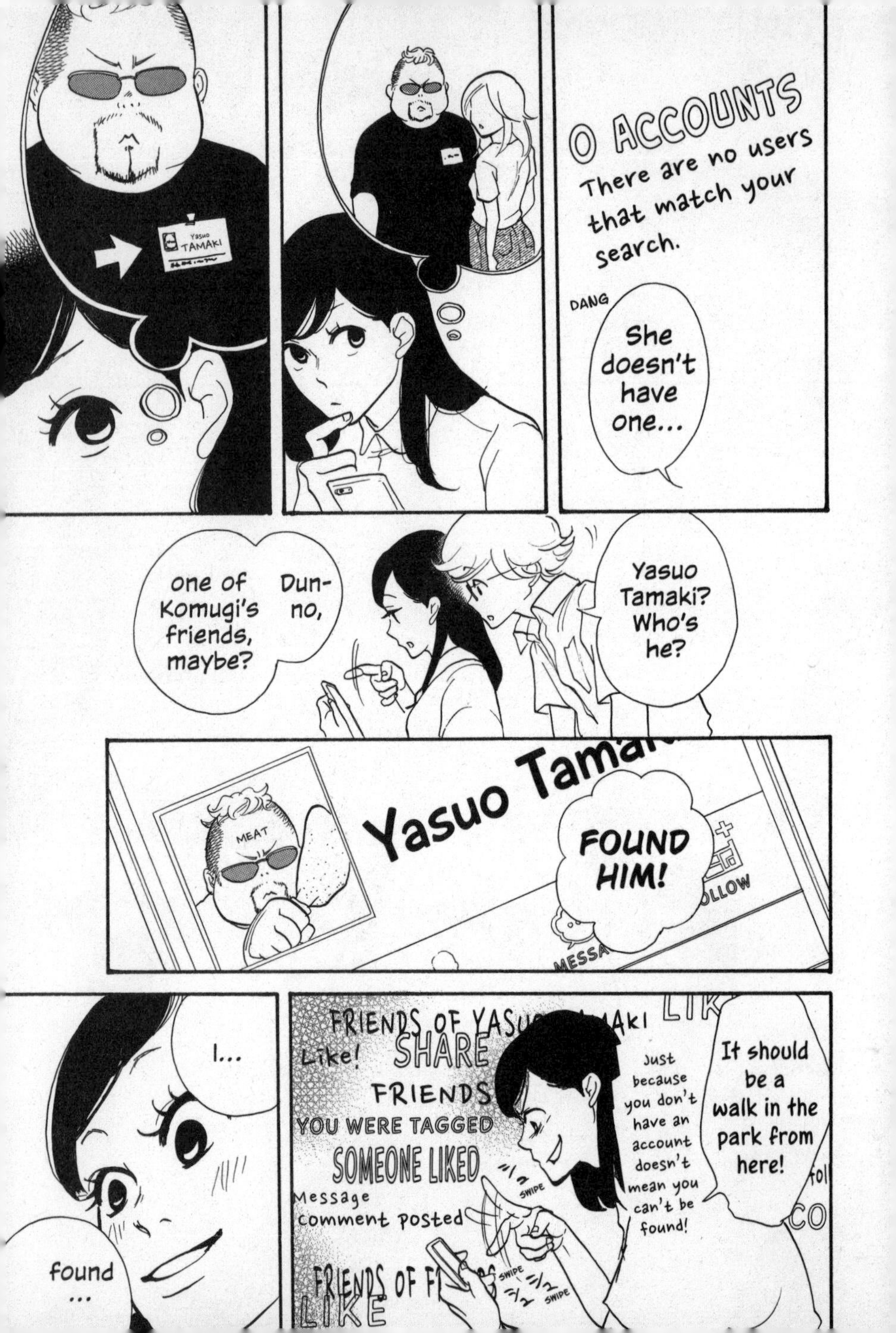
0 ACCOUNTS
There are no users that match your search.
DANG
She doesn't have one...
Yasuo TAMAKI
Yasuo Tamaki? Who's he?
Dun-no, one of Komugi's friends, maybe?
Yasuo Tama
MEAT
FOUND HIM!
It should be a walk in the park from here!
Just because you don't have an account doesn't mean you can't be found!
FRIENDS OF YASU
AKI
Like!
SHARE
FRIENDS
YOU WERE TAGGED
SOMEONE LIKED
Message
comment posted
SWIPE
LIKE
I...
found ...

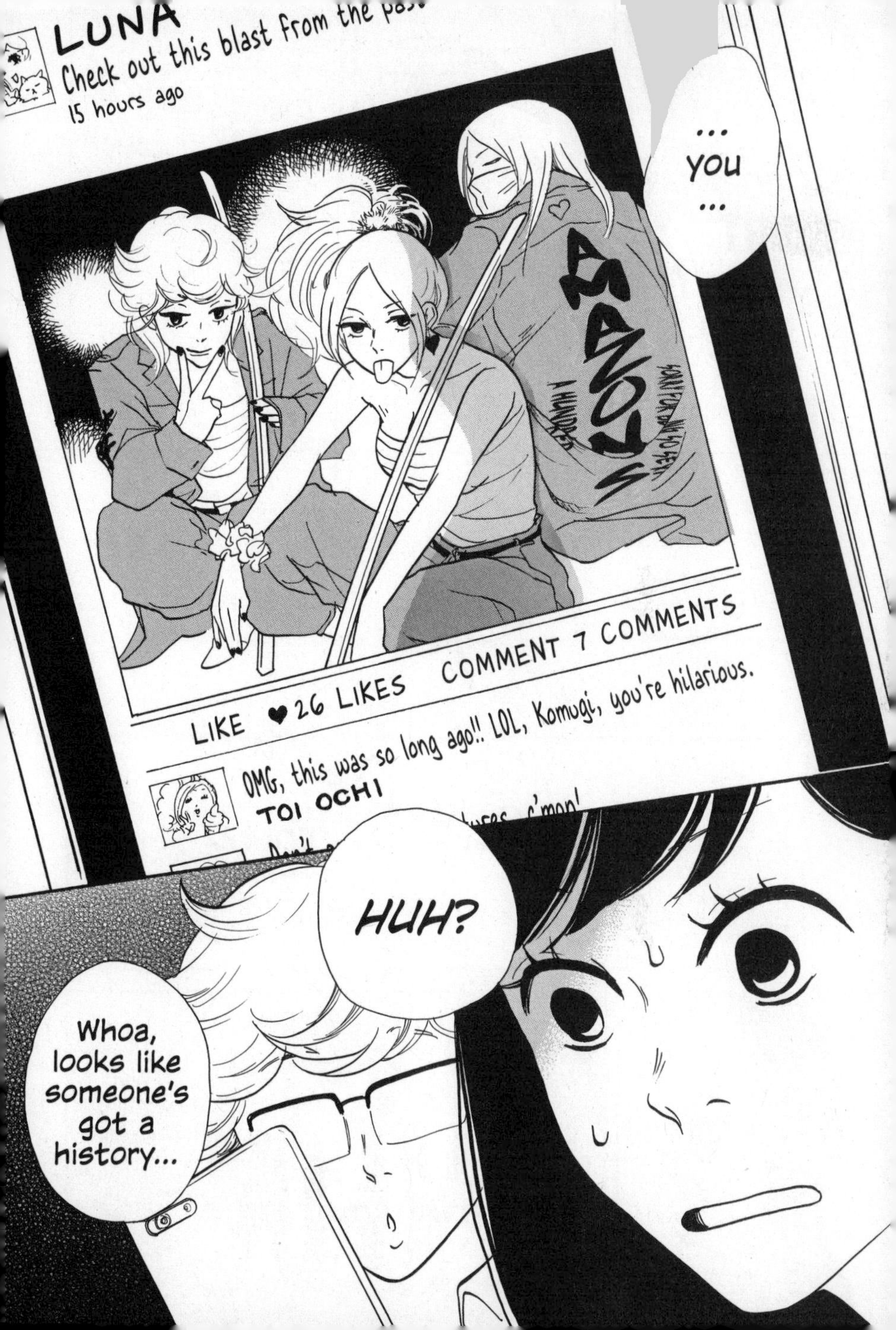
... you ...
LUNA
Check out this blast from the pa
15 hours ago
AMANOYA
LIKE ♥ 26 LIKES COMMENT 7 COMMENTS
OMG, this was so long ago!! LOL, Komugi, you're hilarious.
TOI OCHI
HUH?
Whoa, looks like someone's got a history...

17
ROCKET NIGHT

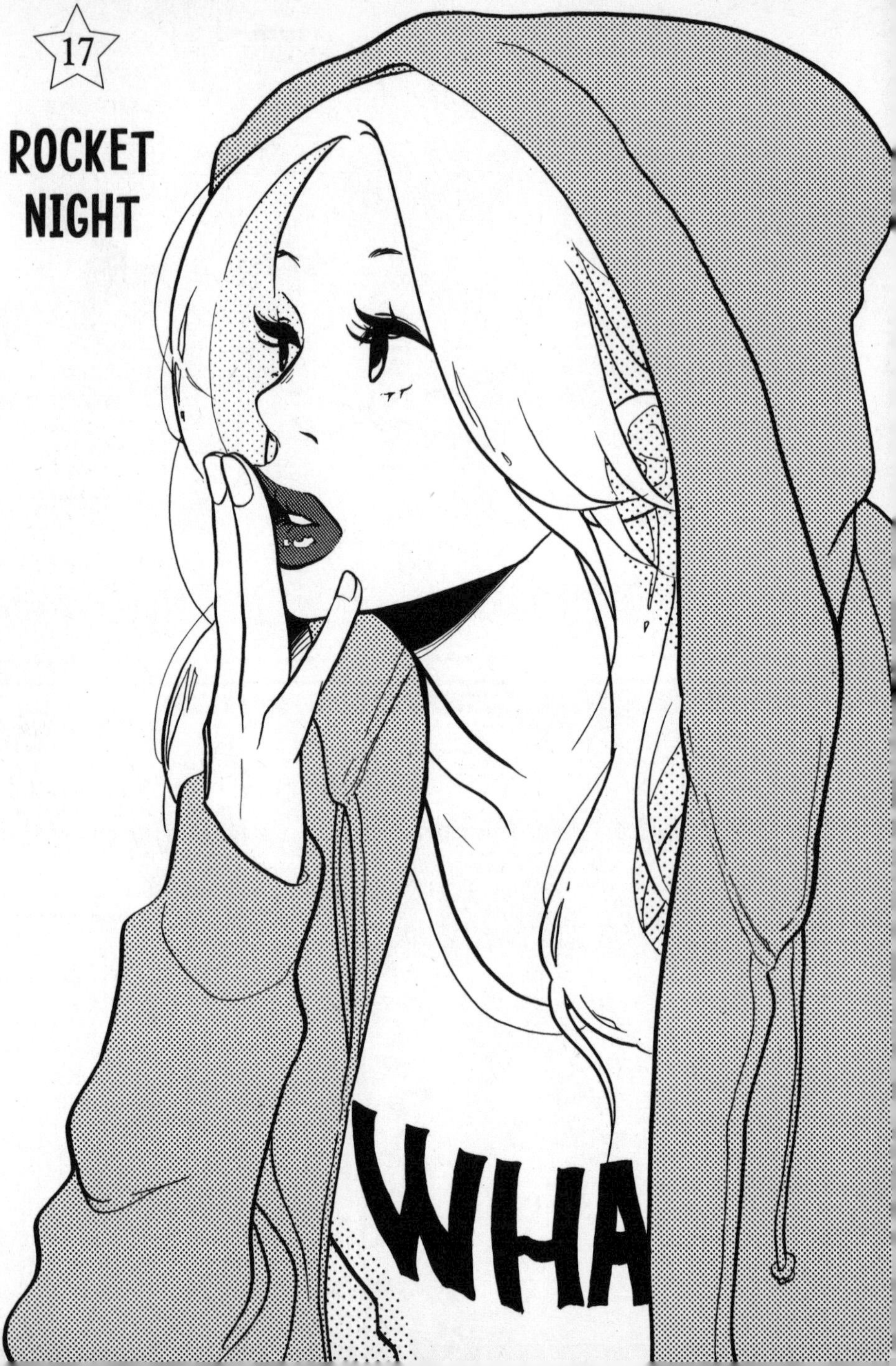
WHA

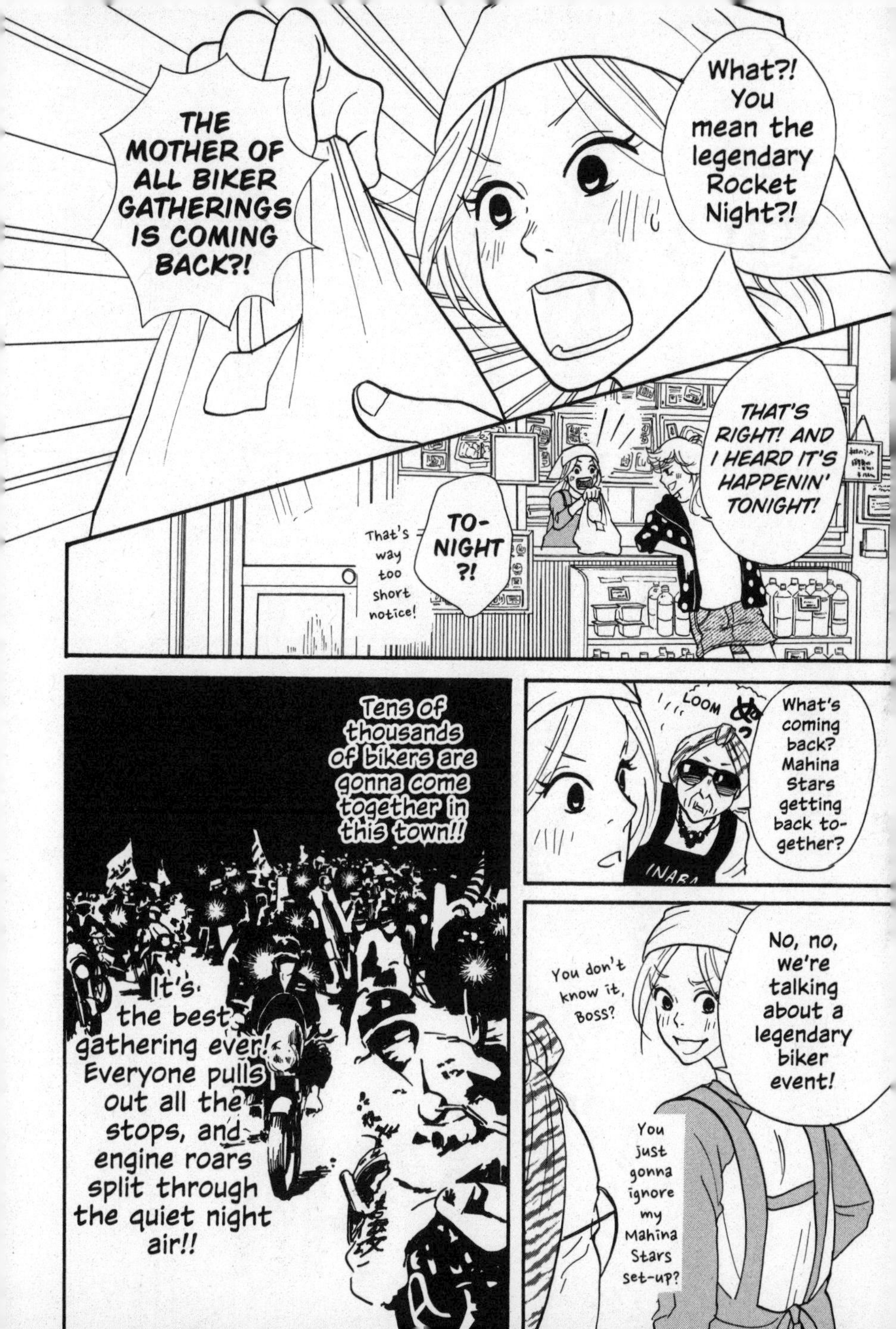
What?! You mean the legendary Rocket Night?!
THE MOTHER OF ALL BIKER GATHERINGS IS COMING BACK?!
THAT'S RIGHT! AND I HEARD IT'S HAPPENIN' TONIGHT!
TO-NIGHT?!
That's way too short notice!
LOOM
What's coming back? Mahina Stars getting back to-gether?
No, no, we're talking about a legendary biker event!
You don't know it, Boss?
You just gonna ignore my Mahina Stars set-up?
Tens of thousands of bikers are gonna come together in this town!!
It's the best gathering ever! Everyone pulls out all the stops, and engine roars split through the quiet night air!!

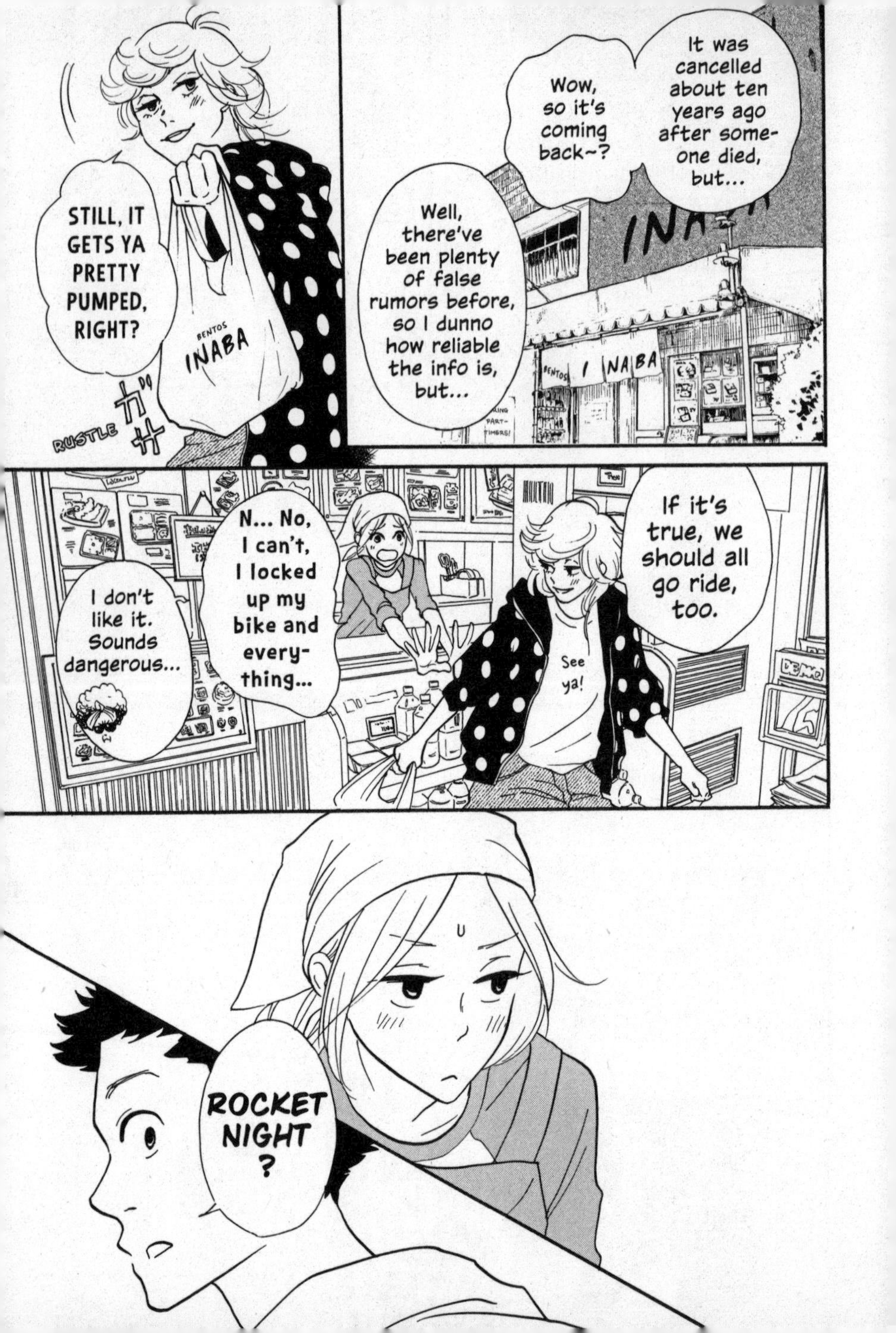
It was cancelled about ten years ago after some-one died, but...
Wow, so it's coming back~?
INABA
Well, there've been plenty of false rumors before, so I dunno how reliable the info is, but...
BENTOS I NA BA
PART-TIMERS!
STILL, IT GETS YA PRETTY PUMPED, RIGHT?
BENTOS INABA
RUSTLE
If it's true, we should all go ride, too.
See ya!
N... No, I can't, I locked up my bike and every-thing...
I don't like it. Sounds dangerous...
ROCKET NIGHT ?

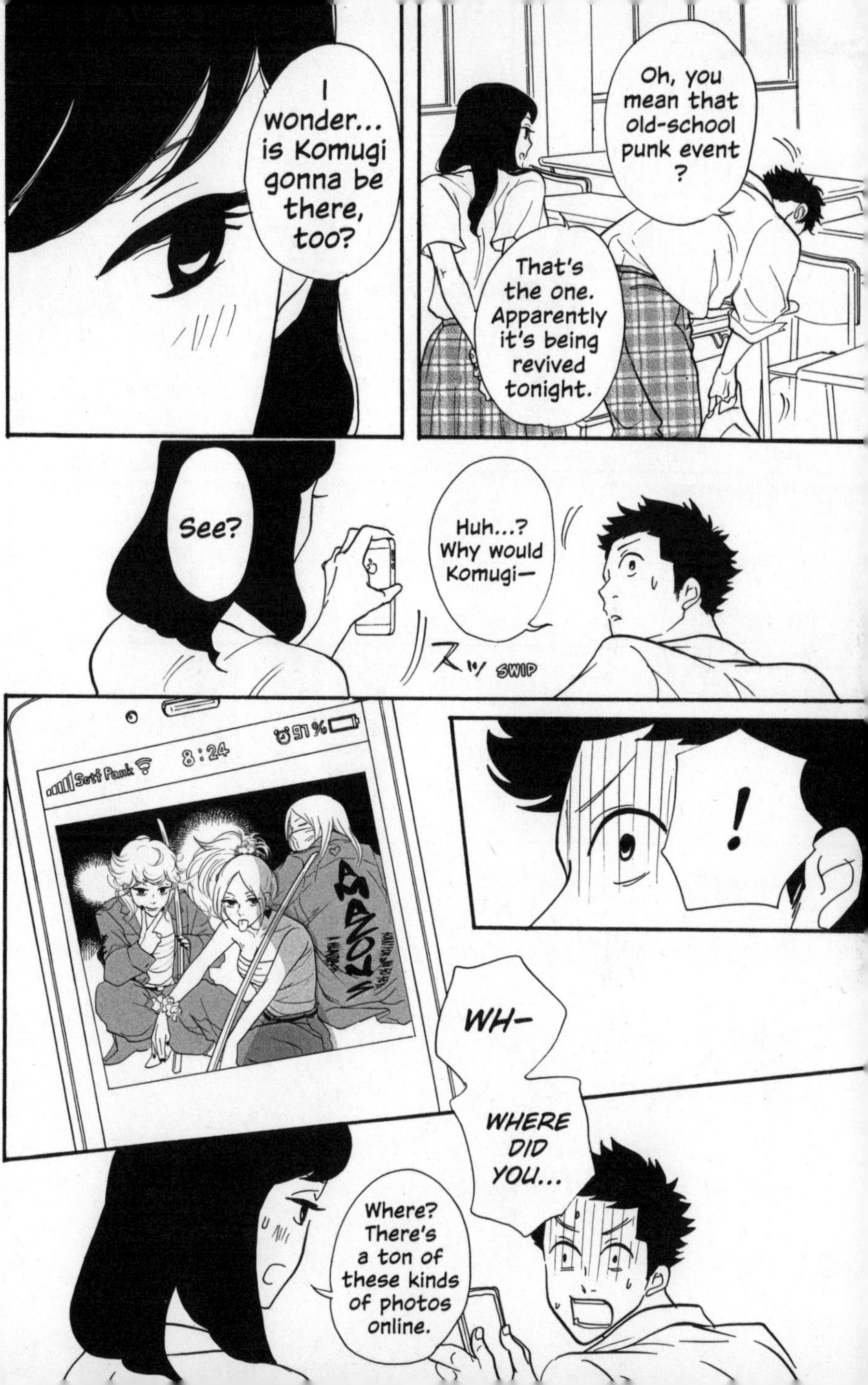
Oh, you mean that old-school punk event?
That's the one. Apparently it's being revived tonight.
I wonder... is Komugi gonna be there, too?
Huh...? Why would Komugi—
See?
スッ SWIP
!
8:24
WH-
WHERE DID YOU...
Where? There's a ton of these kinds of photos online.

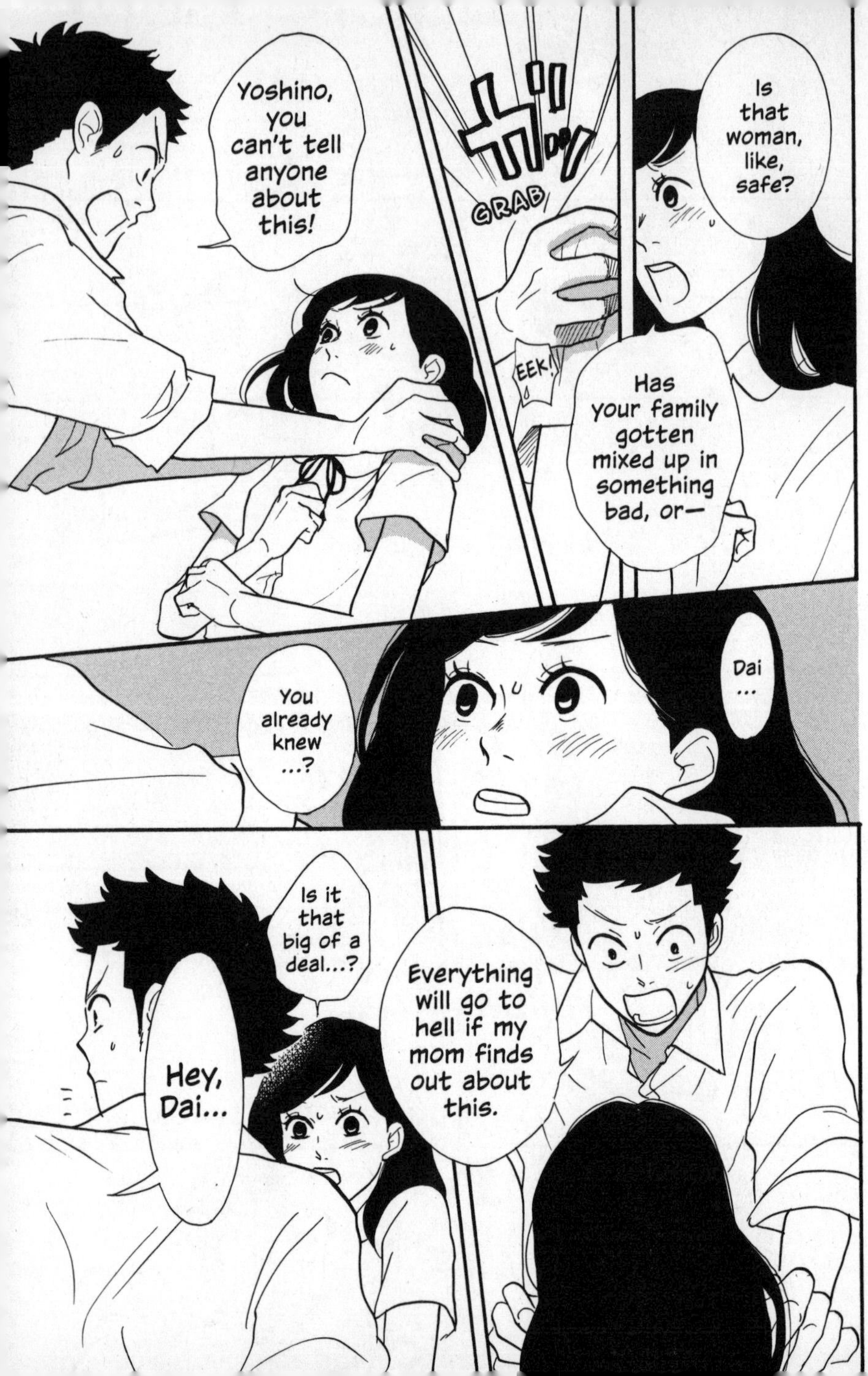

Is that woman, like, safe?
Has your family gotten mixed up in something bad, or—
GRAB
EEK!
Yoshino, you can't tell anyone about this!
Dai...
You already knew...?
Everything will go to hell if my mom finds out about this.
Is it that big of a deal...?
Hey, Dai...

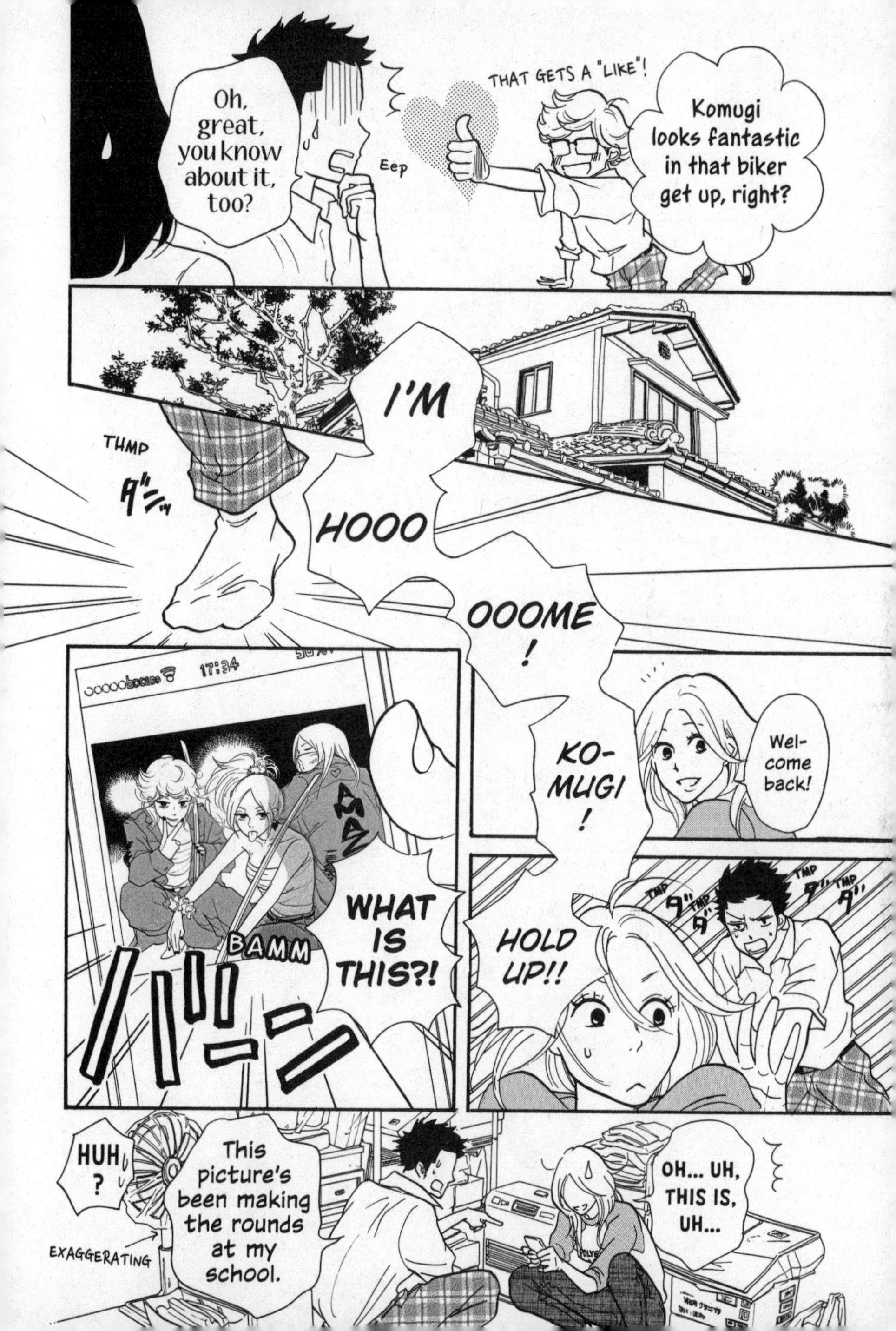
THAT GETS A "LIKE"!
Komugi looks fantastic in that biker get up, right?
Oh, great, you know about it, too?
Eep
I'M HOOOOOOOME!
THMP
Wel-come back!
KO-MUGI!
HOLD UP!!
TMP TMP TMP TMP
17:34
WHAT IS THIS?!
BAMM
OH... UH, THIS IS, UH...
This picture's been making the rounds at my school.
HUH?
EXAGGERATING

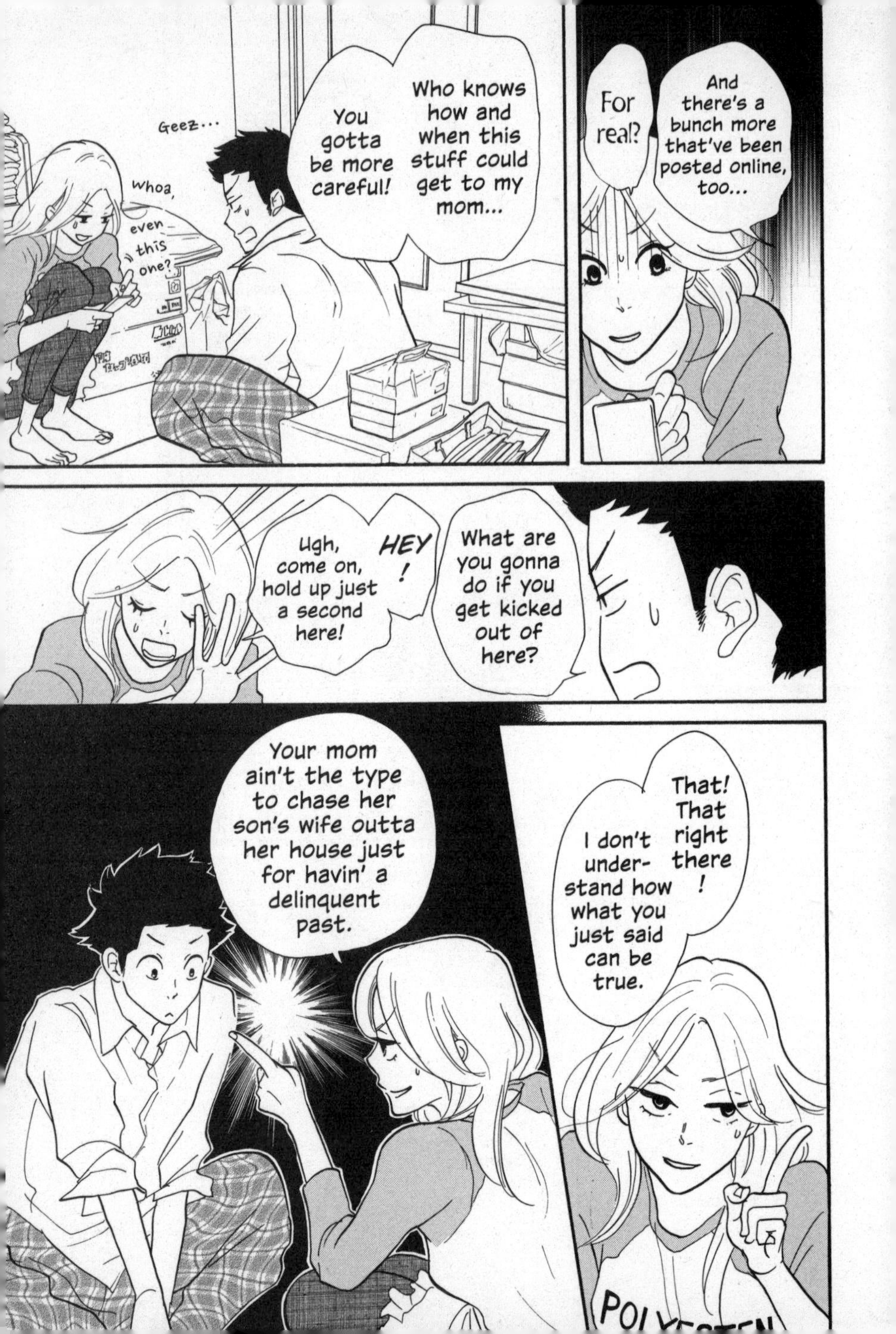
And there's a bunch more that've been posted online, too...
For real?
Who knows how and when this stuff could get to my mom...
You gotta be more careful!
Geez...
Whoa, even this one?
What are you gonna do if you get kicked out of here?
HEY!
Ugh, come on, hold up just a second here!
That! That right there!
I don't understand how what you just said can be true.
Your mom ain't the type to chase her son's wife outta her house just for havin' a delinquent past.

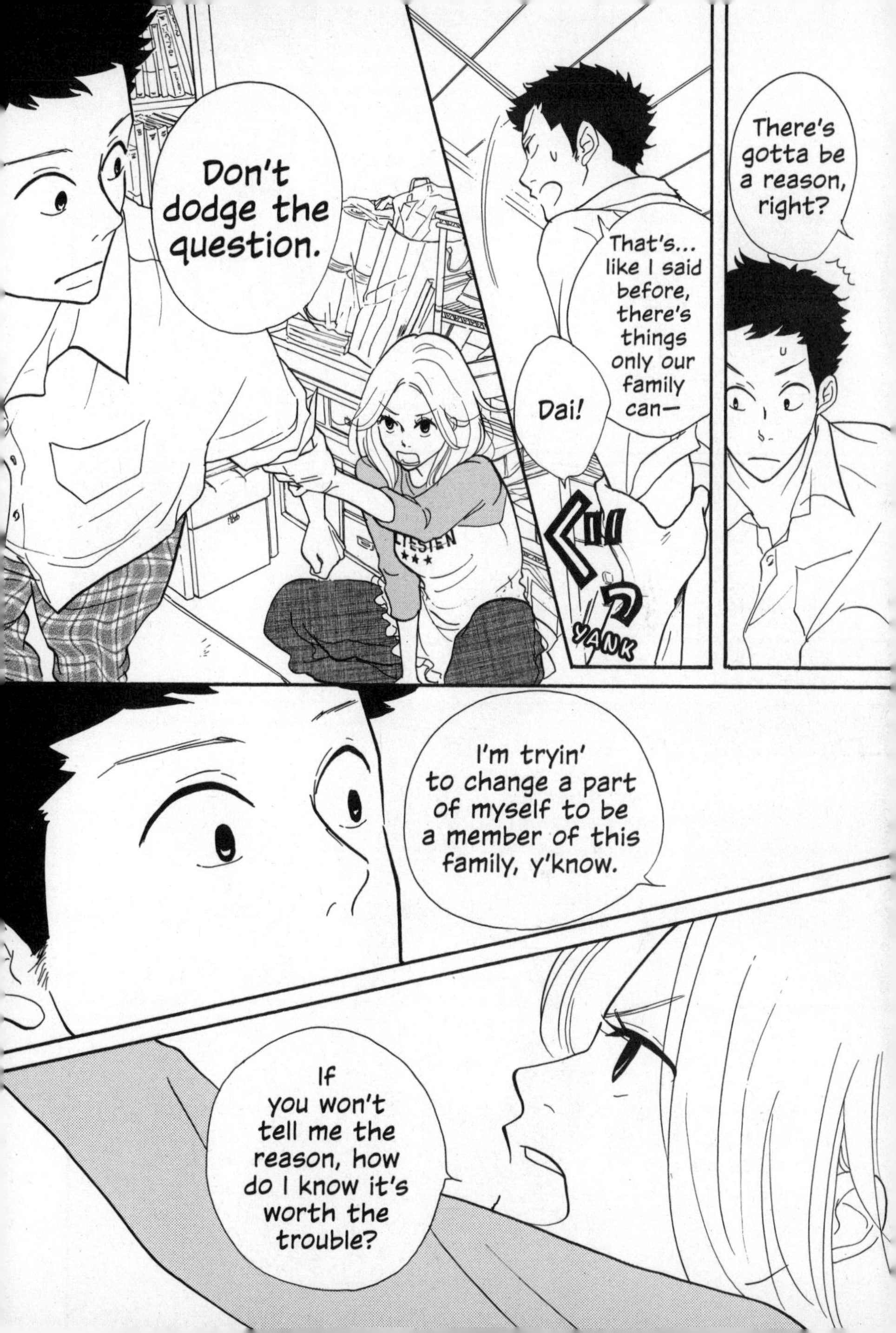
There's gotta be a reason, right?
That's... like I said before, there's things only our family can—
Dai!
YANK
Don't dodge the question.
I'm tryin' to change a part of myself to be a member of this family, y'know.
If you won't tell me the reason, how do I know it's worth the trouble?

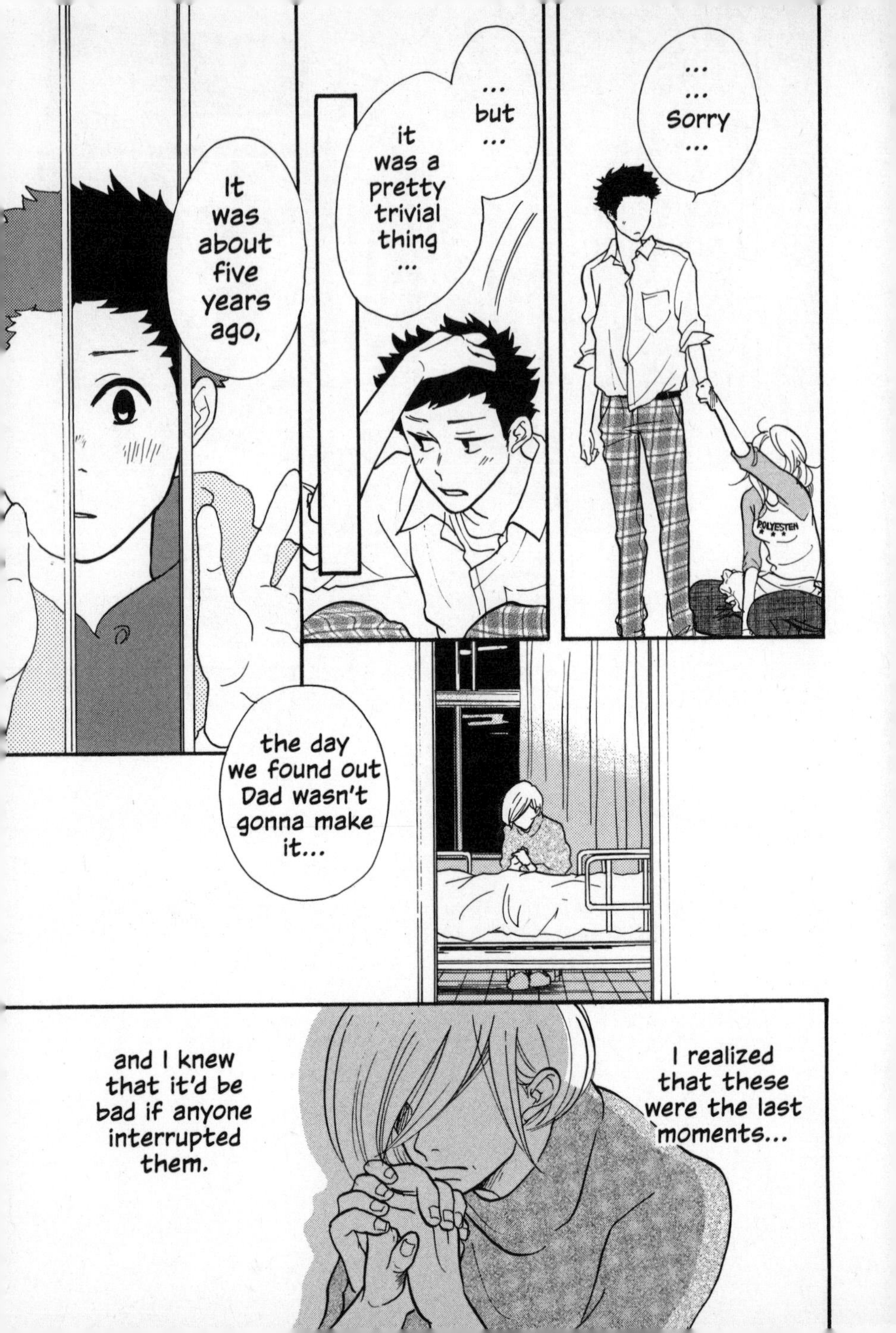
... ... Sorry ...
POLYESTEN
... but ...
it was a pretty trivial thing ...
It was about five years ago,
the day we found out Dad wasn't gonna make it...
I realized that these were the last moments...
and I knew that it'd be bad if anyone interrupted them.

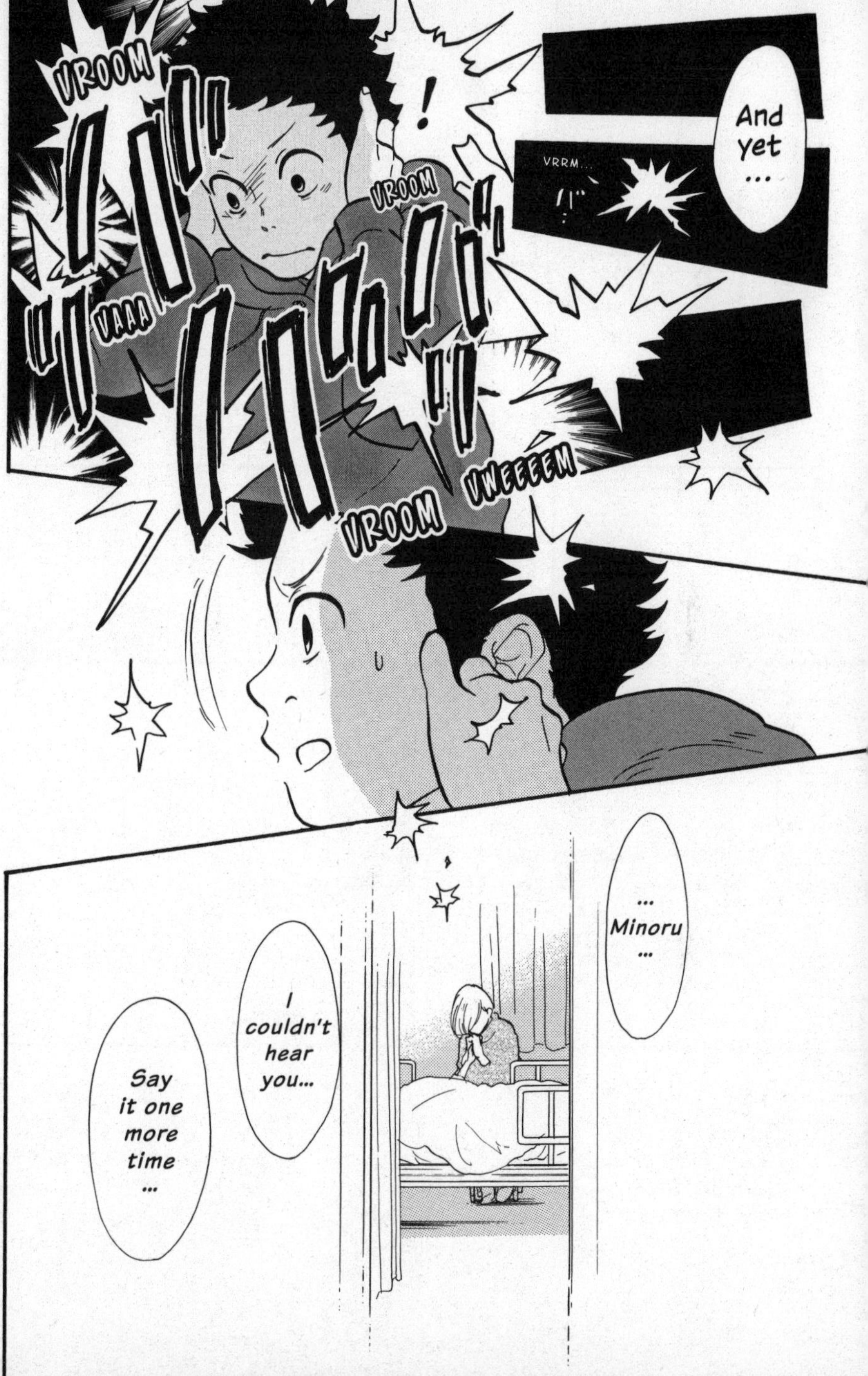
And yet ...
VRRM...
VROOM
VROOM
VAAA
VWEEEEM
VROOM
... Minoru ...
I couldn't hear you...
Say it one more time ...

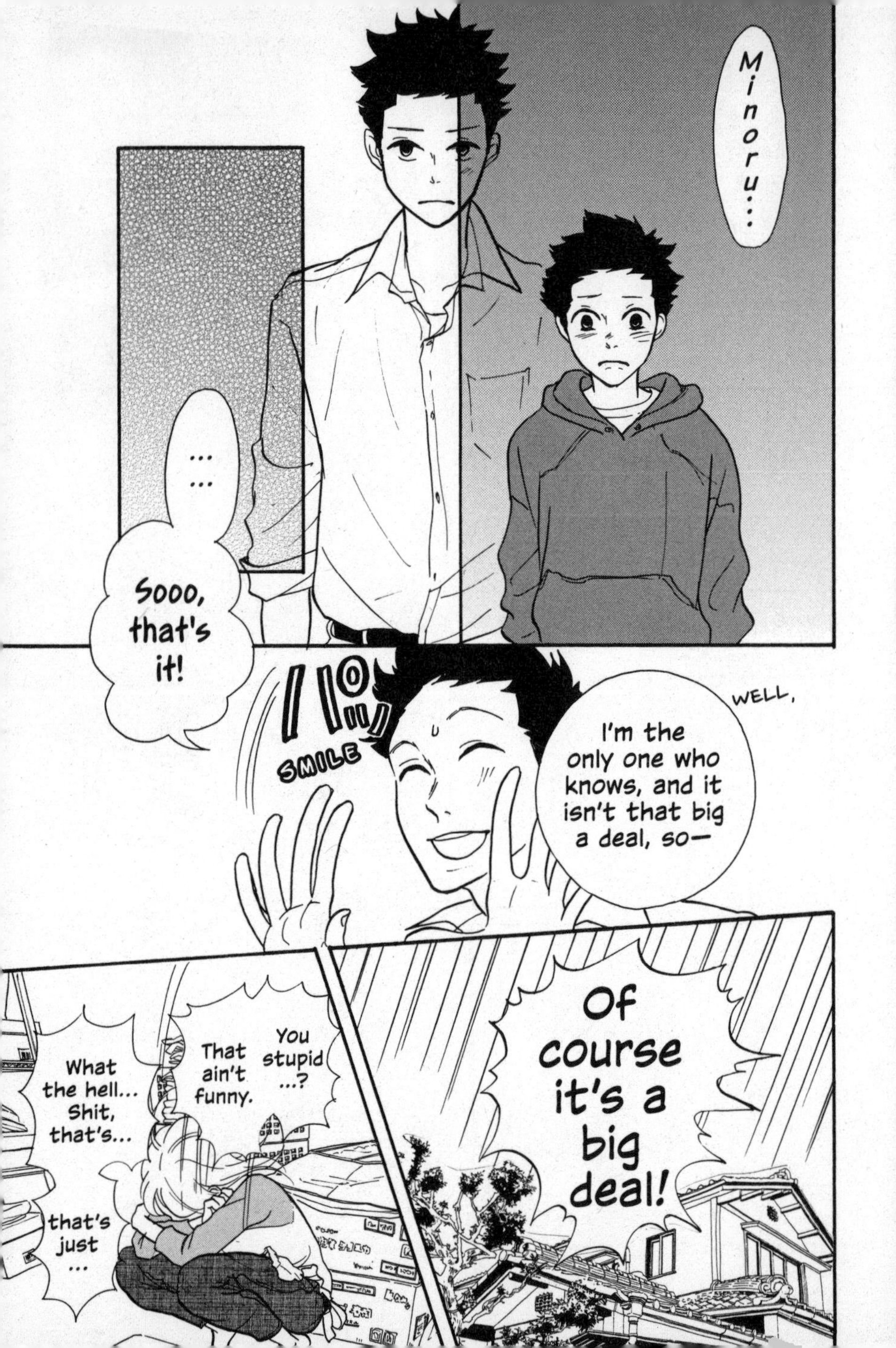
Minoru...
......
Sooo, that's it!
WELL,
I'm the only one who knows, and it isn't that big a deal, so—
SMILE
Of course it's a big deal!
You stupid ...?
That ain't funny.
What the hell... Shit, that's...
that's just ...

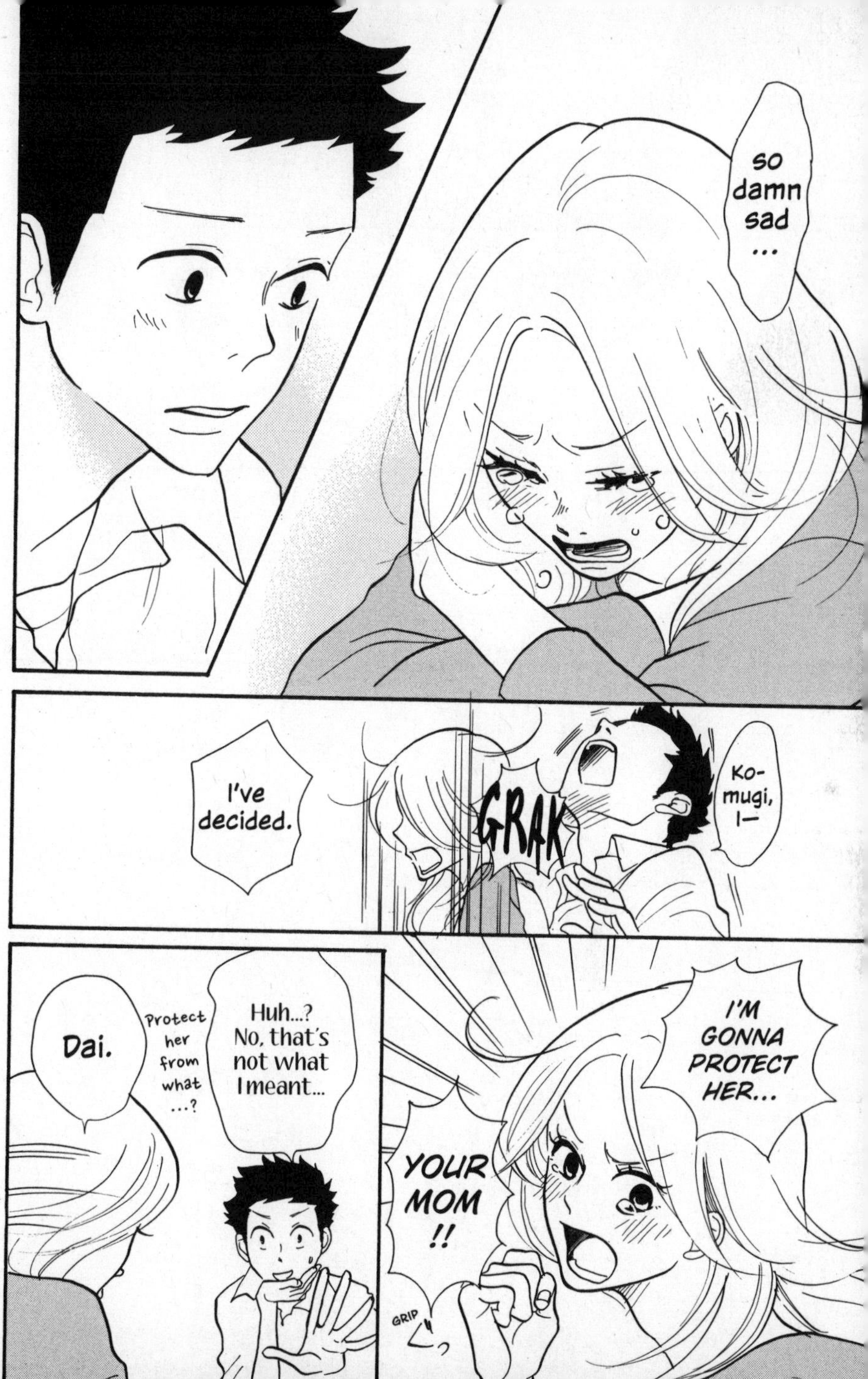
so damn sad ...
Ko-mugi, I—
GRAK
I've decided.
I'M GONNA PROTECT HER...
YOUR MOM !!
GRIP
Huh...? No, that's not what I meant...
Protect her from what ...?
Dai.

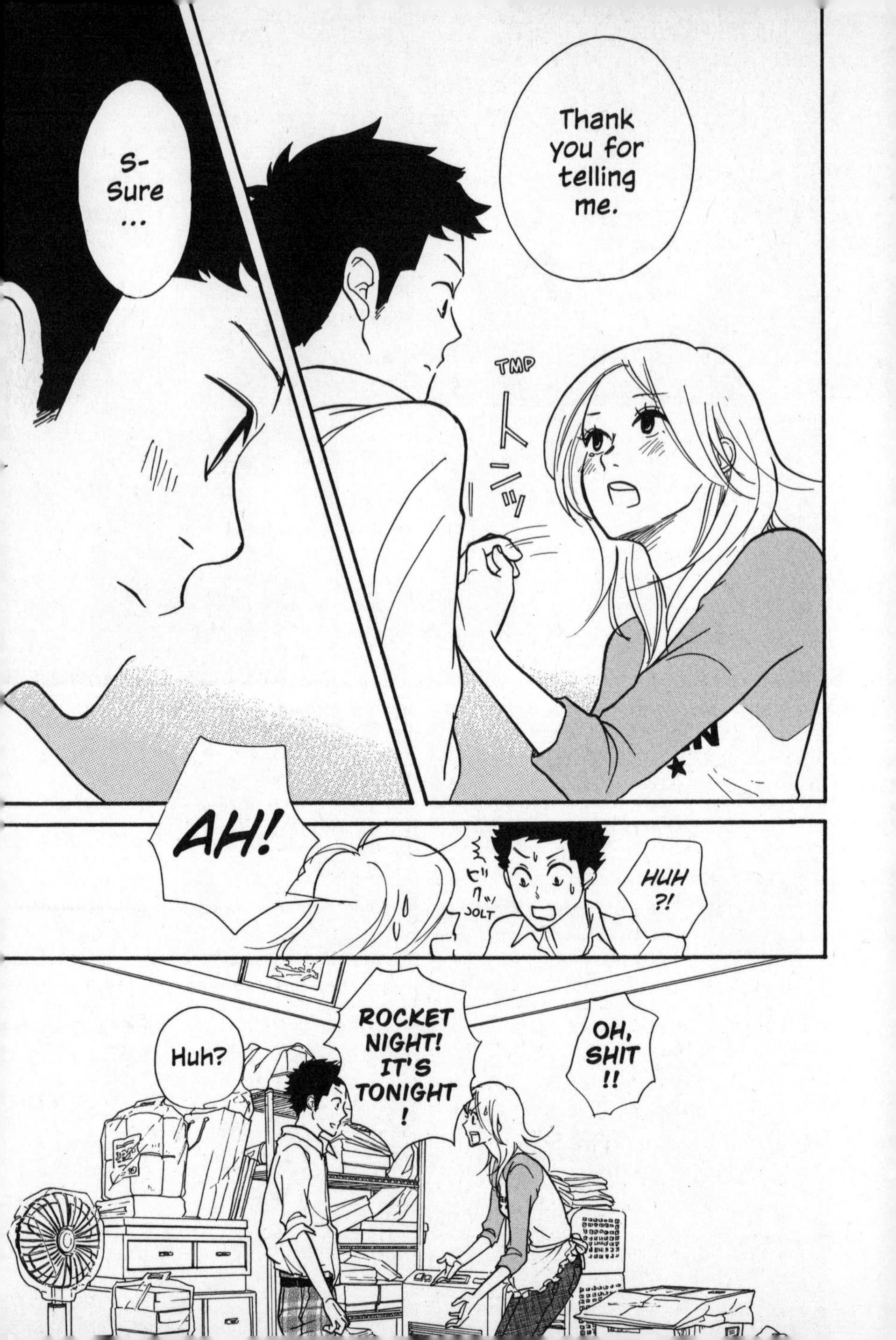
Thank you for telling me.
TMP
S-Sure ...
AH!
JOLT
HUH ?!
OH, SHIT !!
ROCKET NIGHT! IT'S TONIGHT !
Huh?

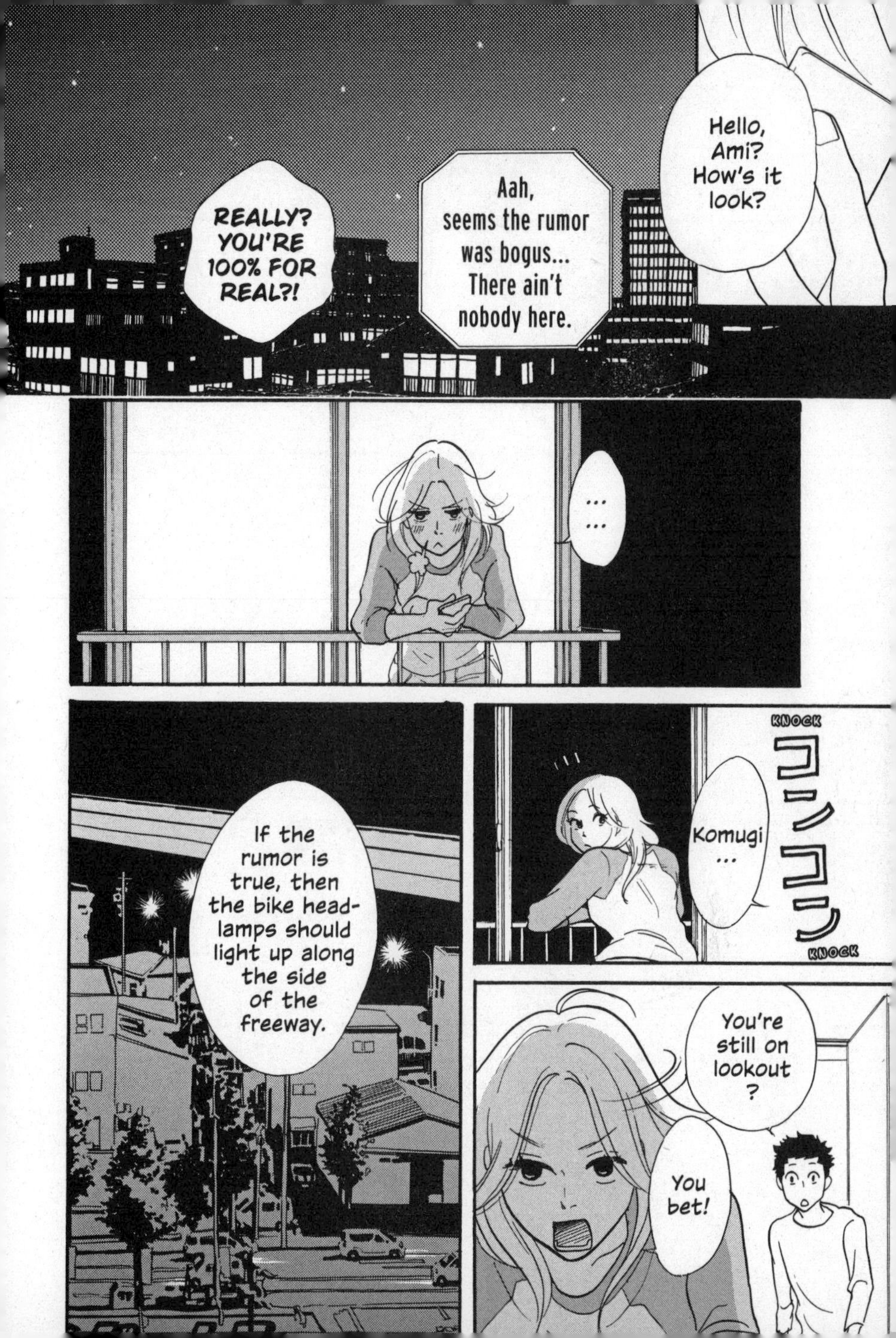
Hello, Ami? How's it look?
Aah, seems the rumor was bogus... There ain't nobody here.
REALLY? YOU'RE 100% FOR REAL?!
... ...
KNOCK
コンコン
KNOCK
Komugi ...
You're still on lookout ?
You bet!
If the rumor is true, then the bike head-lamps should light up along the side of the freeway.

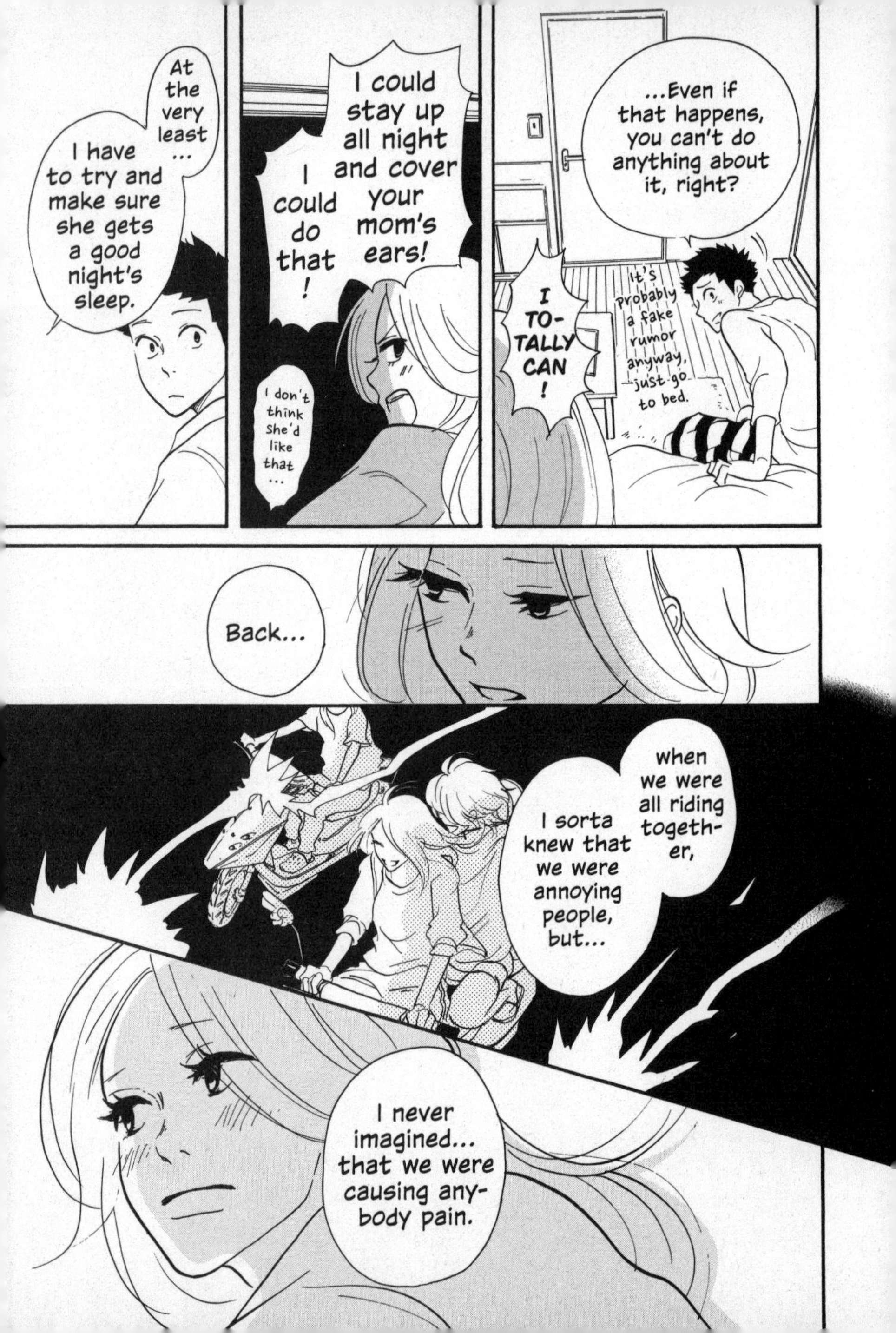
...Even if that happens, you can't do anything about it, right?
It's probably a fake rumor anyway, just go to bed.
I TO-TALLY CAN!
I could stay up all night and cover your mom's ears!
I could do that!
I don't think she'd like that...
At the very least...
I have to try and make sure she gets a good night's sleep.
Back...
when we were all riding together,
I sorta knew that we were annoying people, but...
I never imagined... that we were causing any-body pain.

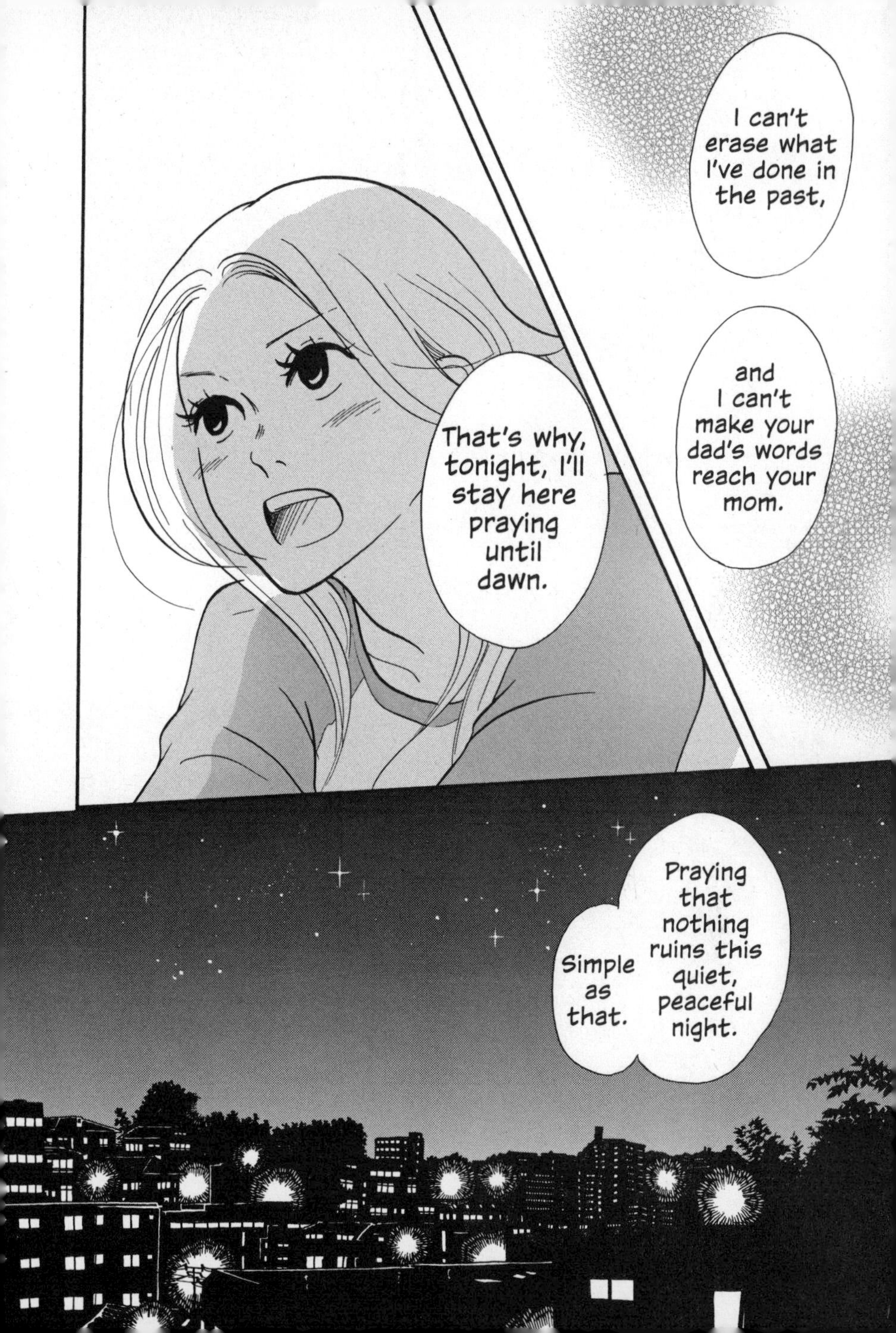
I can't erase what I've done in the past,
and I can't make your dad's words reach your mom.
That's why, tonight, I'll stay here praying until dawn.
Praying that nothing ruins this quiet, peaceful night.
Simple as that.

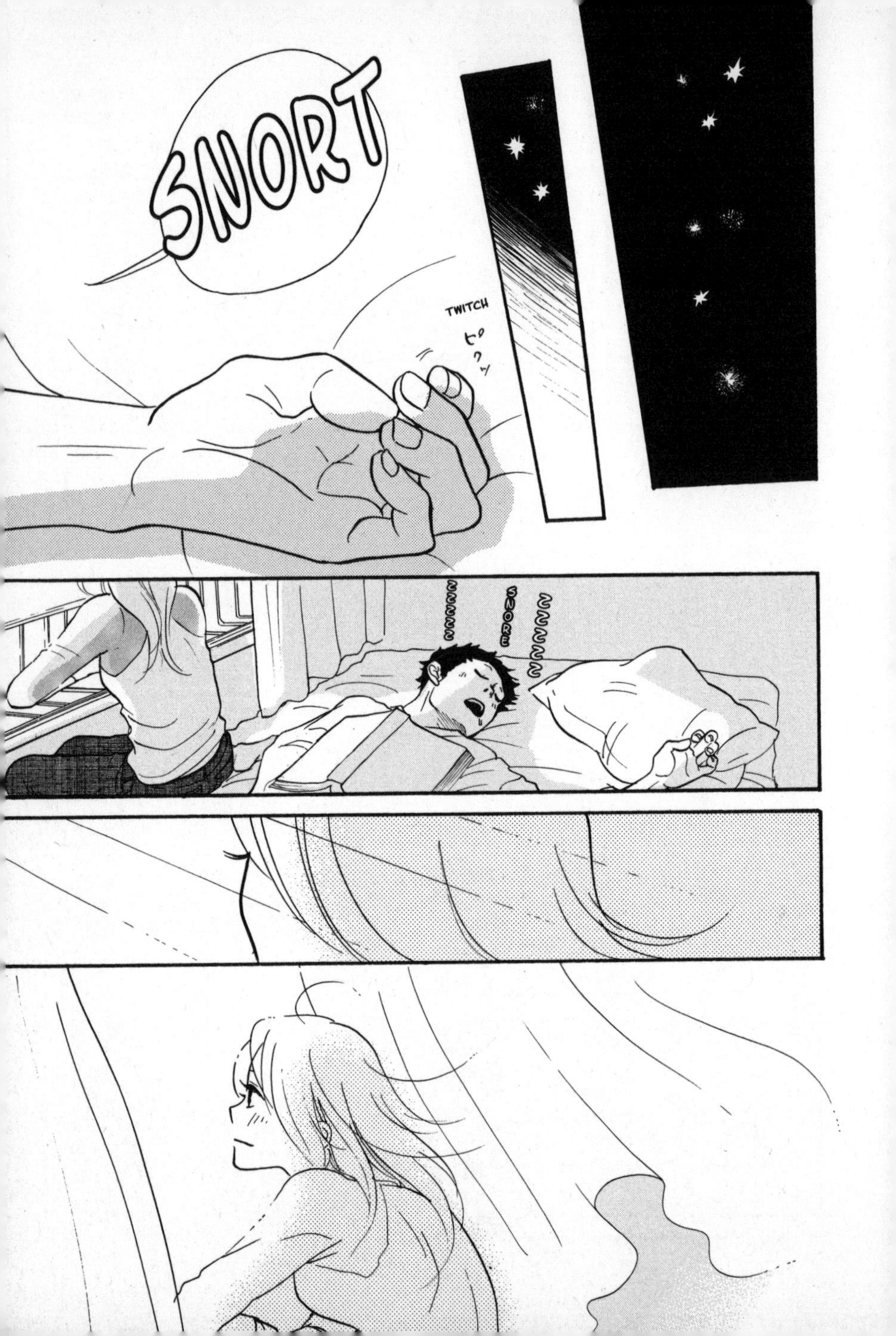
TWITCH
ピクッ
SNORT
ZZZZZZ
SNORE
ZZZZZ

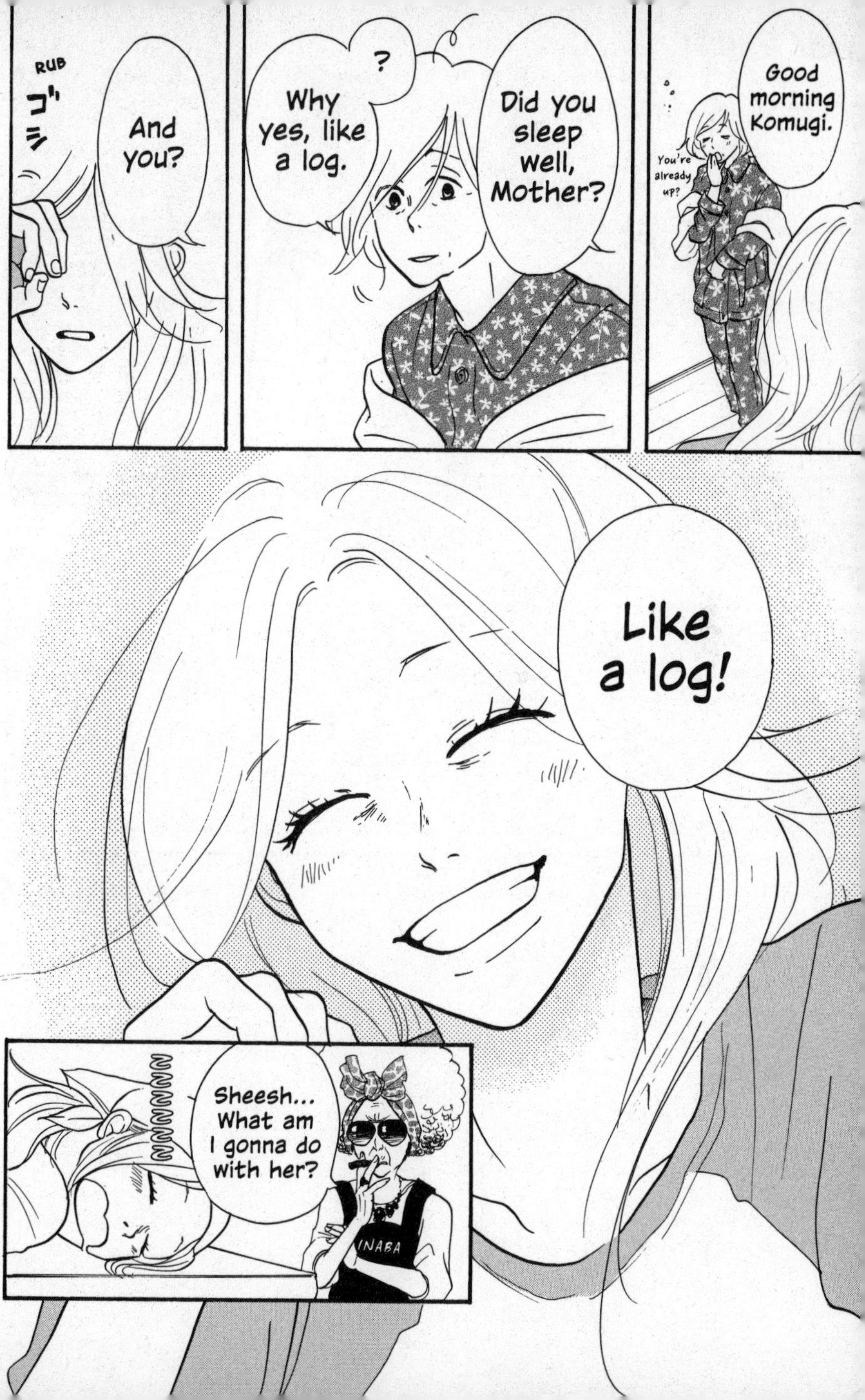
Good morning Komugi.
You're already up?
Did you sleep well, Mother?
?
Why yes, like a log.
And you?
RUB
ゴシ
Like a log!
Sheesh... What am I gonna do with her?
INABA

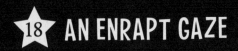

18 AN ENRAPT GAZE

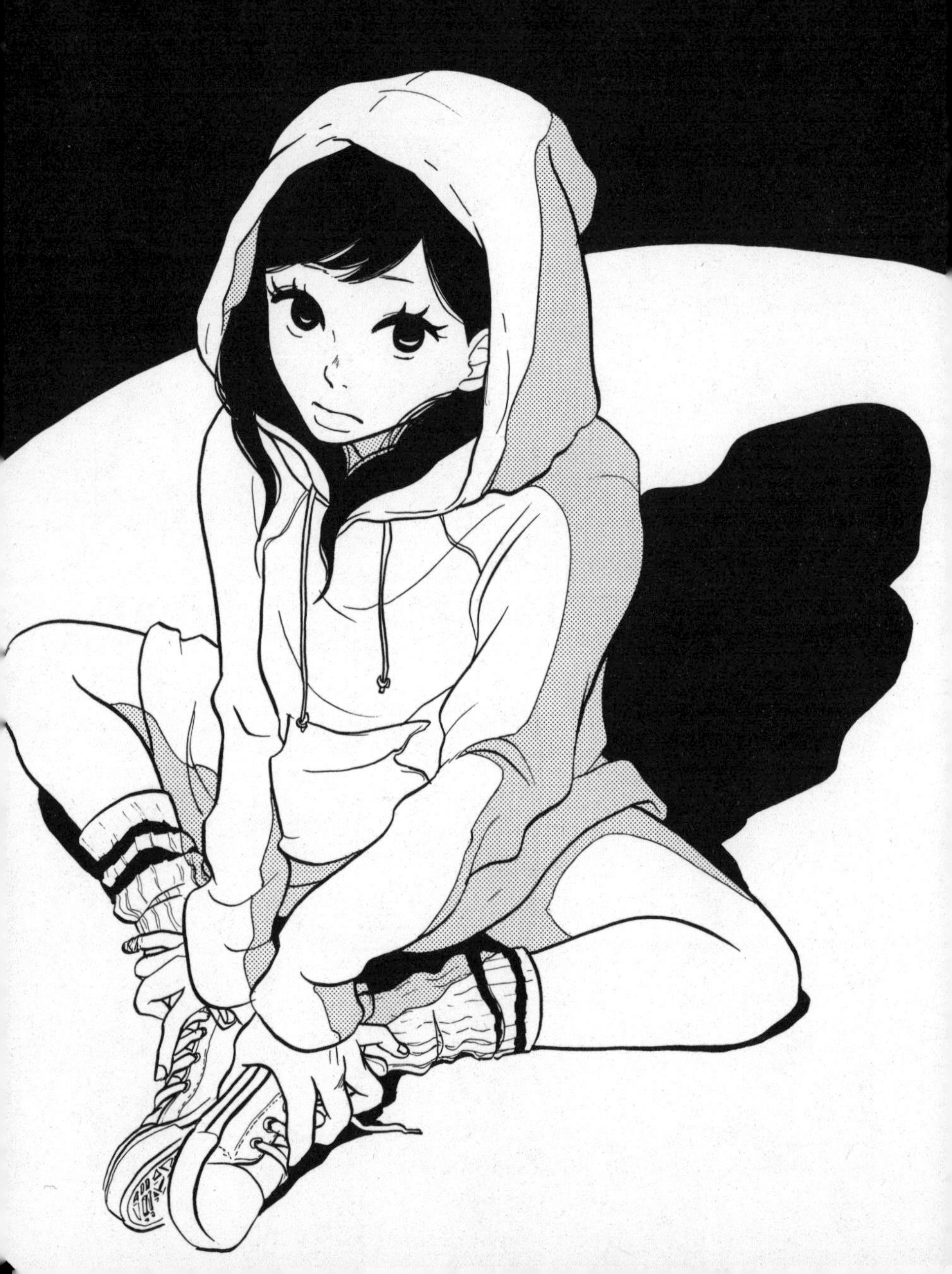

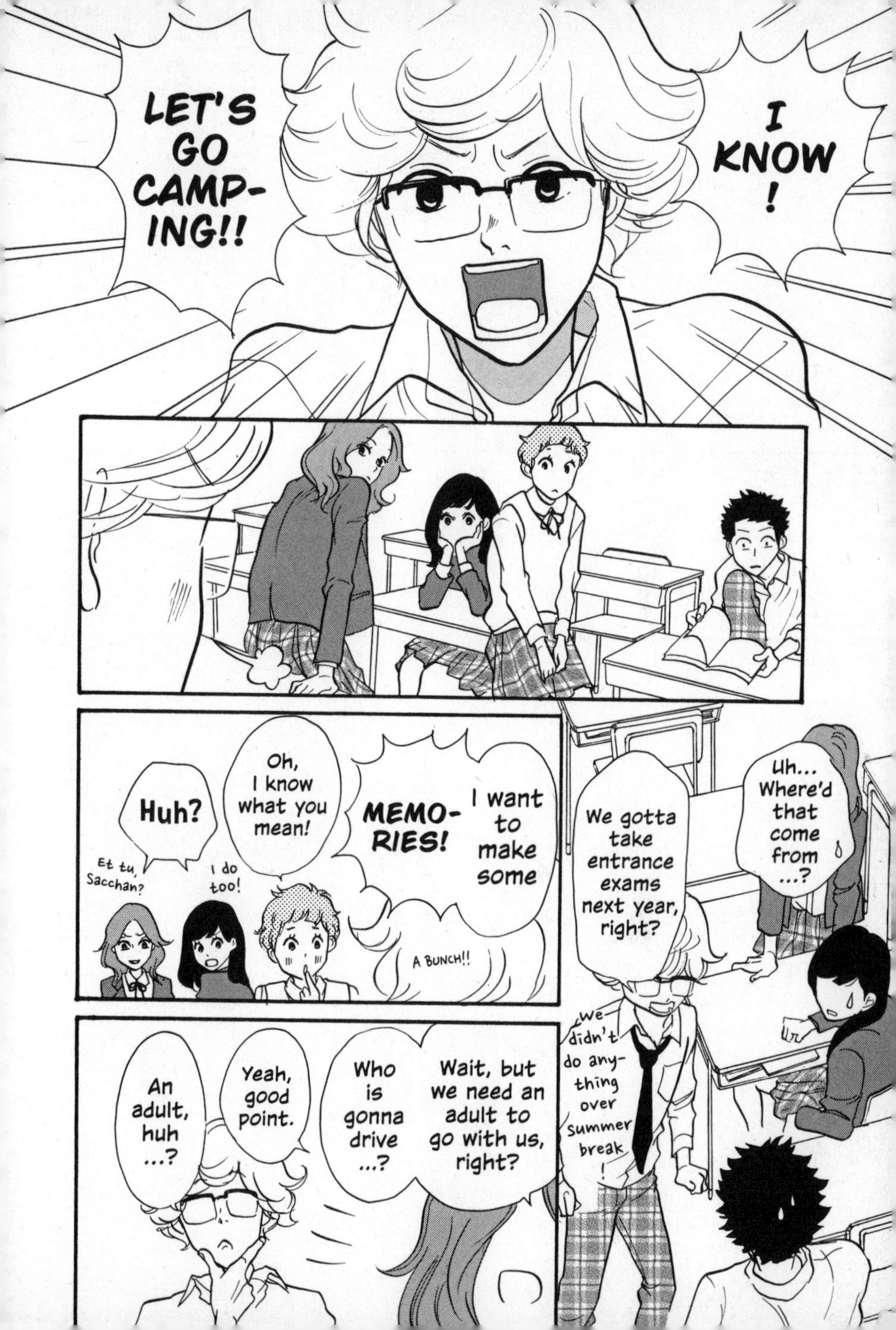

I KNOW!
LET'S GO CAMPING!!
Uh... Where'd that come from...?
We gotta take entrance exams next year, right?
We didn't do anything over summer break!
I want to make some MEMORIES!
A BUNCH!!
Oh, I know what you mean!
I do too!
Huh?
Et tu, Sacchan?
Wait, but we need an adult to go with us, right?
Who is gonna drive...?
Yeah, good point.
An adult, huh...?

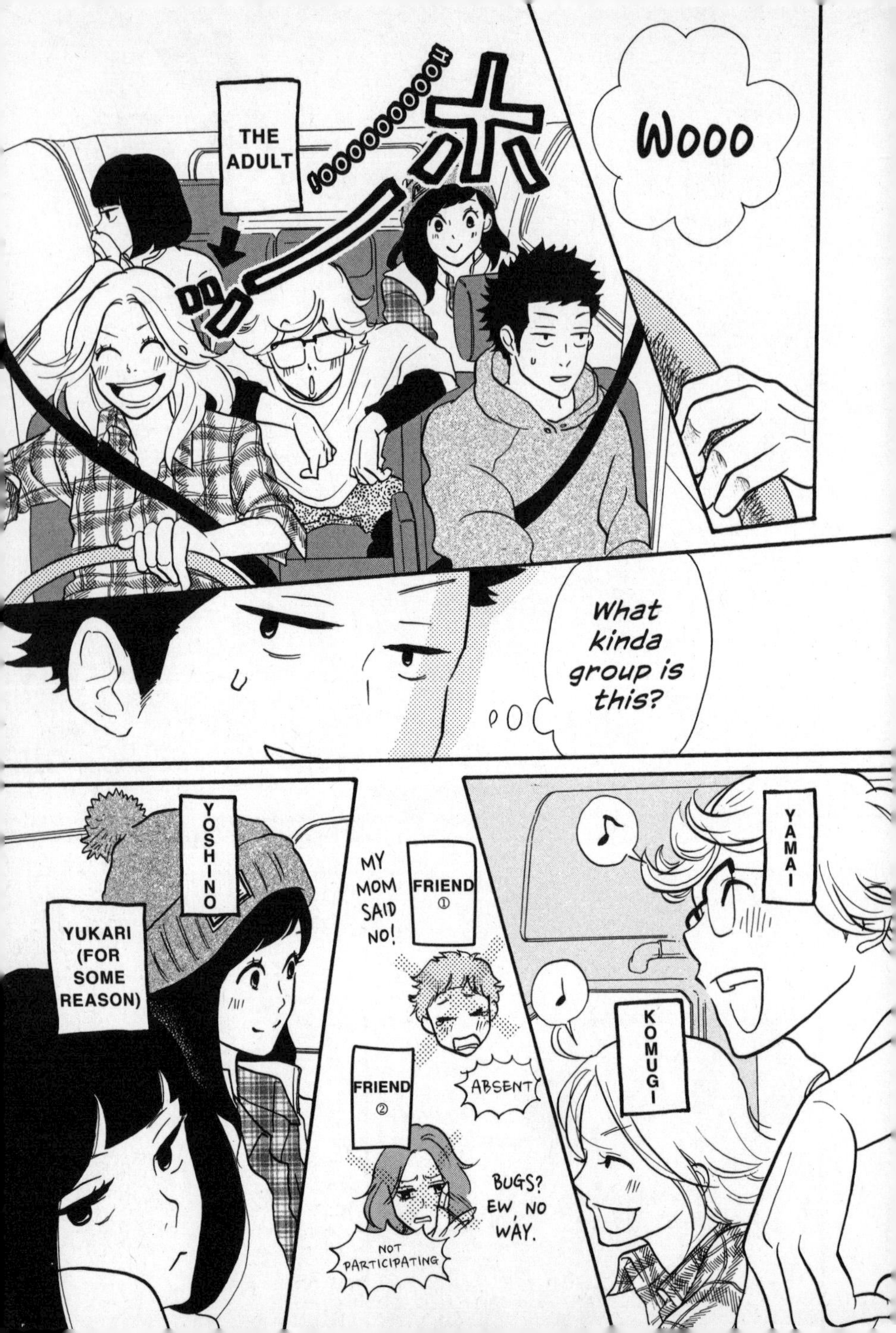

Wooo
THE ADULT
HOOOOOOOOO!
What kinda group is this?
YAMAI
KOMUGI
YOSHINO
YUKARI (FOR SOME REASON)
FRIEND ①
MY MOM SAID NO!
ABSENT
FRIEND ②
BUGS? EW, NO WAY.
NOT PARTICIPATING

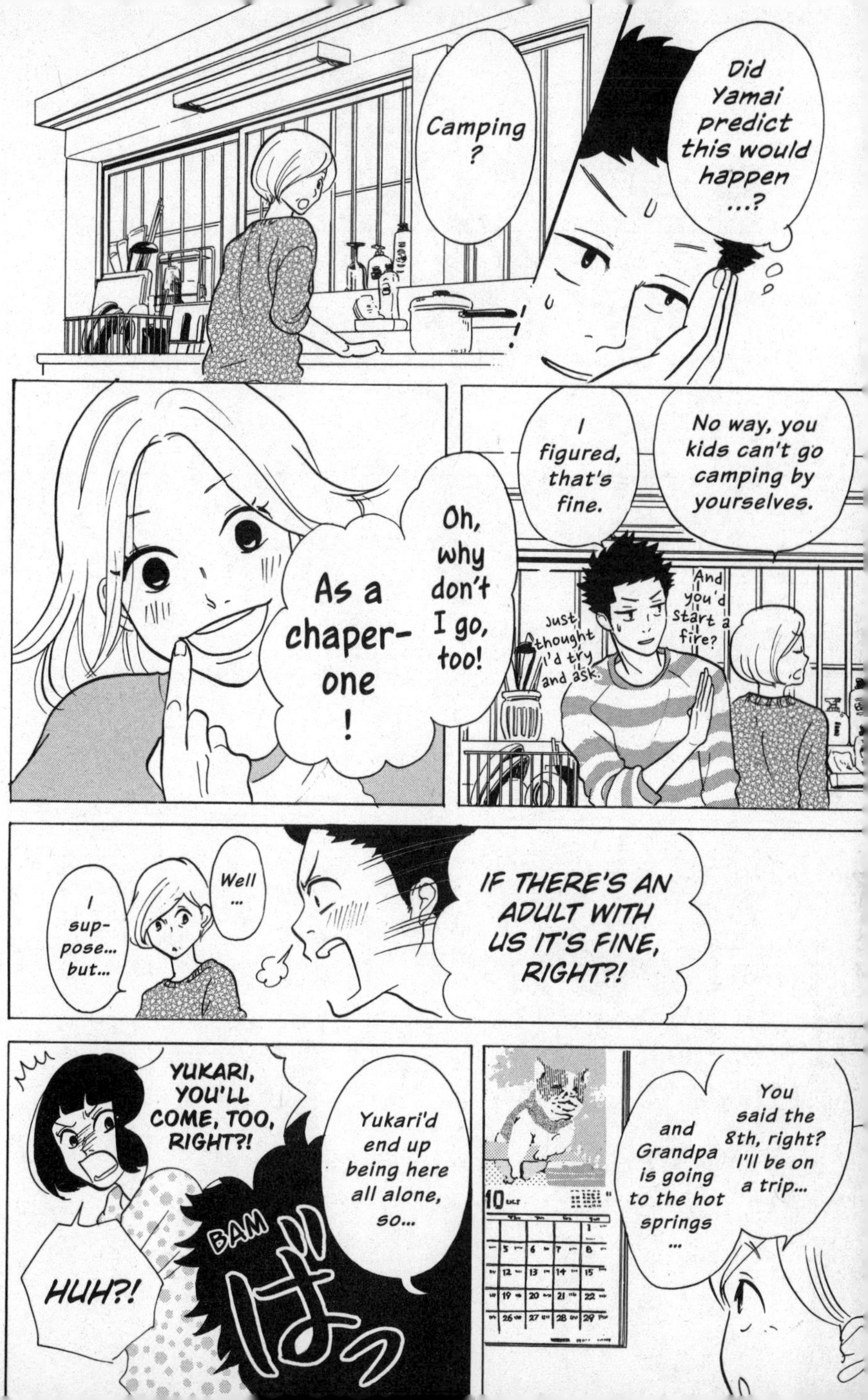
Did Yamai predict this would happen ...?
Camping?
No way, you kids can't go camping by yourselves.
I figured, that's fine.
And you'd start a fire?
Just thought I'd try and ask.
Oh, why don't I go, too!
As a chaper-one!
IF THERE'S AN ADULT WITH US IT'S FINE, RIGHT?!
Well ...
I sup-pose... but...
You said the 8th, right? I'll be on a trip...
and Grandpa is going to the hot springs ...
Yukari'd end up being here all alone, so...
YUKARI, YOU'LL COME, TOO, RIGHT?!
BAM
ばっ
HUH?!

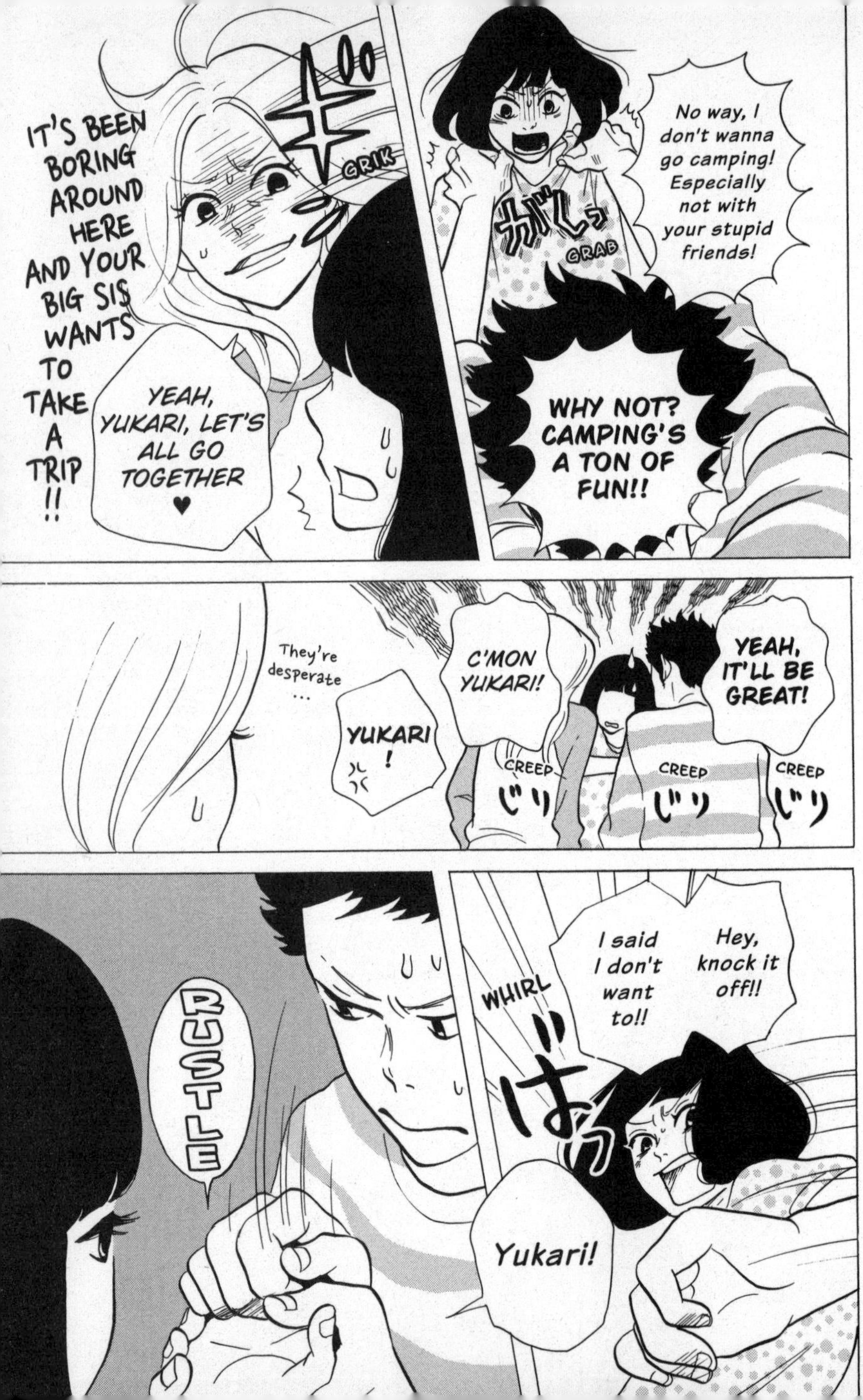
No way, I don't wanna go camping! Especially not with your stupid friends!
ガしっ
GRAB
WHY NOT? CAMPING'S A TON OF FUN!!
GRIK
IT'S BEEN BORING AROUND HERE AND YOUR BIG SIS WANTS TO TAKE A TRIP!!
YEAH, YUKARI, LET'S ALL GO TOGETHER ♥
YEAH, IT'LL BE GREAT!
CREEP
じり
CREEP
じり
C'MON YUKARI!
CREEP
じり
YUKARI!
They're desperate...
Hey, knock it off!!
I said I don't want to!!
WHIRL
ばっ
Yukari!
RUSTLE

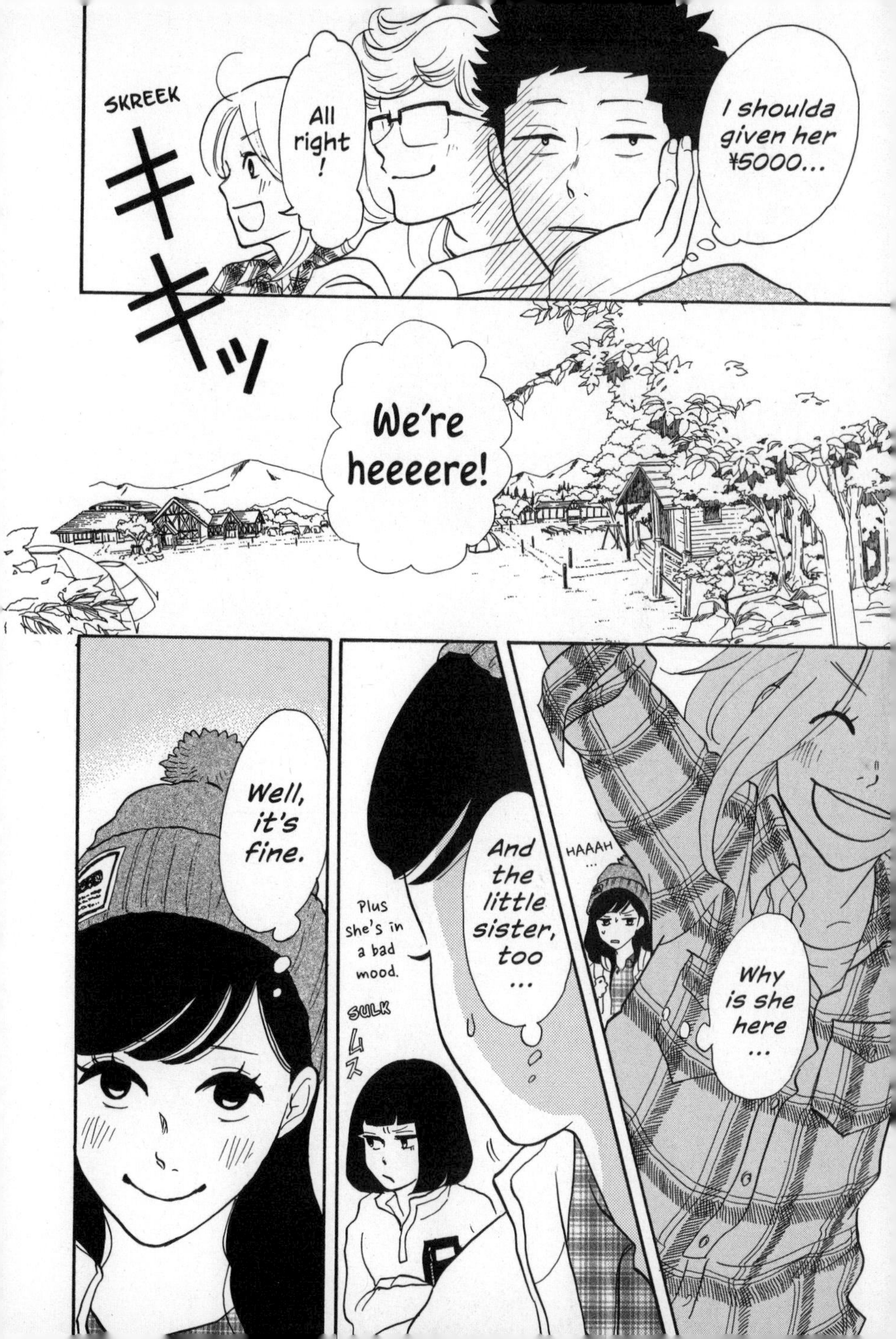
I shoulda given her ¥5000...
All right!
SKREEK
キキッ
We're heeeere!
Why is she here ...
HAAAH ...
And the little sister, too ...
Plus she's in a bad mood.
SULK
ムス
Well, it's fine.

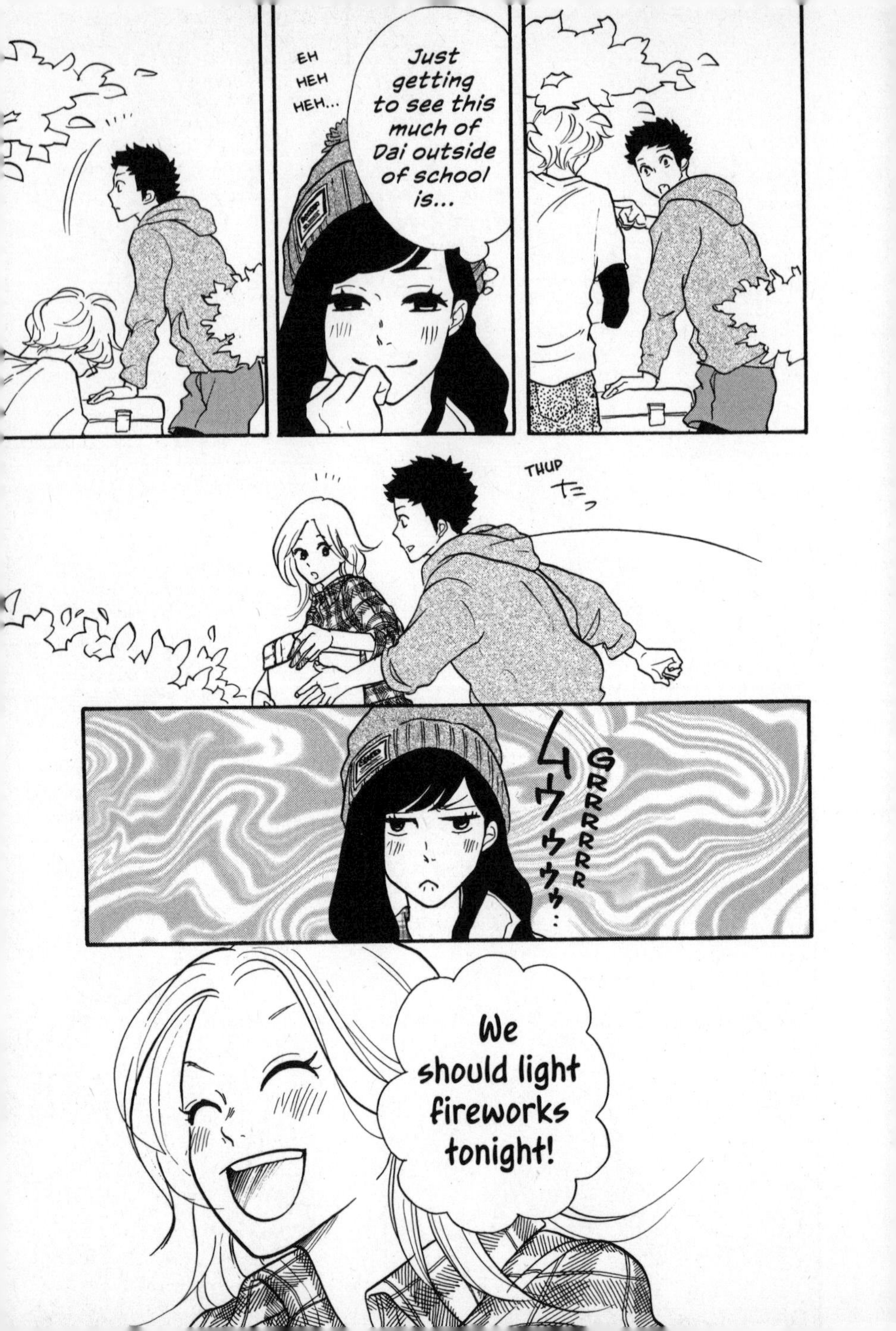

Just getting to see this much of Dai outside of school is...
EH HEH HEH...
THUP
GRRRRRR
We should light fireworks tonight!

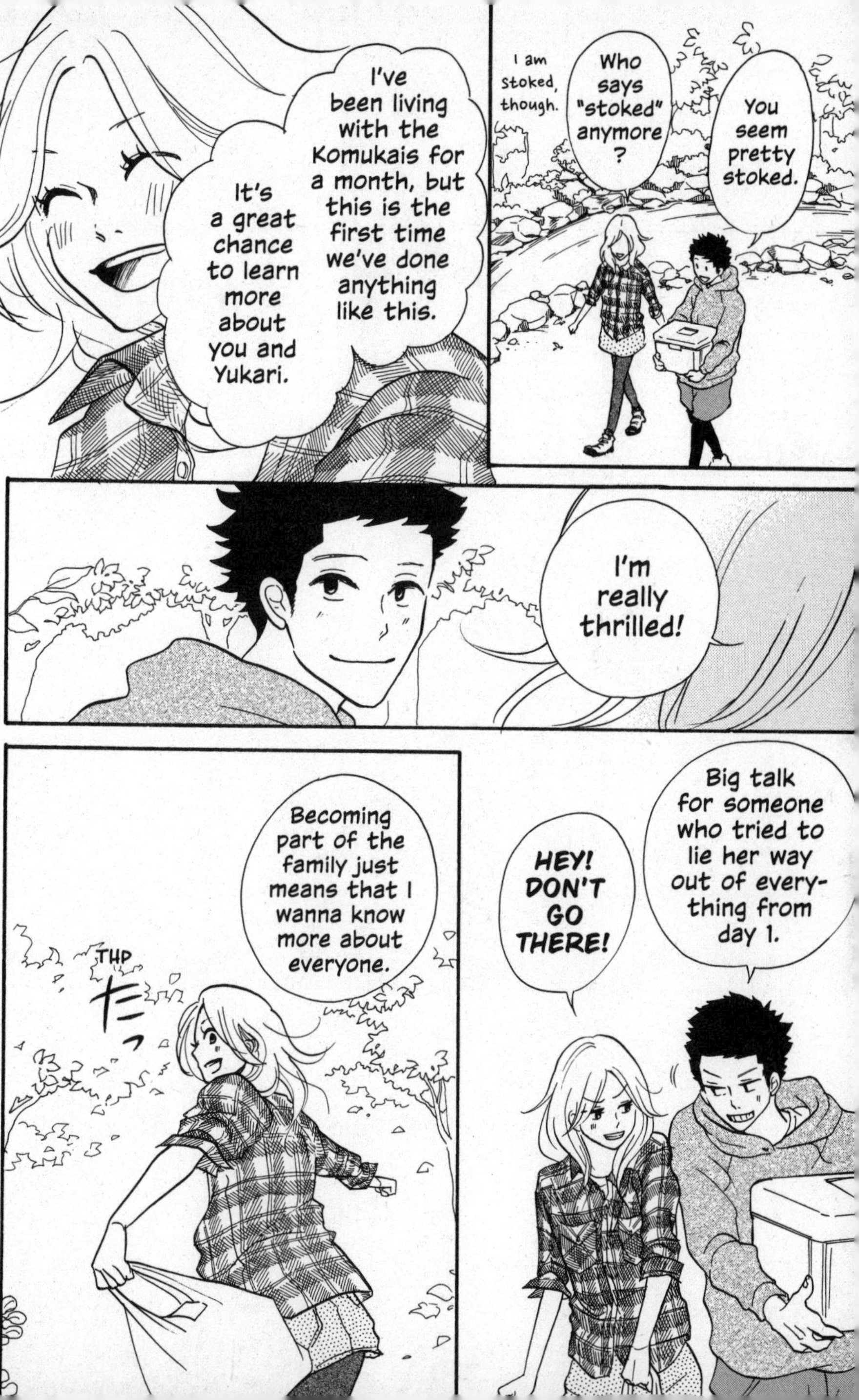
You seem pretty stoked.
Who says "stoked" anymore?
I am stoked, though.
I've been living with the Komukais for a month, but this is the first time we've done anything like this.
It's a great chance to learn more about you and Yukari.
I'm really thrilled!
Big talk for someone who tried to lie her way out of every-thing from day 1.
HEY! DON'T GO THERE!
Becoming part of the family just means that I wanna know more about everyone.
THP

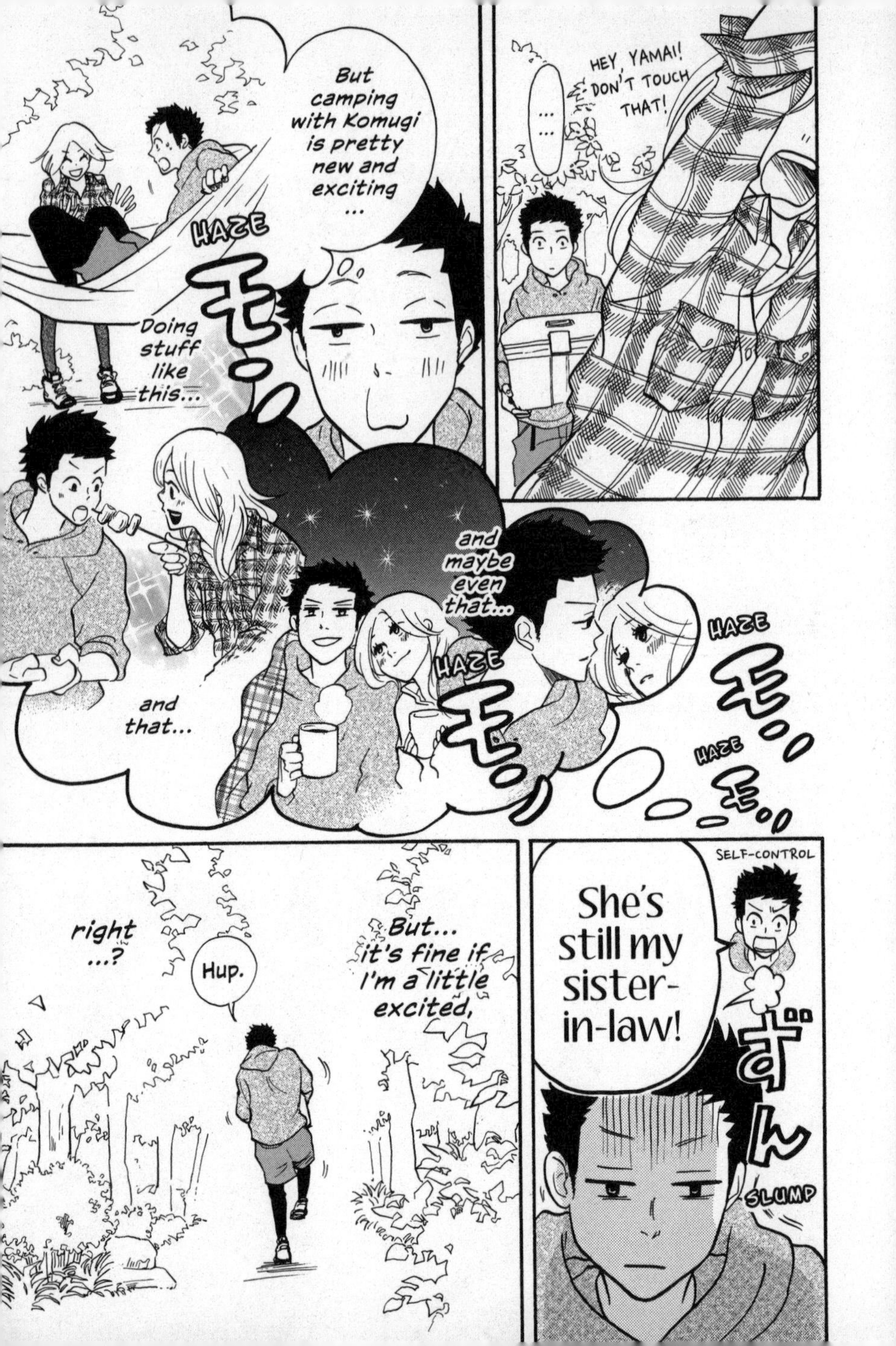
HEY, YAMAI! DON'T TOUCH THAT!
……
But camping with Komugi is pretty new and exciting ...
HAZE
モ
Doing stuff like this...
and that...
and maybe even that...
HAZE
モ
HAZE
モ
HAZE
モ
SELF-CONTROL
She's still my sister-in-law!
ずん
SLUMP
But... it's fine if I'm a little excited,
Hup.
right ...?

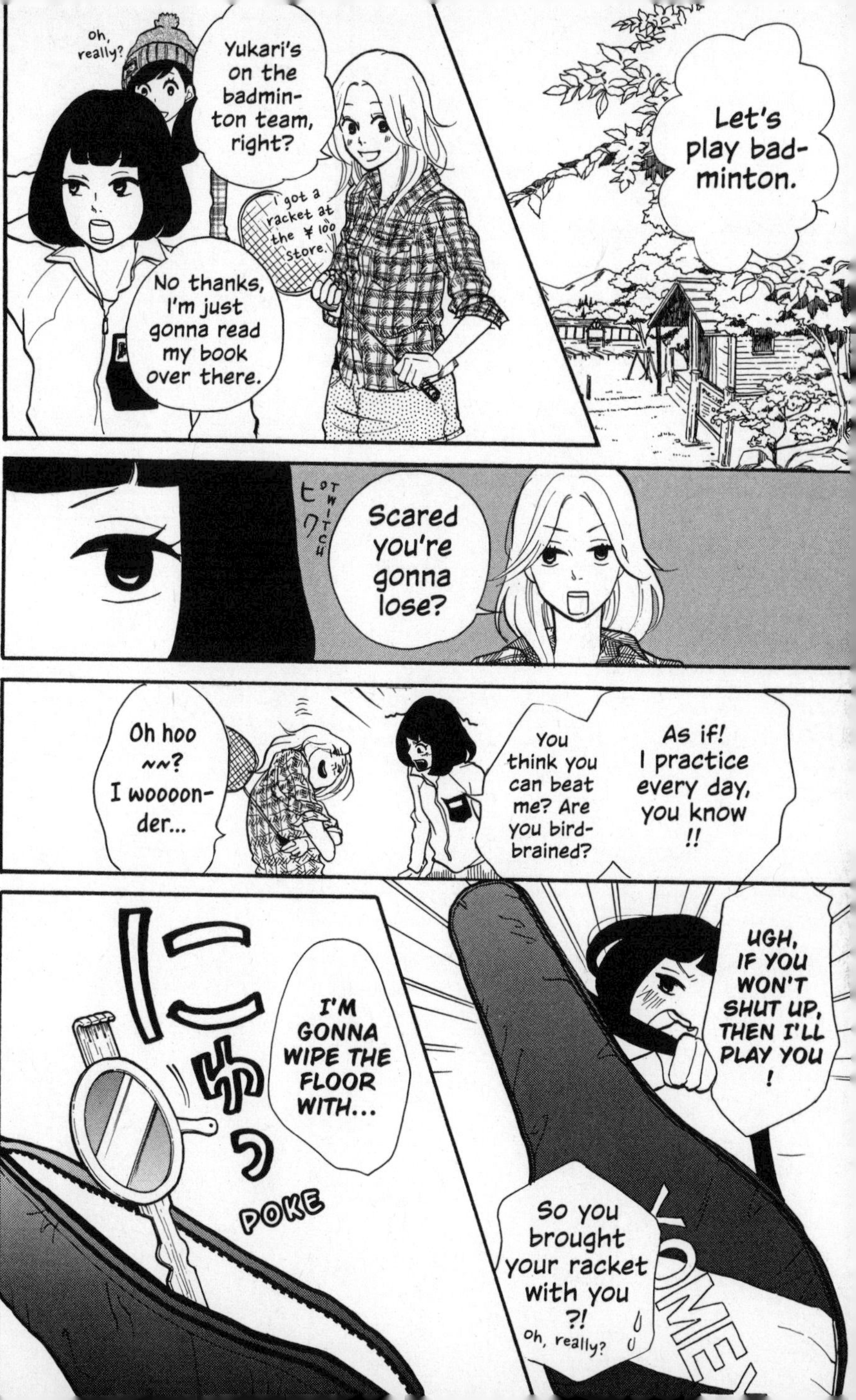
Let's play badminton.
Yukari's on the badminton team, right?
oh, really?
I got a racket at the ¥100 store.
No thanks, I'm just gonna read my book over there.
Scared you're gonna lose?
ピク
TWITCH
As if! I practice every day, you know!!
You think you can beat me? Are you bird-brained?
Oh hoo ~~? I wooooonder...
UGH, IF YOU WON'T SHUT UP, THEN I'LL PLAY YOU!
So you brought your racket with you?!
oh, really?
I'M GONNA WIPE THE FLOOR WITH...
ゆっ
POKE

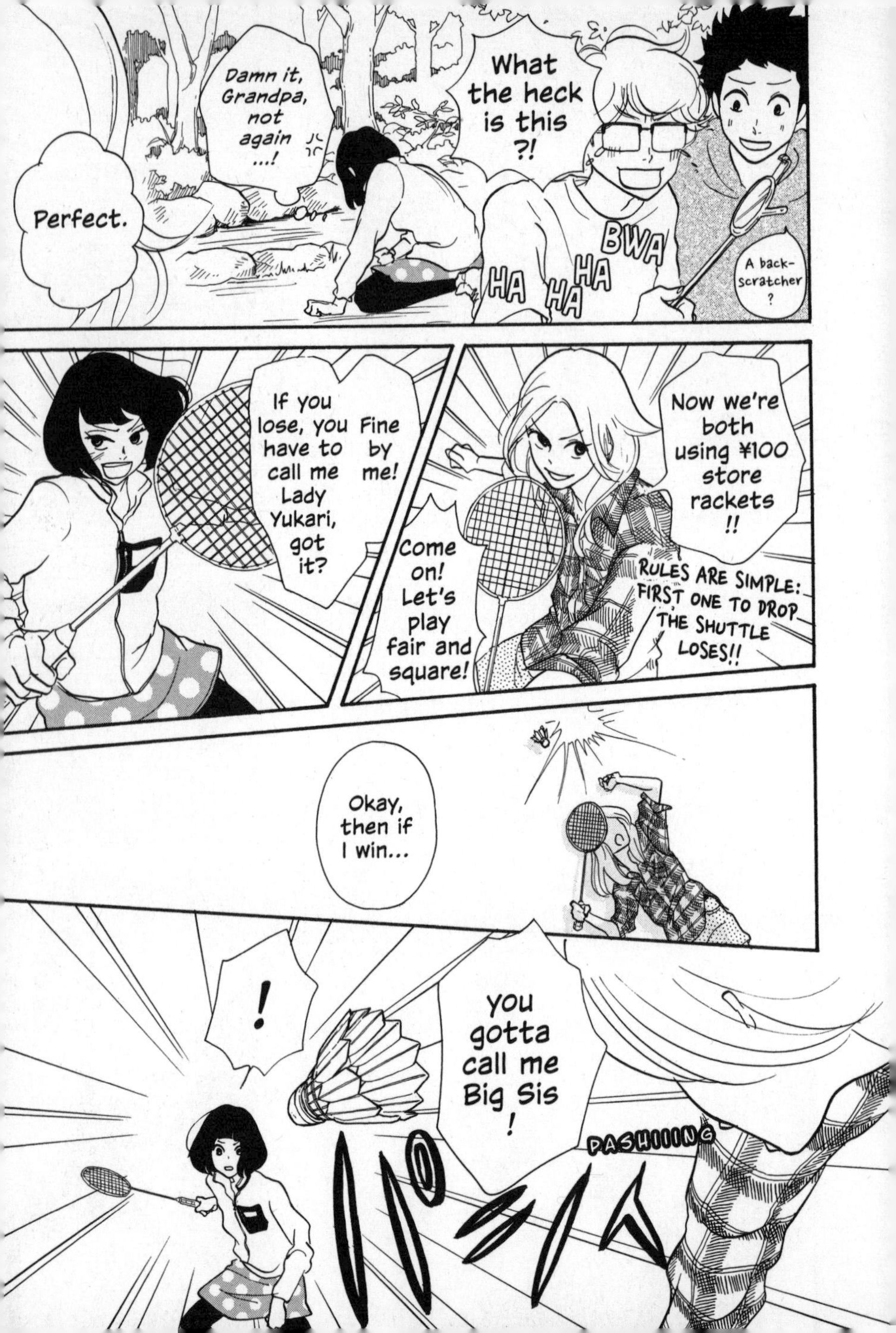
What the heck is this ?!
A back-scratcher ?
BWA HA HA HA HA
Damn it, Grandpa, not again ...!
Perfect.
Now we're both using ¥100 store rackets !!
RULES ARE SIMPLE: FIRST ONE TO DROP THE SHUTTLE LOSES!!
Come on! Let's play fair and square!
Fine by me!
If you lose, you have to call me Lady Yukari, got it?
Okay, then if I win...
You gotta call me Big Sis !
PASHIIING
!

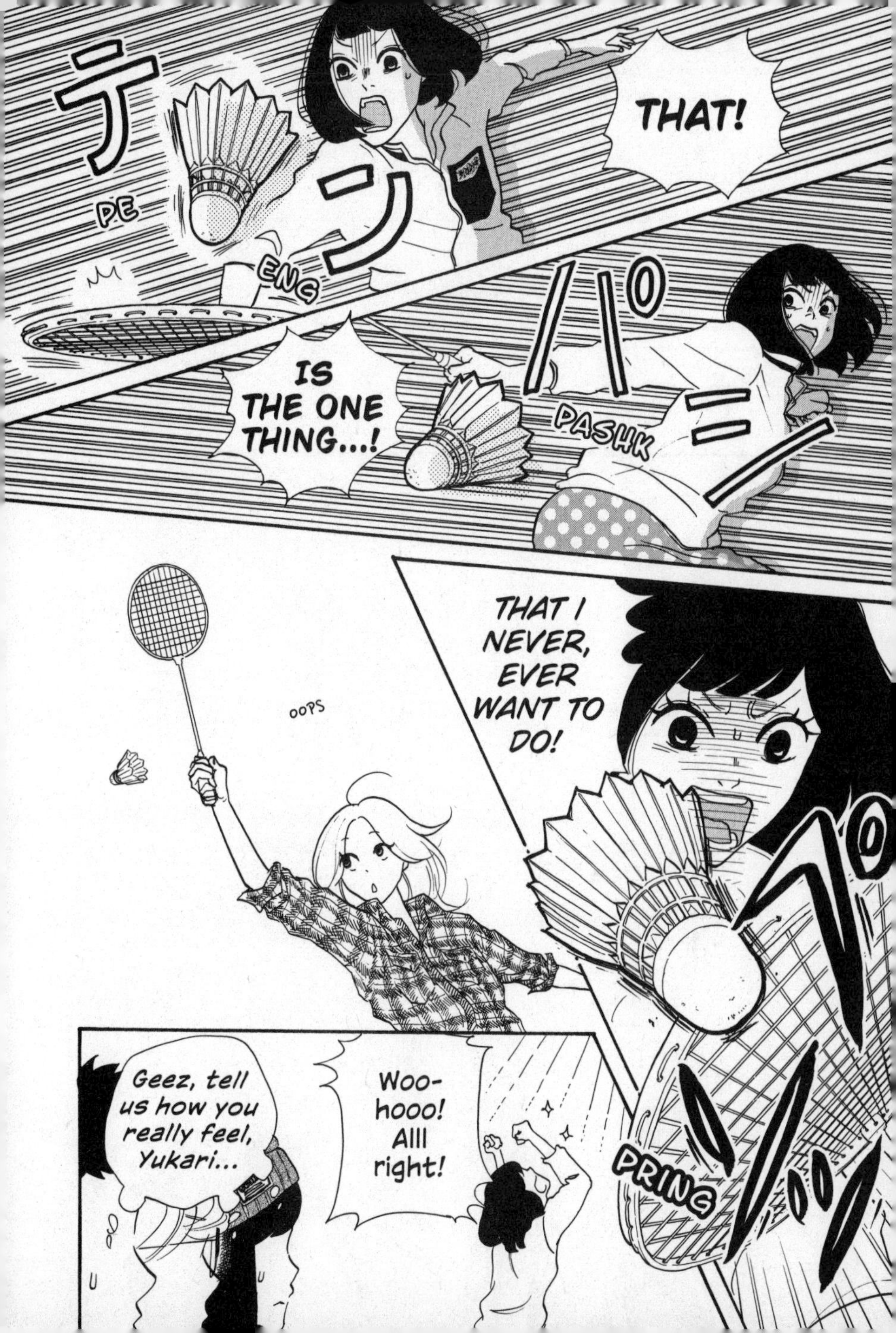
THAT!
テン
PE
ENG
パ
IS THE ONE THING...!
PASHK
THAT I NEVER, EVER WANT TO DO!
パ
PRING
OOPS
Woo-hooo! Alll right!
Geez, tell us how you really feel, Yukari...

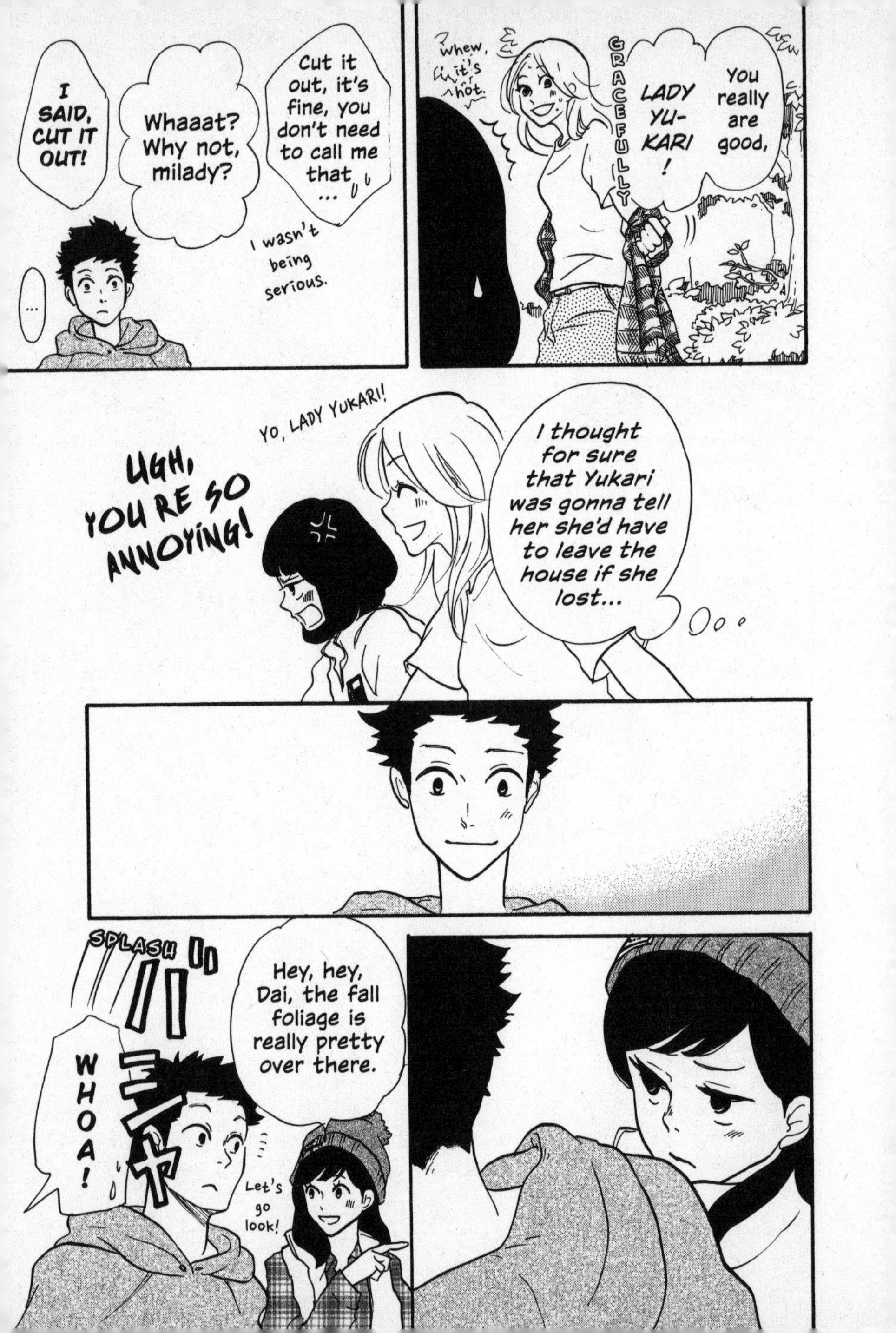
You really are good,
LADY YUKARI!
GRACEFULLY
whew, it's hot.
Cut it out, it's fine, you don't need to call me that ...
I wasn't being serious.
Whaaat? Why not, milady?
I SAID, CUT IT OUT!
...
I thought for sure that Yukari was gonna tell her she'd have to leave the house if she lost...
YO, LADY YUKARI!
UGH, YOU RE SO ANNOYING!
Hey, hey, Dai, the fall foliage is really pretty over there.
Let's go look!
SPLASH
WHOA!

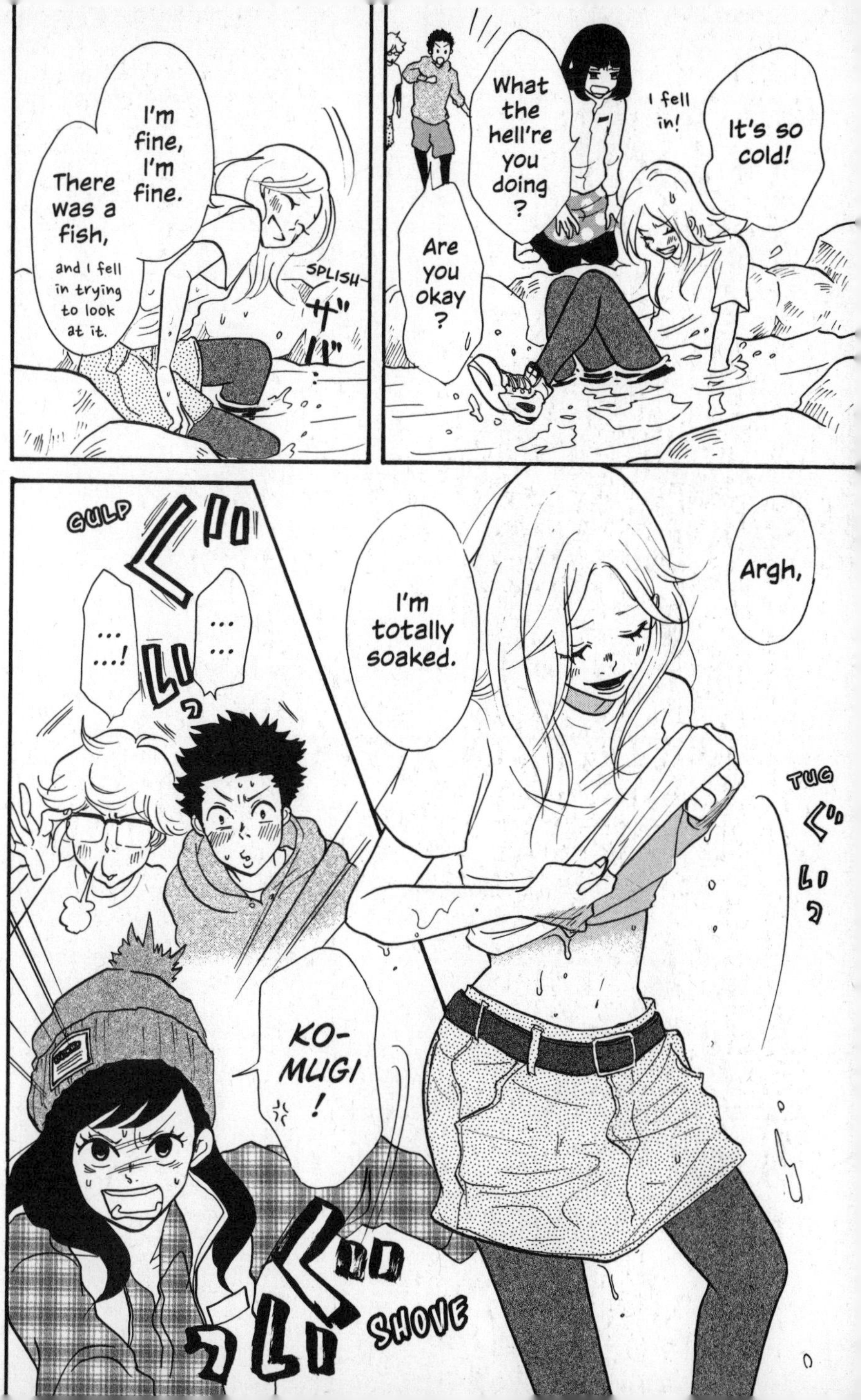
It's so cold!
I fell in!
What the hell're you doing?
Are you okay?
SPLISH
I'm fine, I'm fine.
There was a fish,
and I fell in trying to look at it.
Argh,
I'm totally soaked.
TUG
GULP
... ...
... ...!
KO-MUGI!
SHOVE

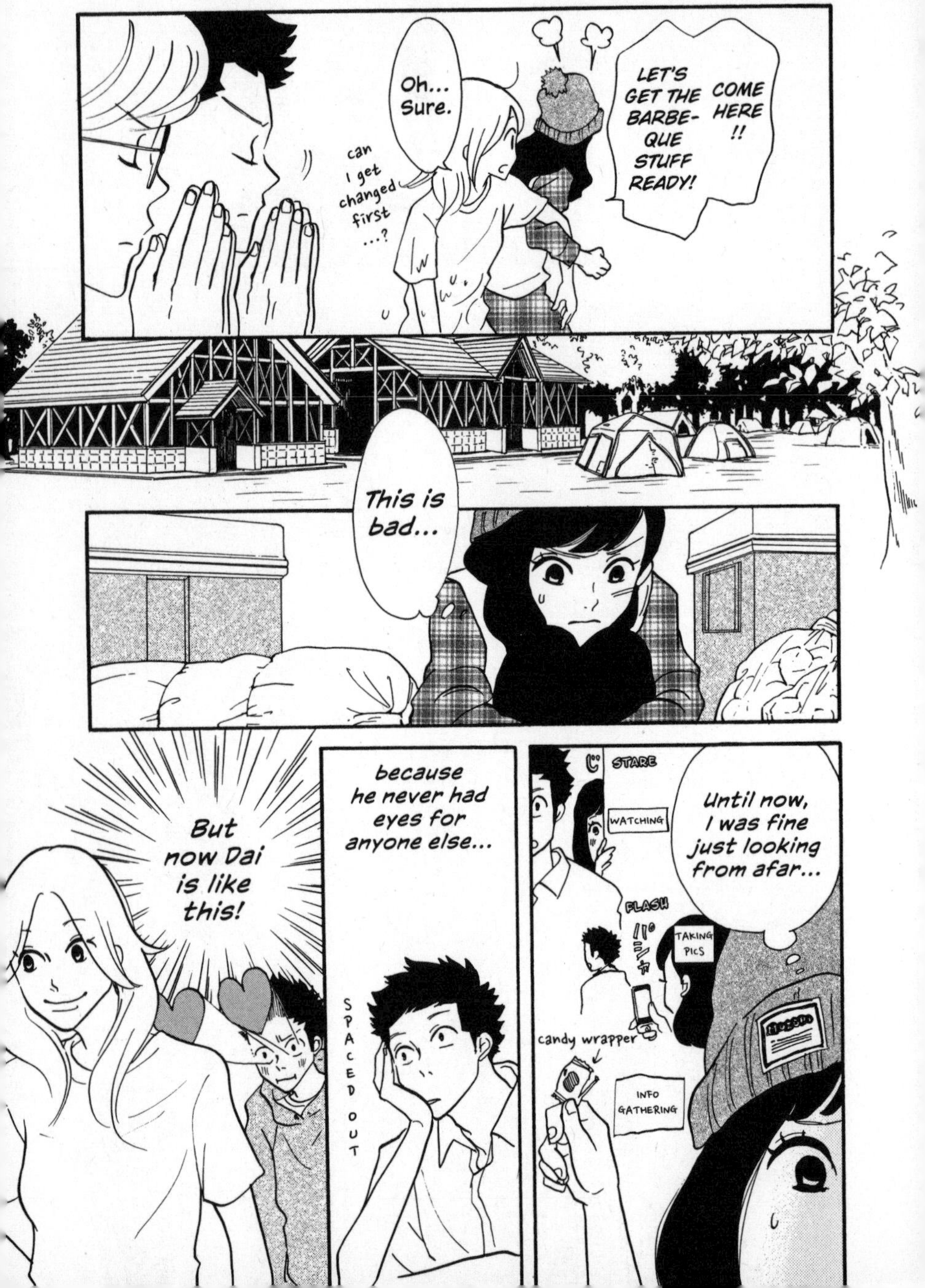
COME HERE!!
LET'S GET THE BARBE-QUE STUFF READY!
Oh... Sure.
can I get changed first...?
This is bad...
Until now, I was fine just looking from afar...
STARE
WATCHING
FLASH
TAKING PICS
candy wrapper
INFO GATHERING
because he never had eyes for anyone else...
SPACED OUT
But now Dai is like this!

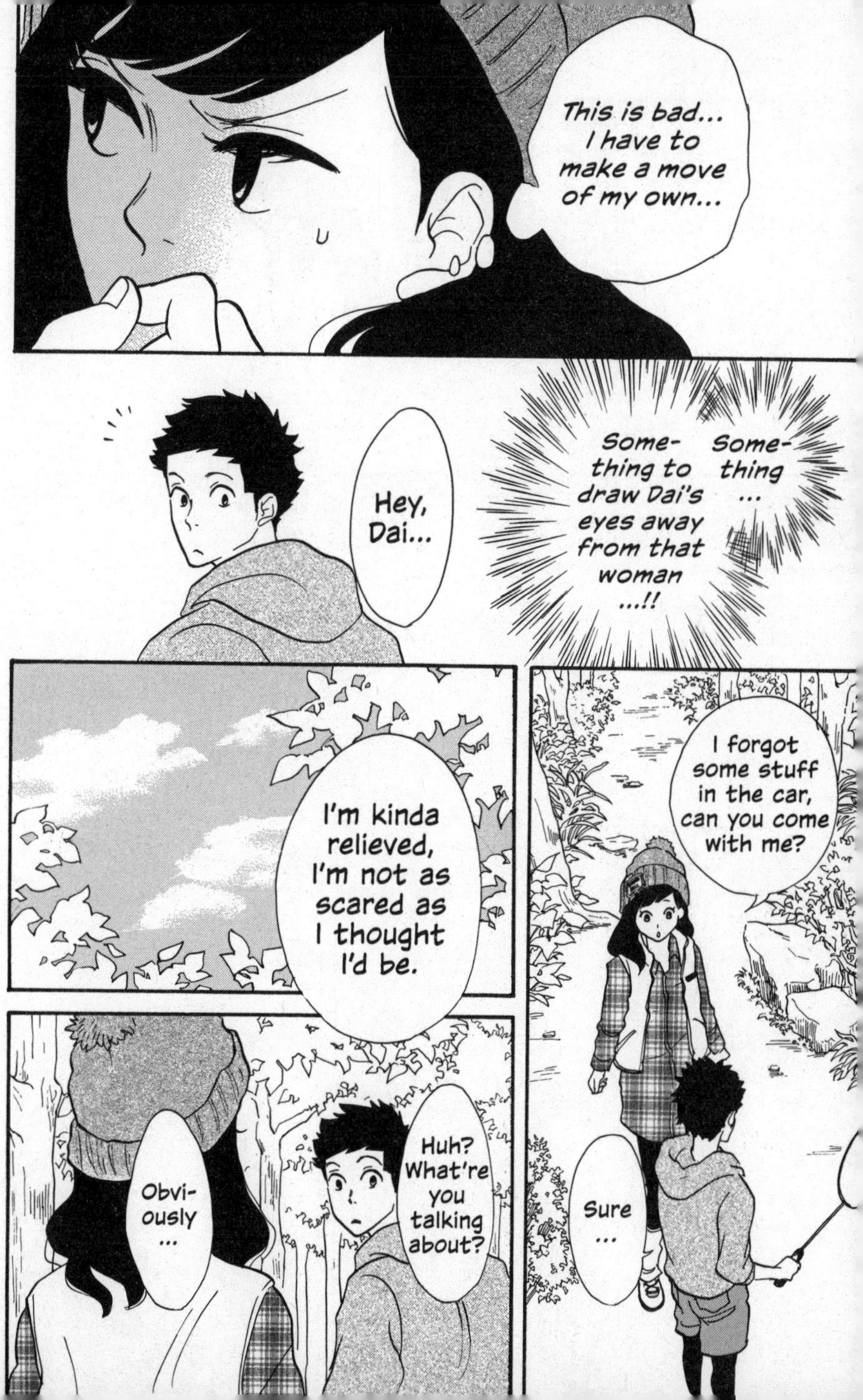
This is bad... I have to make a move of my own...
Something...
Something to draw Dai's eyes away from that woman...!!
Hey, Dai...
I forgot some stuff in the car, can you come with me?
Sure...
I'm kinda relieved, I'm not as scared as I thought I'd be.
Huh? What're you talking about?
Obviously...

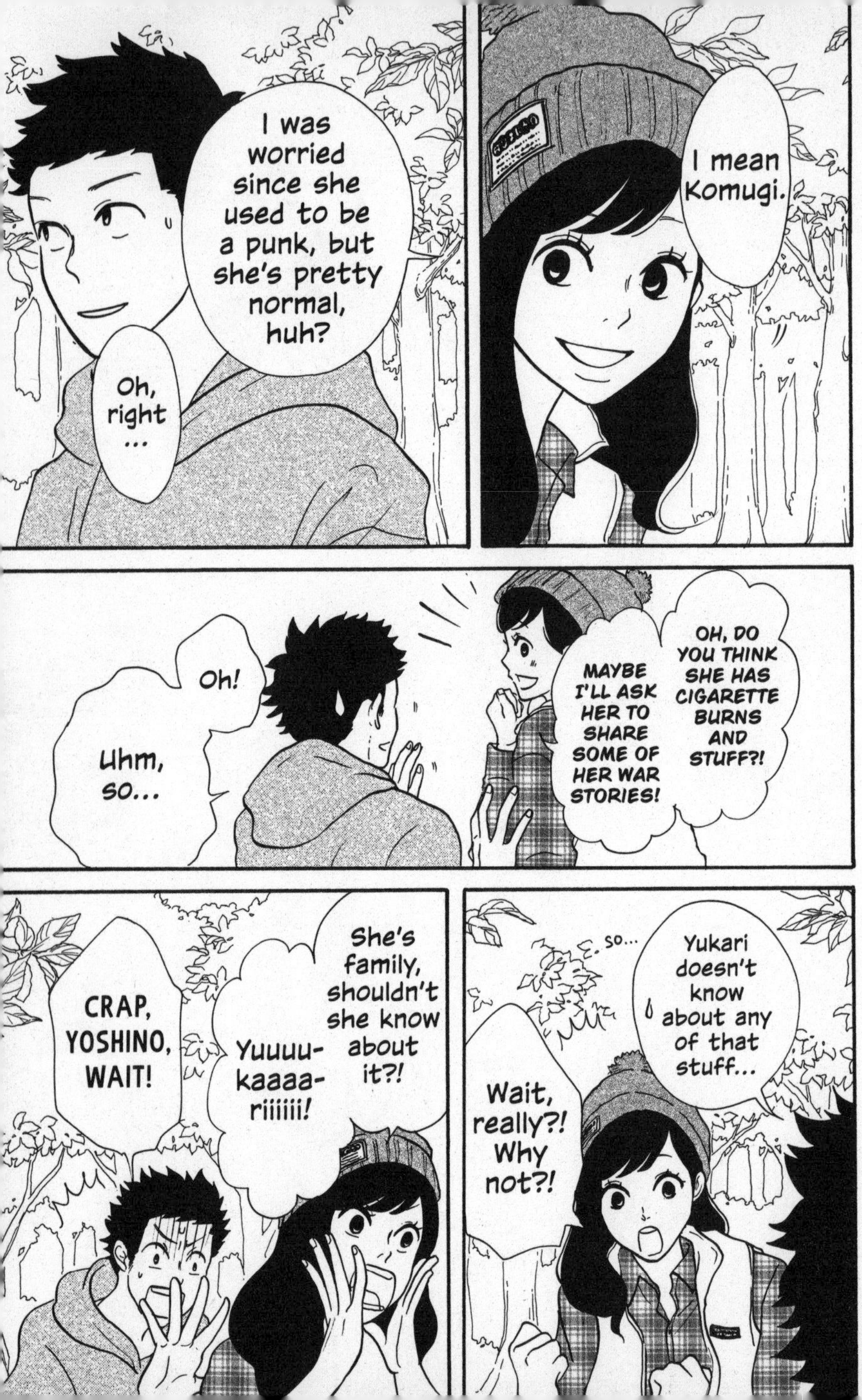
I mean Komugi.
I was worried since she used to be a punk, but she's pretty normal, huh?
Oh, right ...
OH, DO YOU THINK SHE HAS CIGARETTE BURNS AND STUFF?!
MAYBE I'LL ASK HER TO SHARE SOME OF HER WAR STORIES!
Oh!
Uhm, so...
Yukari doesn't know about any of that stuff...
so...
Wait, really?! Why not?!
She's family, shouldn't she know about it?!
Yuuuu-kaaaa-riiiiiii!
CRAP, YOSHINO, WAIT!

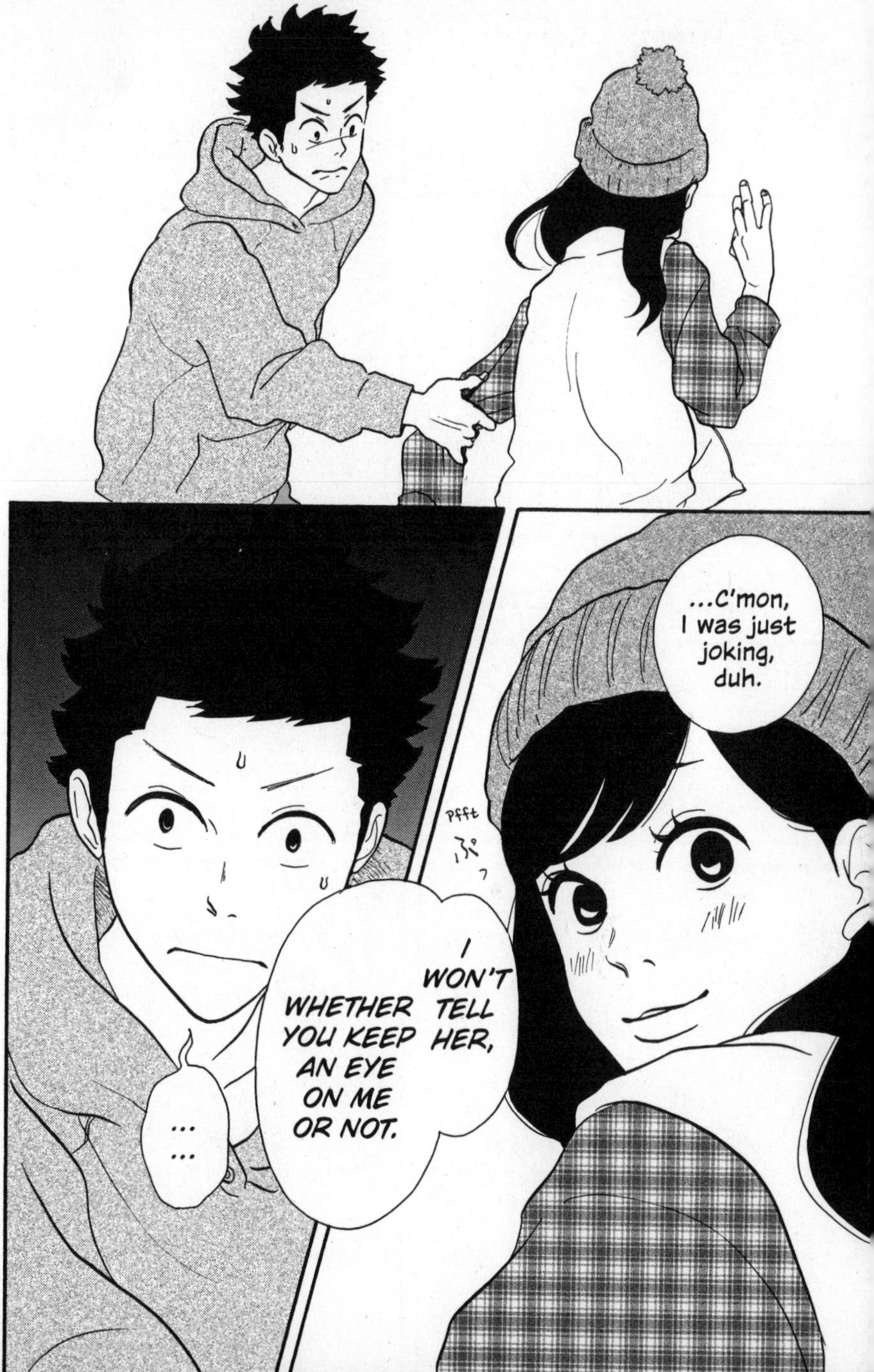
...C'mon, I was just joking, duh.
pfft
ぷっ
I WON'T TELL HER, WHETHER YOU KEEP AN EYE ON ME OR NOT.
... ...

19 CAMP SCANDALOUS

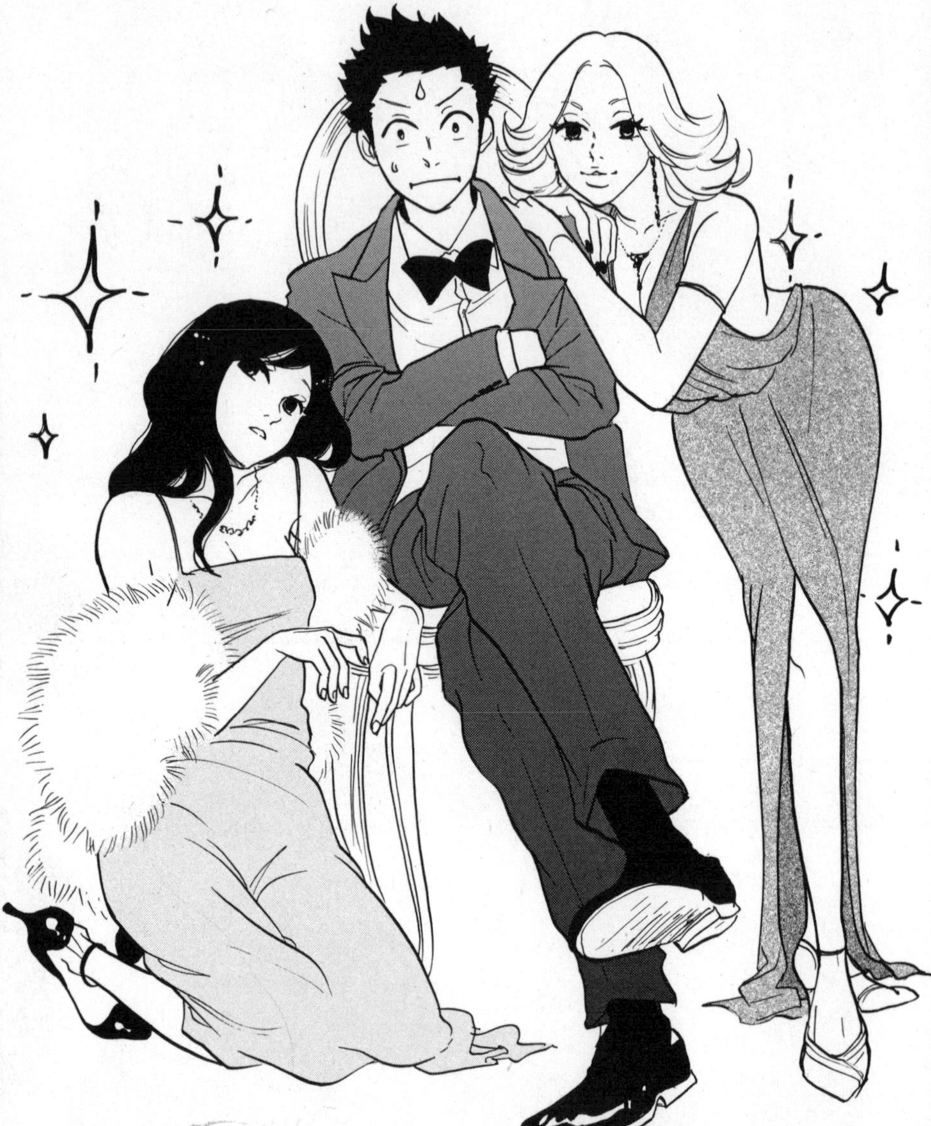

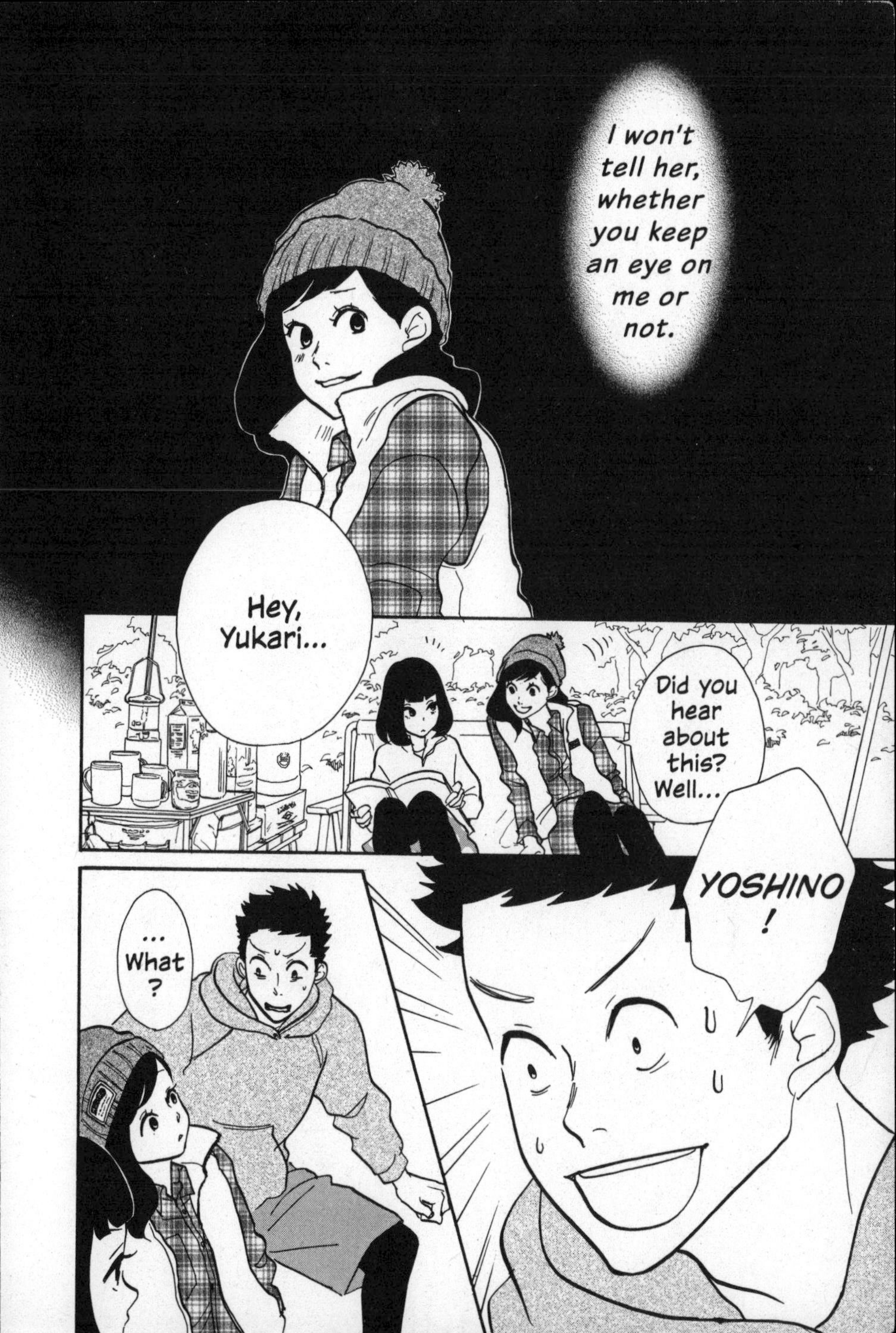
I won't tell her, whether you keep an eye on me or not.
Hey, Yukari...
Did you hear about this? Well...
YOSHINO!
...What?

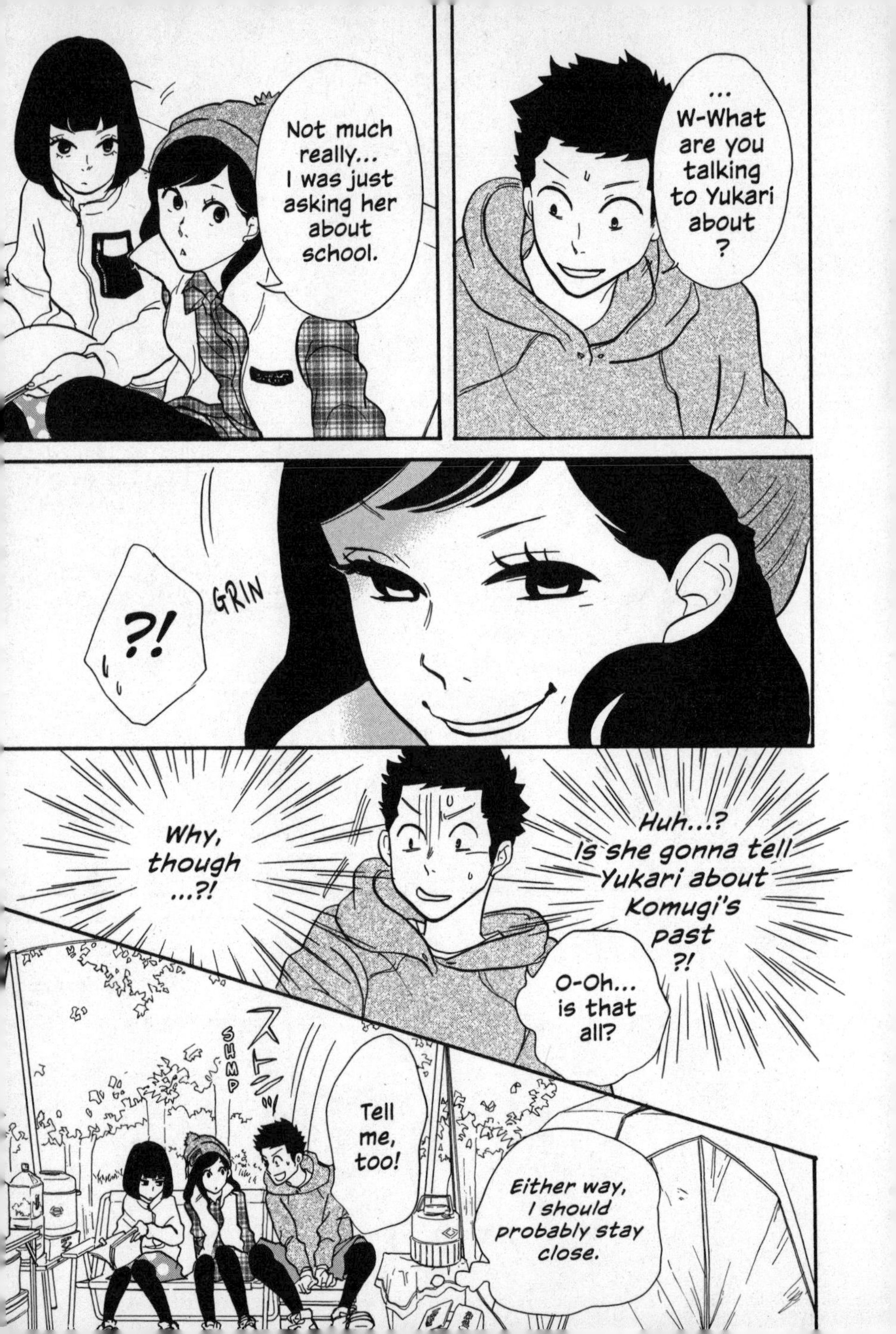

... W-What are you talking to Yukari about ?
Not much really... I was just asking her about school.
GRIN
?!
Huh...? Is she gonna tell Yukari about Komugi's past ?!
Why, though ...?!
O-Oh... is that all?
Either way, I should probably stay close.
Tell me, too!
SHMP

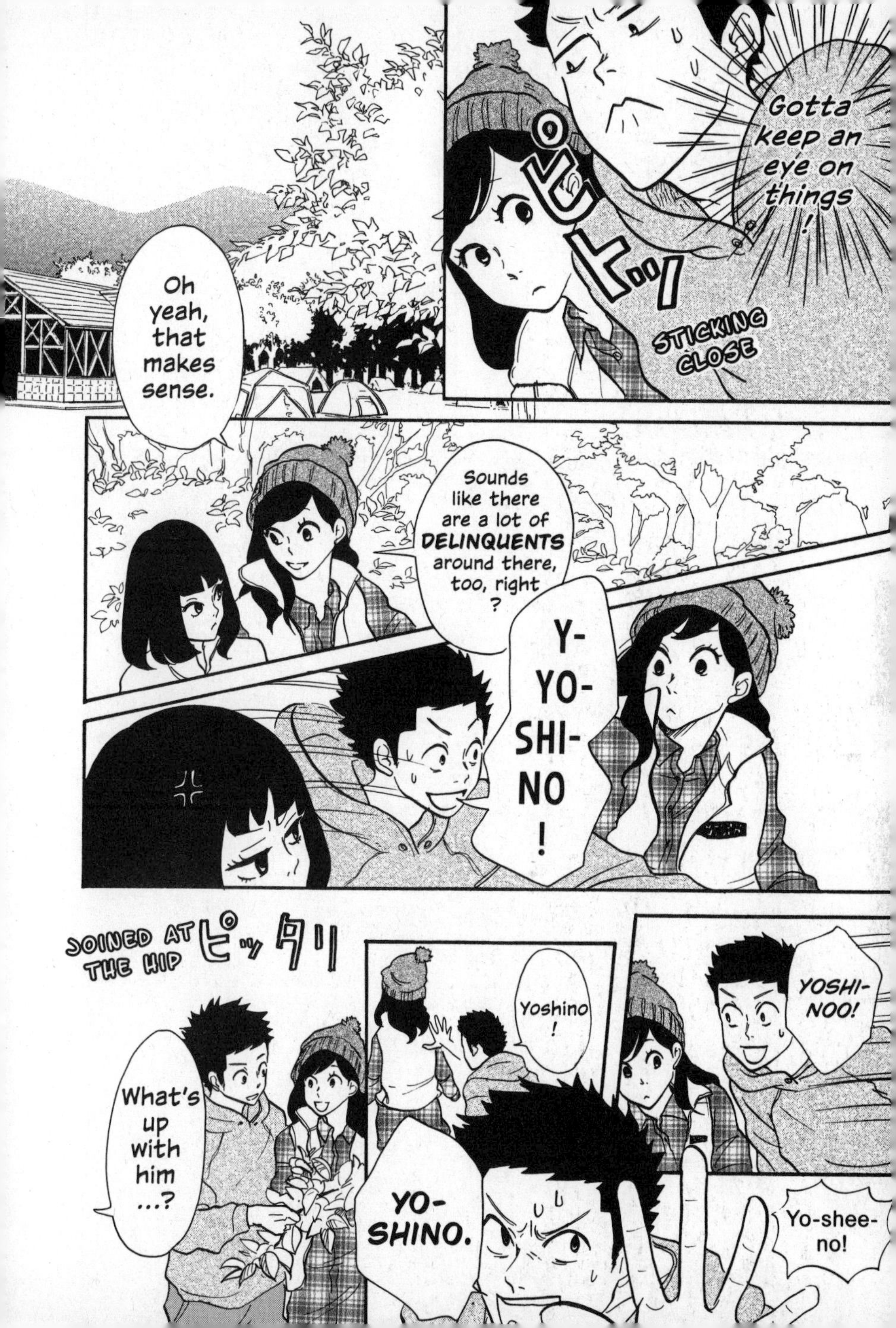
Gotta keep an eye on things!
ピト
STICKING CLOSE
Oh yeah, that makes sense.
Sounds like there are a lot of **DELINQUENTS** around there, too, right?
Y-YO-SHI-NO!
YOSHI-NOO!
Yoshino!
Yo-shee-no!
YO-SHINO.
JOINED AT THE HIP
ピッタリ
What's up with him...?

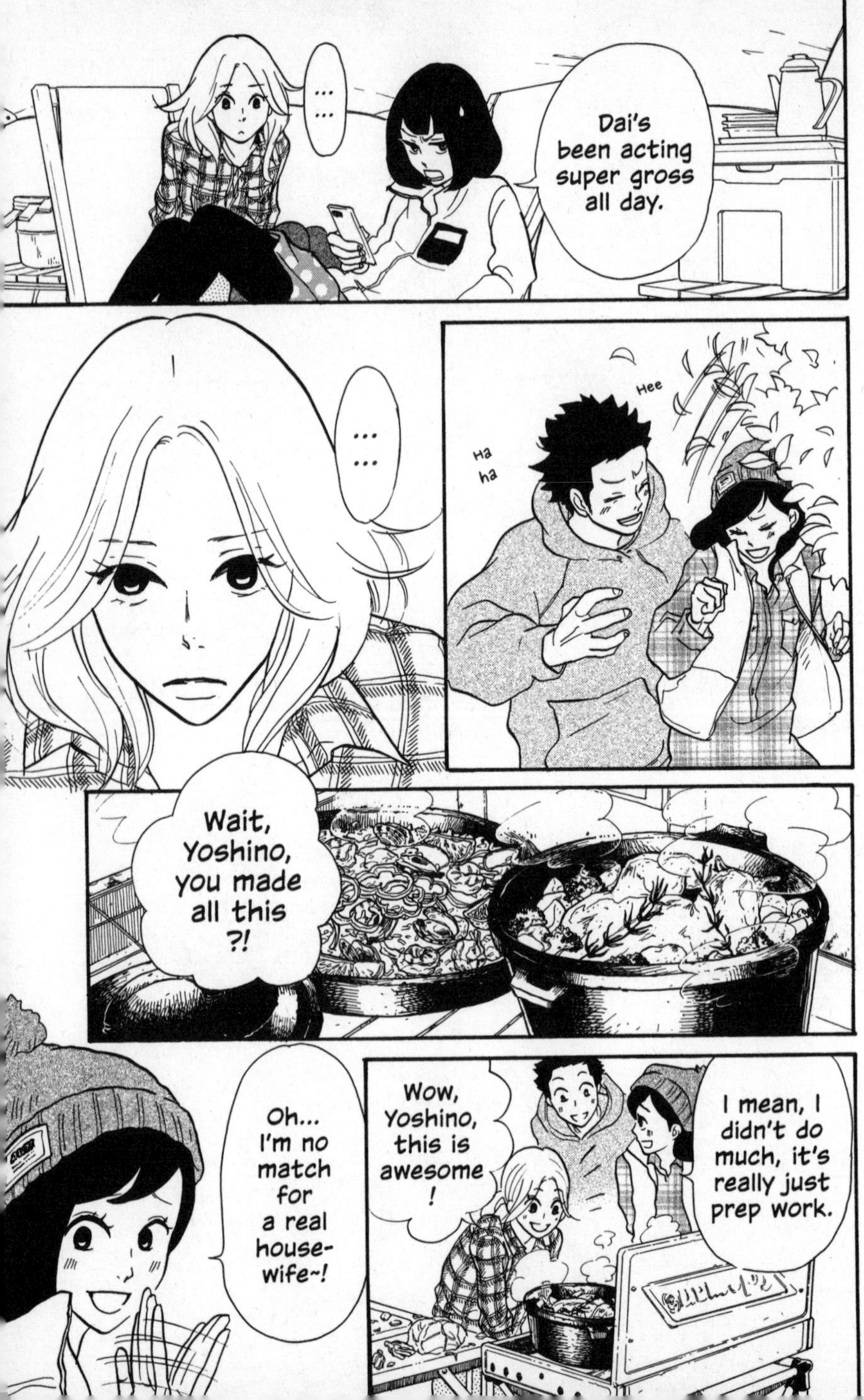

Dai's been acting super gross all day.
……
Hee
Ha ha
……
Wait, Yoshino, you made all this?!
I mean, I didn't do much, it's really just prep work.
Wow, Yoshino, this is awesome!
Oh... I'm no match for a real housewife~!

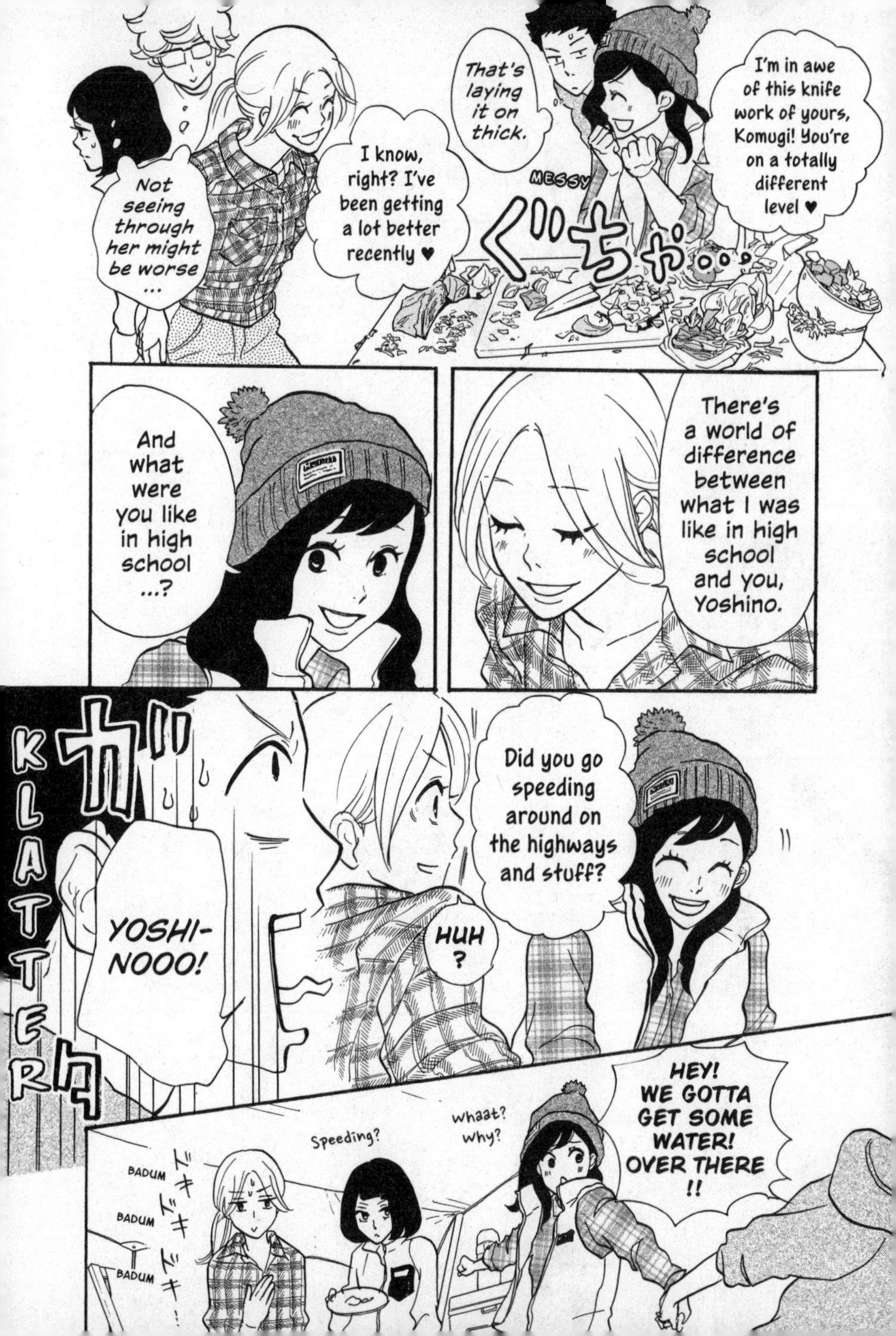
I'm in awe of this knife work of yours, Komugi! You're on a totally different level ♥
That's laying it on thick.
MESSY
I know, right? I've been getting a lot better recently ♥
Not seeing through her might be worse ...
There's a world of difference between what I was like in high school and you, Yoshino.
And what were you like in high school ...?
Did you go speeding around on the highways and stuff?
HUH ?
YOSHI-NOOO!
KLATTER
HEY! WE GOTTA GET SOME WATER! OVER THERE !!
Whaat? Why?
Speeding?
BADUM
BADUM
BADUM

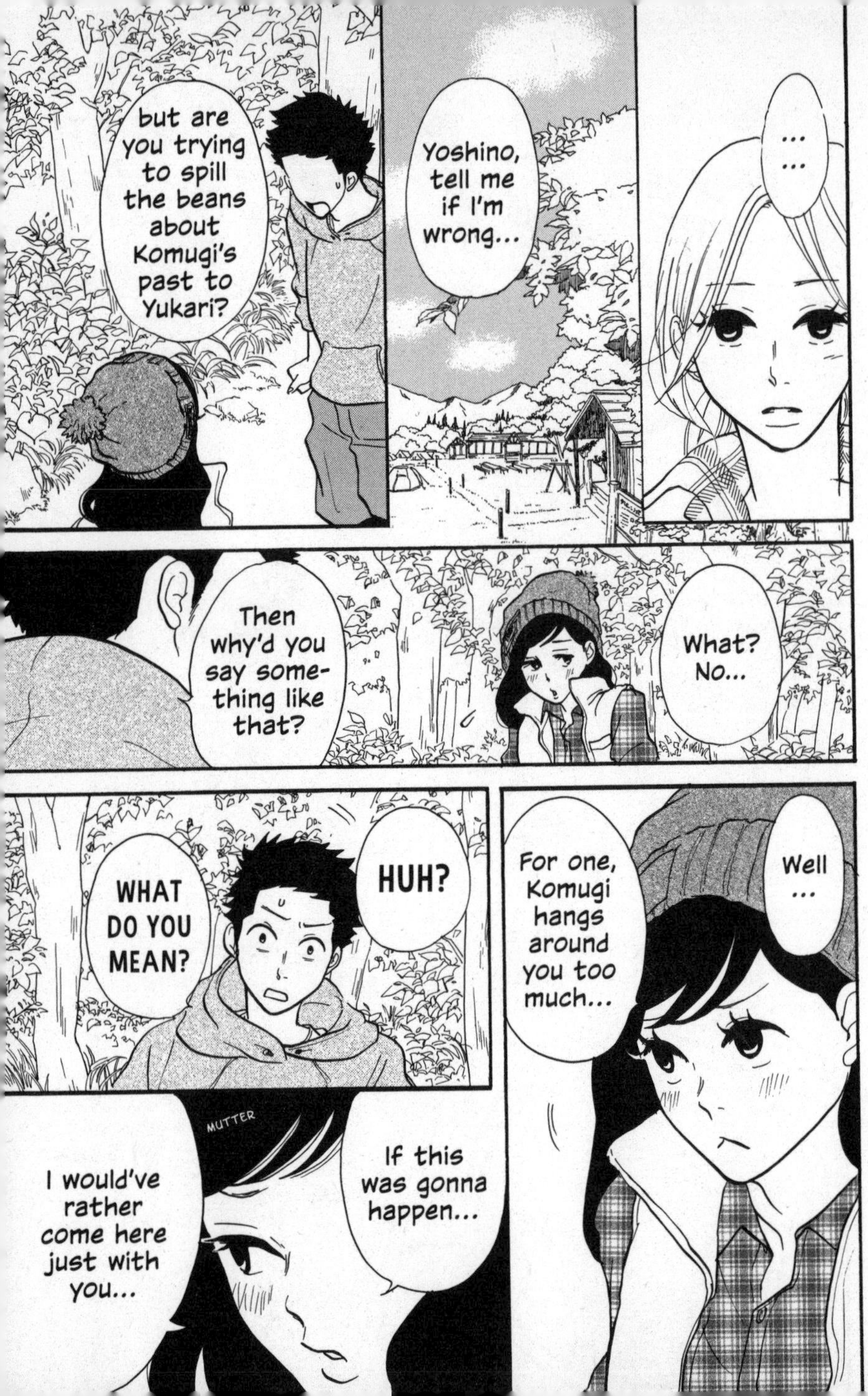
... ...
Yoshino, tell me if I'm wrong...
but are you trying to spill the beans about Komugi's past to Yukari?
What? No...
Then why'd you say some-thing like that?
Well ...
For one, Komugi hangs around you too much...
HUH?
WHAT DO YOU MEAN?
MUTTER
If this was gonna happen...
I would've rather come here just with you...

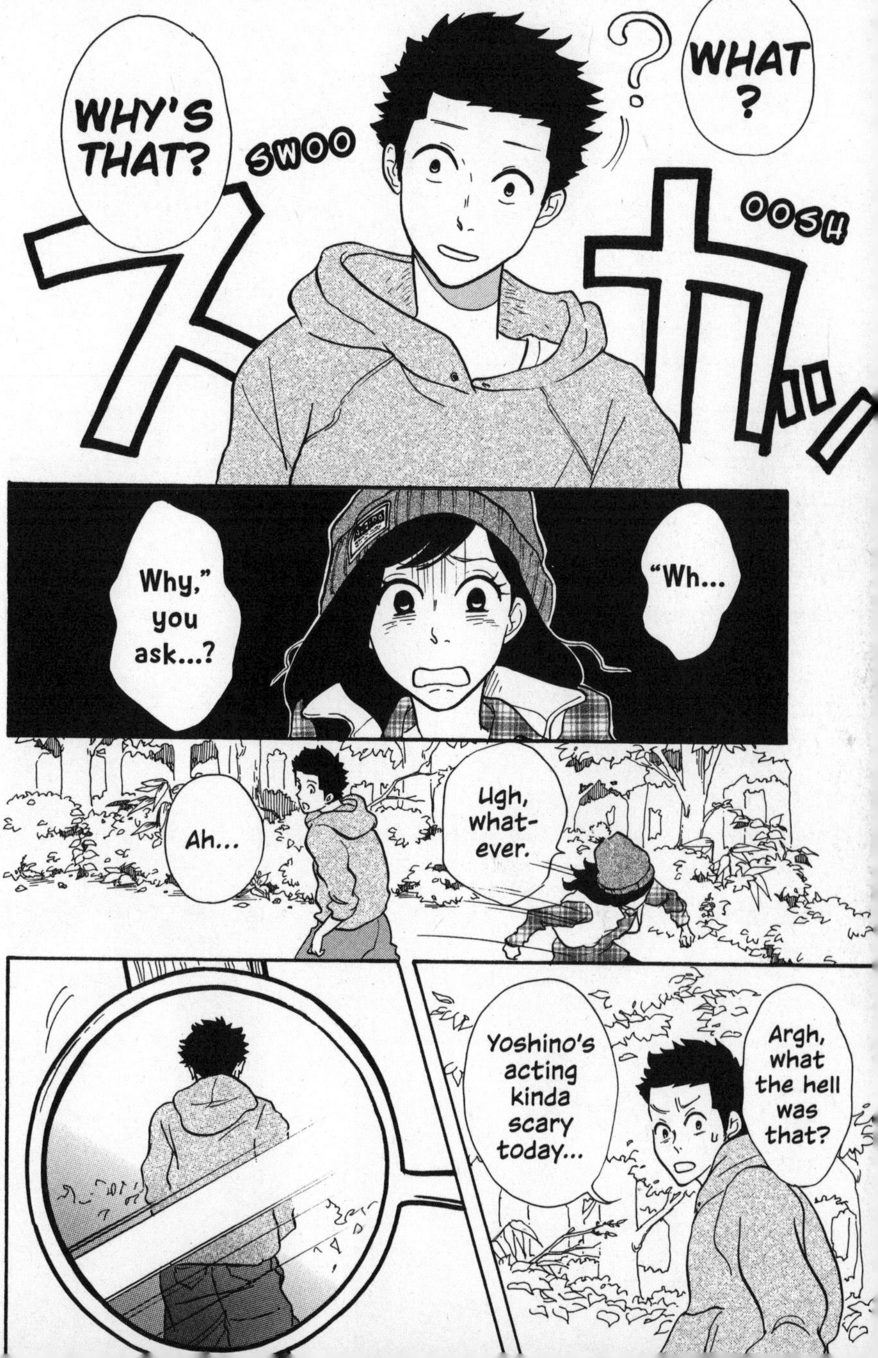
WHAT ?
WHY'S THAT?
SWOO
OOSH
"Wh...
Why," you ask...?
Ugh, what-ever.
Ah...
Argh, what the hell was that?
Yoshino's acting kinda scary today...

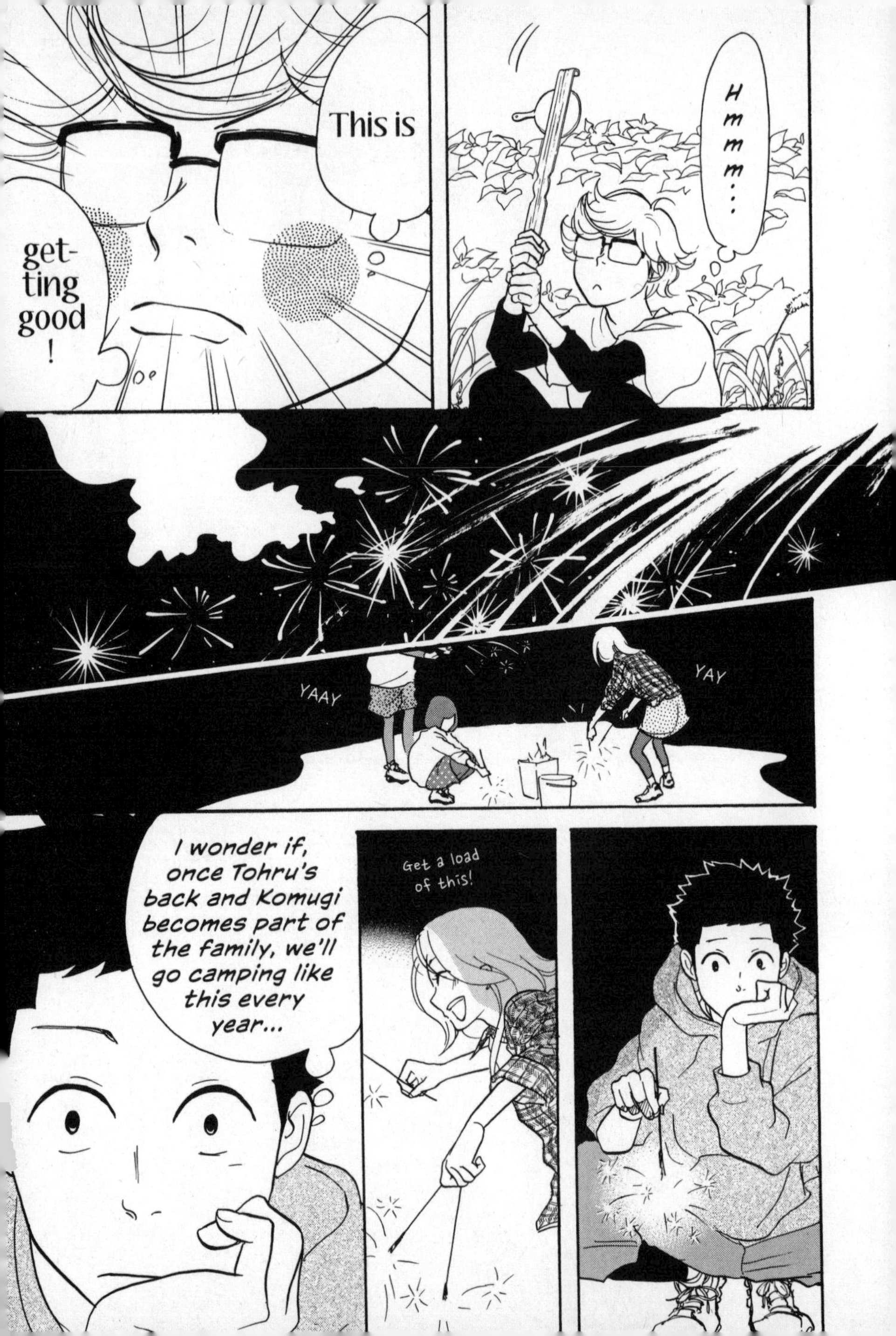
Hmmm...
This is getting good!
YAY
YAAY
Get a load of this!
I wonder if, once Tohru's back and Komugi becomes part of the family, we'll go camping like this every year...

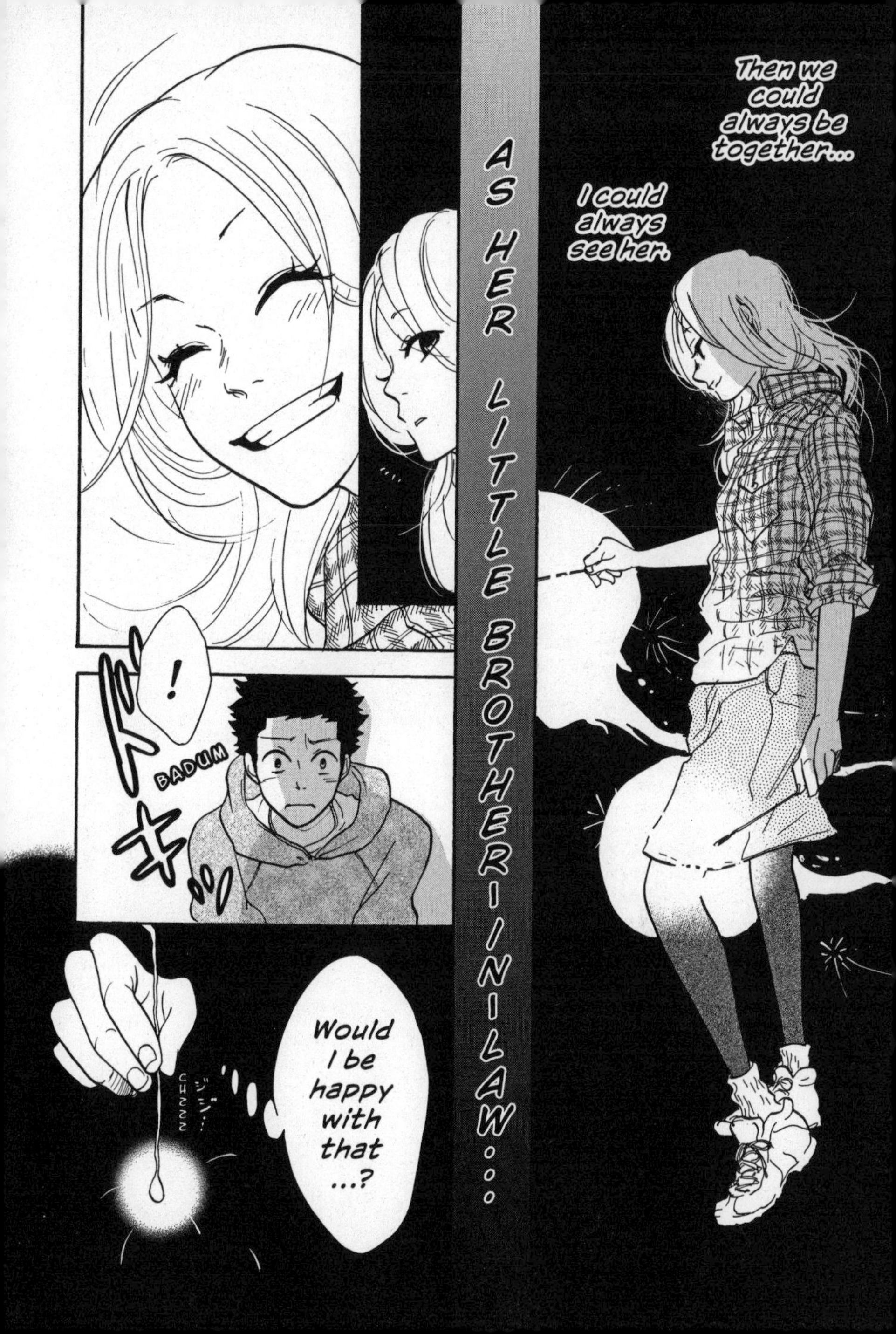
Then we could always be together...
I could always see her.
AS HER LITTLE BROTHER-IN-LAW...
!
BADUM
Would I be happy with that ...?
CHZZZ

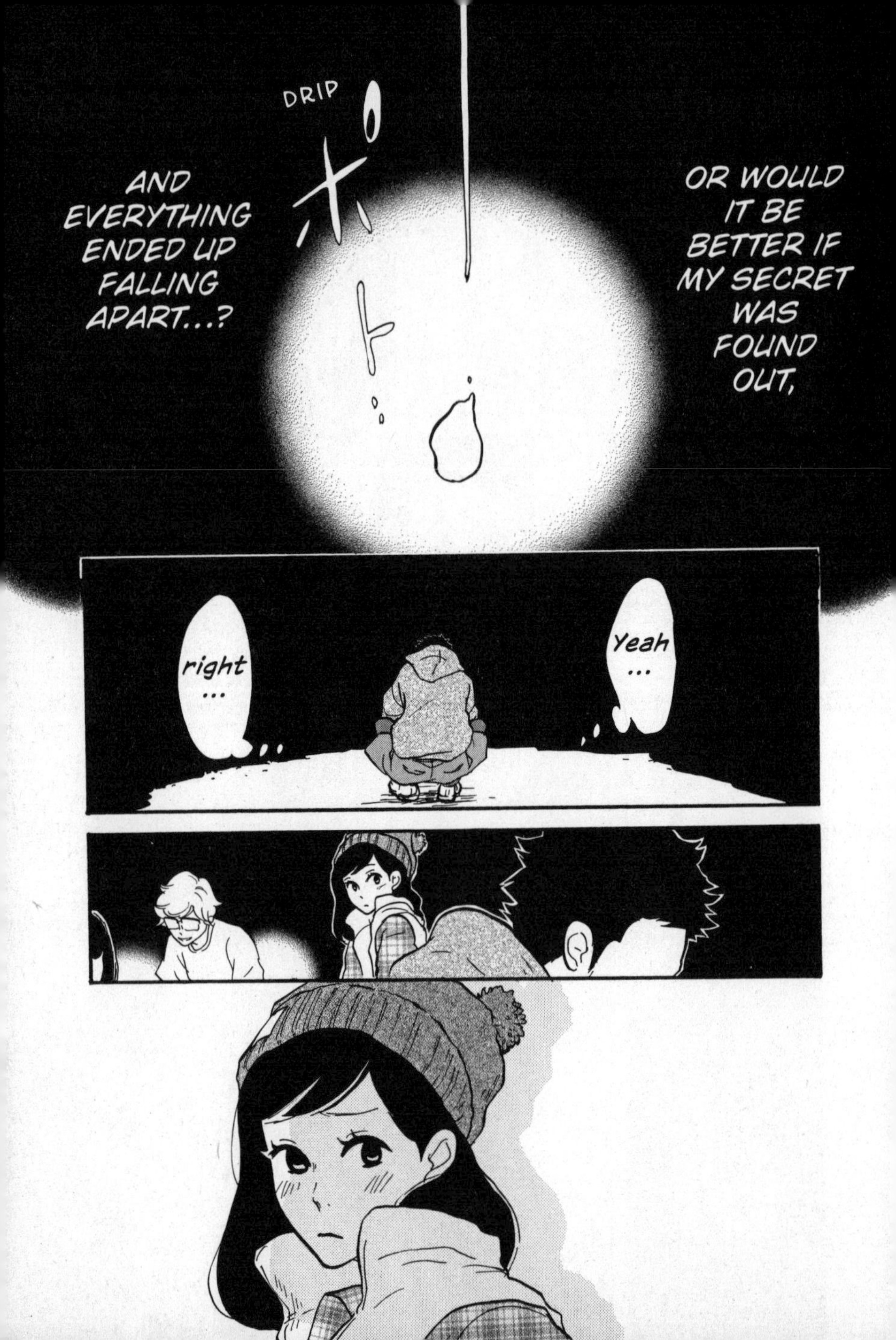
OR WOULD IT BE BETTER IF MY SECRET WAS FOUND OUT,
DRIP
ポト
AND EVERYTHING ENDED UP FALLING APART...?
Yeah...
right...

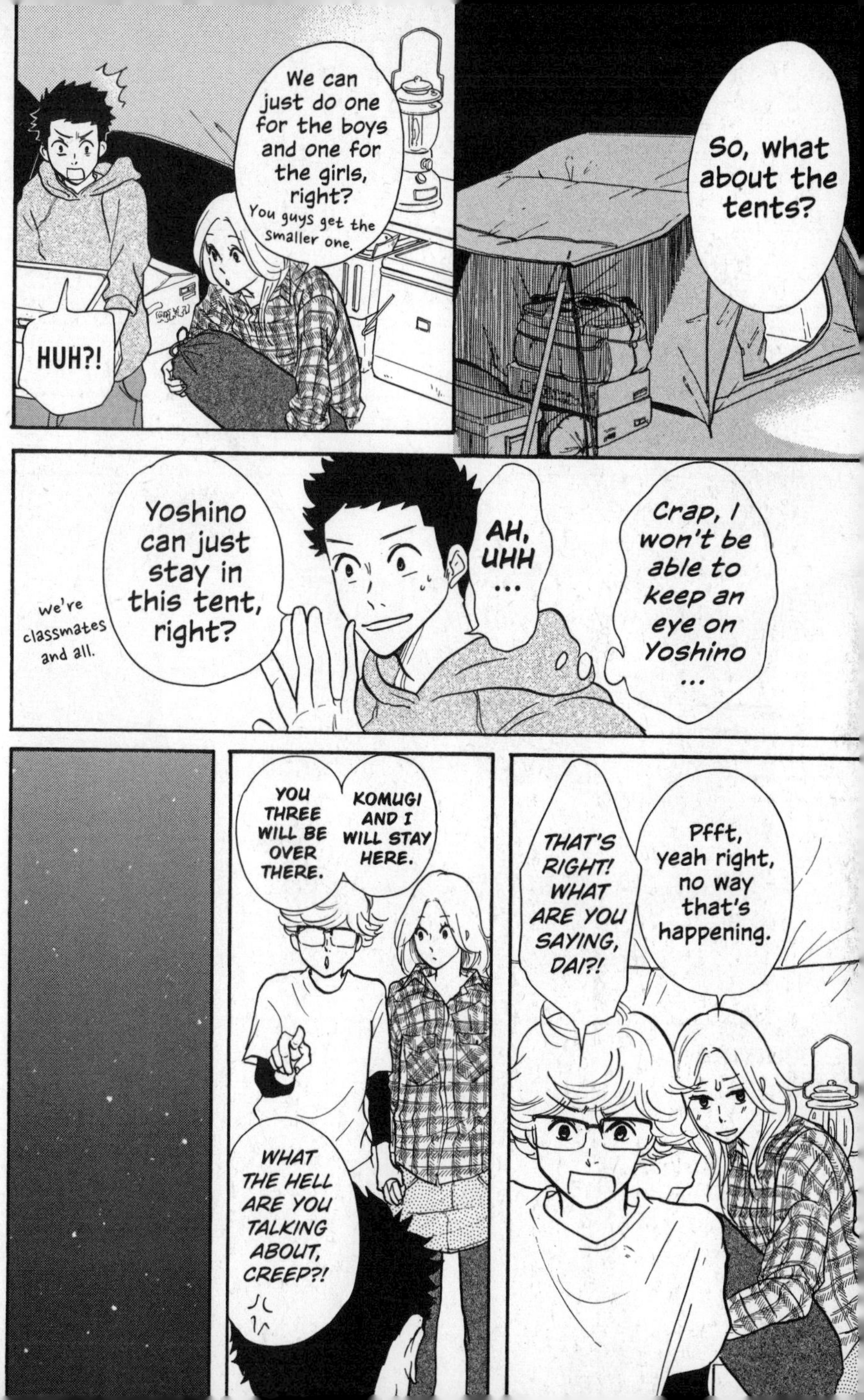
So, what about the tents?
We can just do one for the boys and one for the girls, right?
You guys get the smaller one.
HUH?!
Crap, I won't be able to keep an eye on Yoshino ...
AH, UHH ...
Yoshino can just stay in this tent, right?
we're classmates and all.
Pfft, yeah right, no way that's happening.
THAT'S RIGHT! WHAT ARE YOU SAYING, DAI?!
KOMUGI AND I WILL STAY HERE.
YOU THREE WILL BE OVER THERE.
WHAT THE HELL ARE YOU TALKING ABOUT, CREEP?!

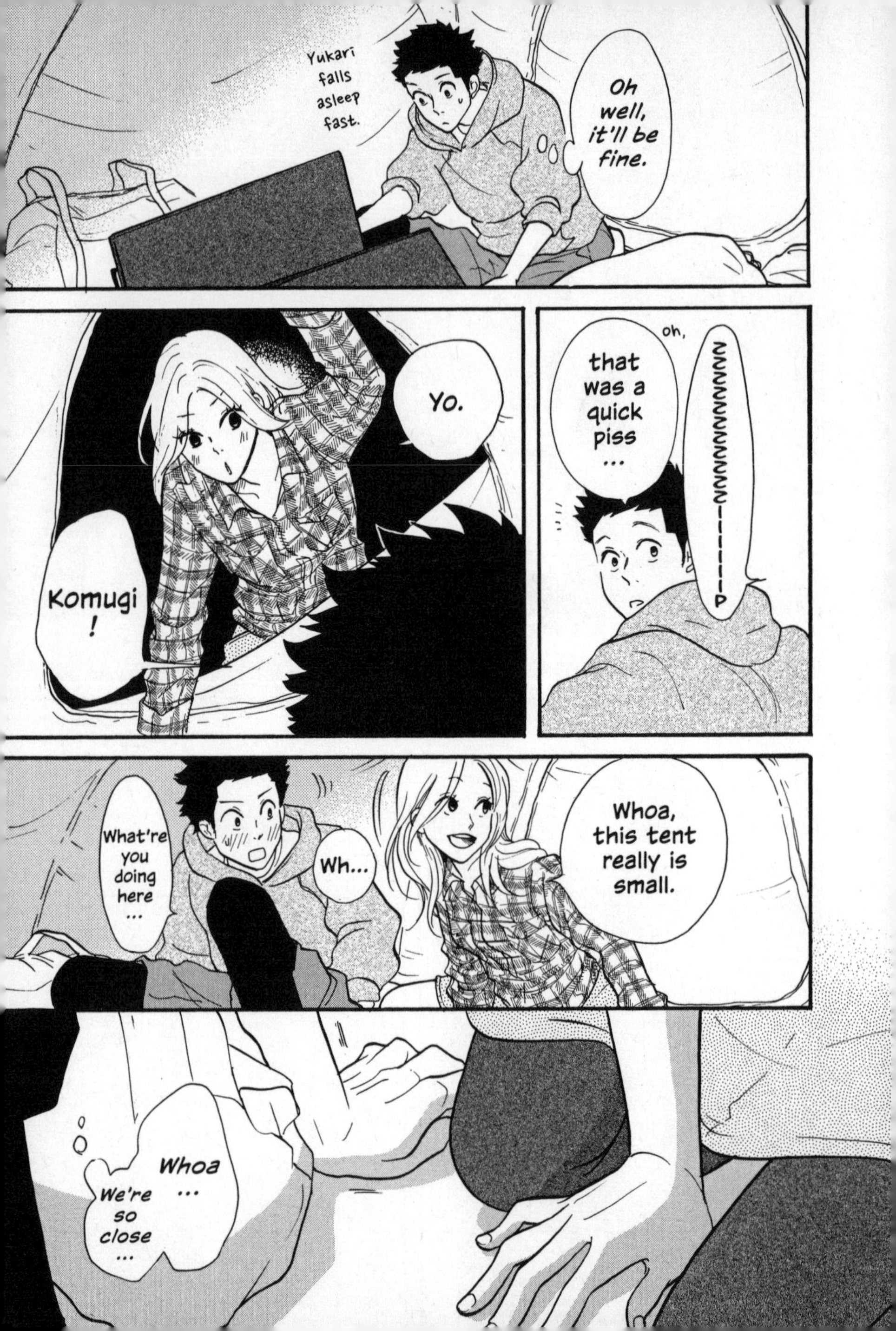
Oh well, it'll be fine.
Yukari falls asleep fast.
ZZZZZZZZZZZZ-----P
oh, that was a quick piss ...
Yo.
Komugi!
Whoa, this tent really is small.
Wh...
What're you doing here ...
Whoa ...
We're so close ...

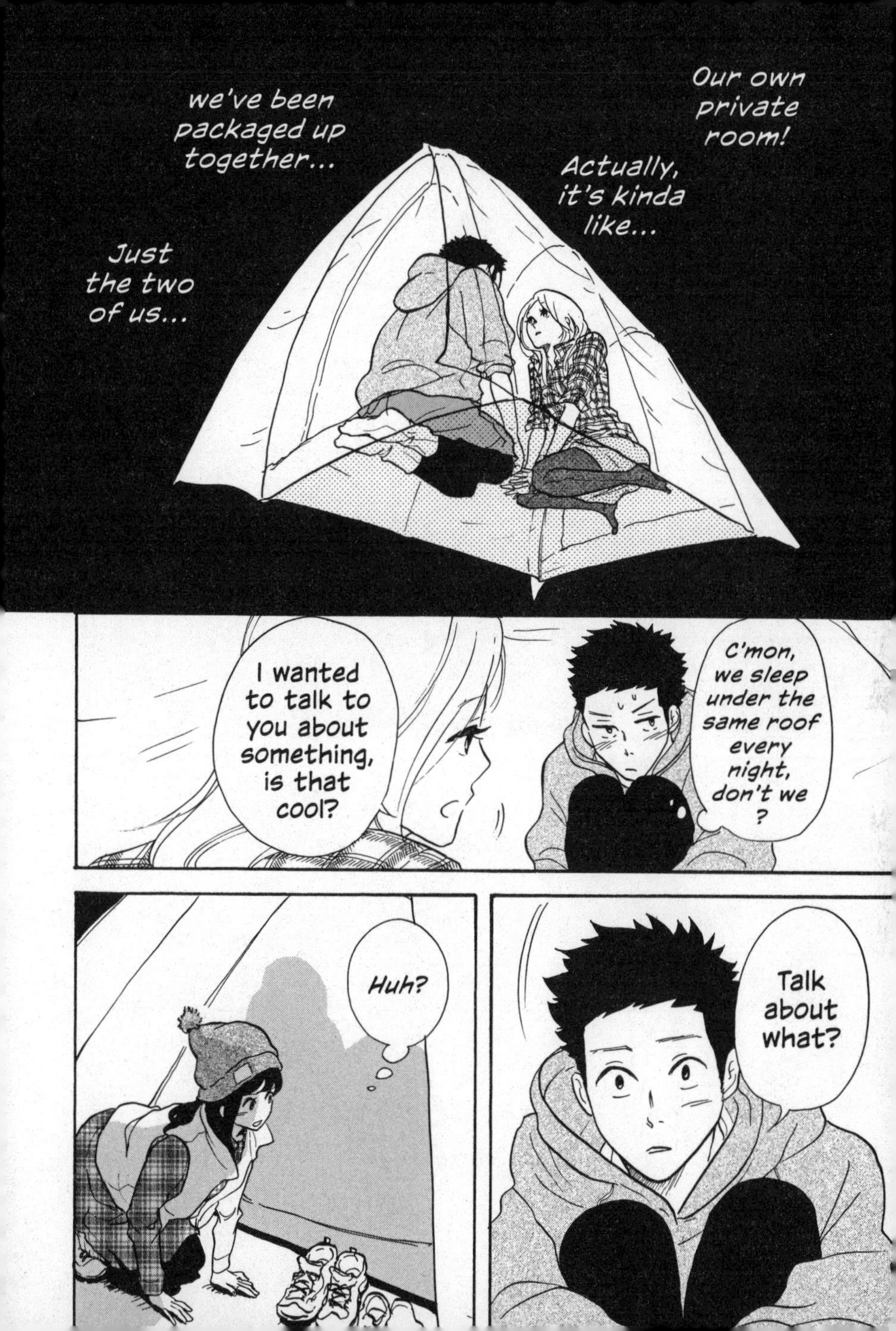
Just the two of us...
we've been packaged up together...
Actually, it's kinda like...
Our own private room!
C'mon, we sleep under the same roof every night, don't we ?
I wanted to talk to you about something, is that cool?
Talk about what?
Huh?

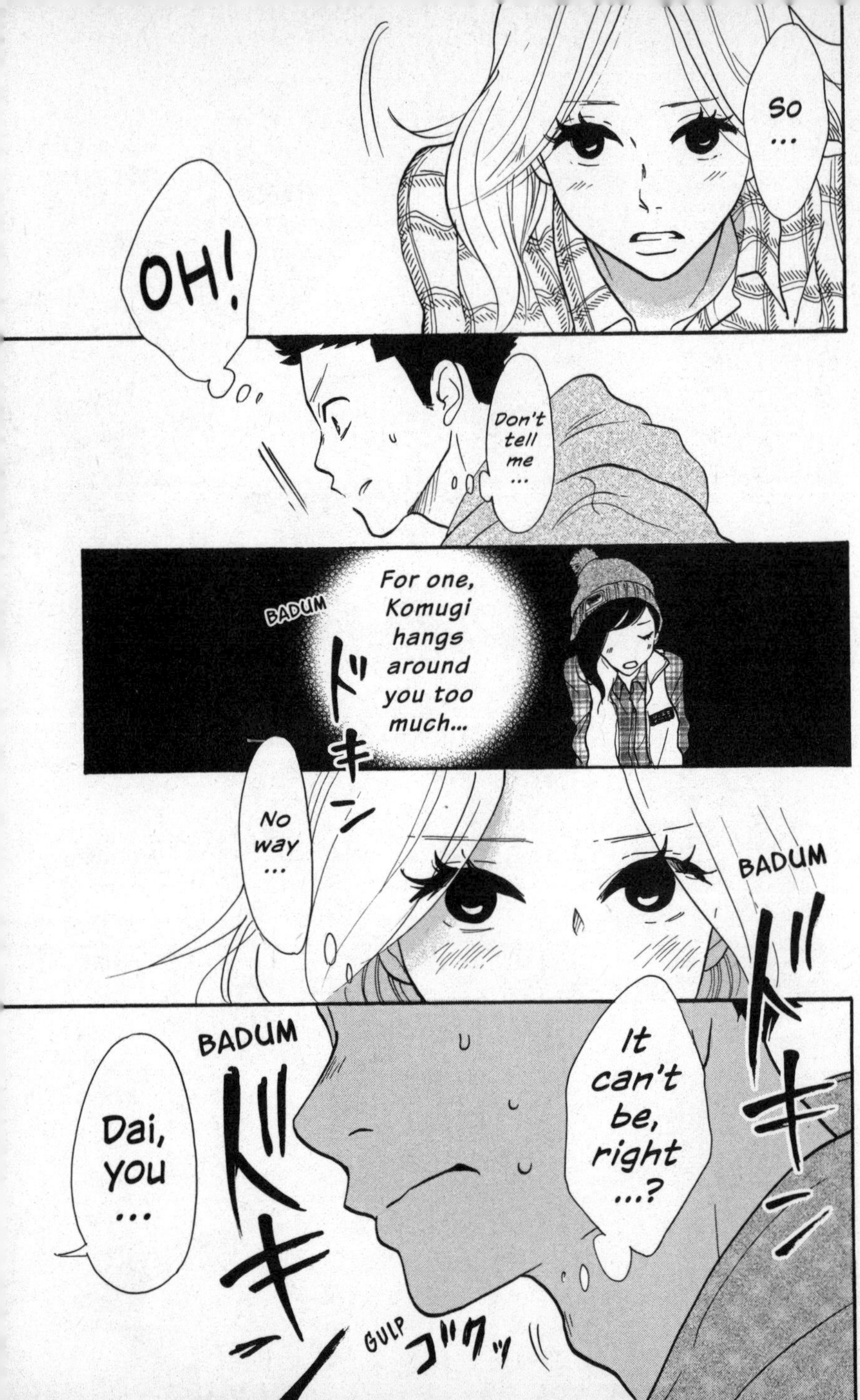

So ...
OH!
Don't tell me ...
BADUM
ドキン
For one, Komugi hangs around you too much...
No way ...
BADUM
ドキーン
It can't be, right ...?
BADUM
ドキーン
Dai, you ...
GULP
ゴクッ

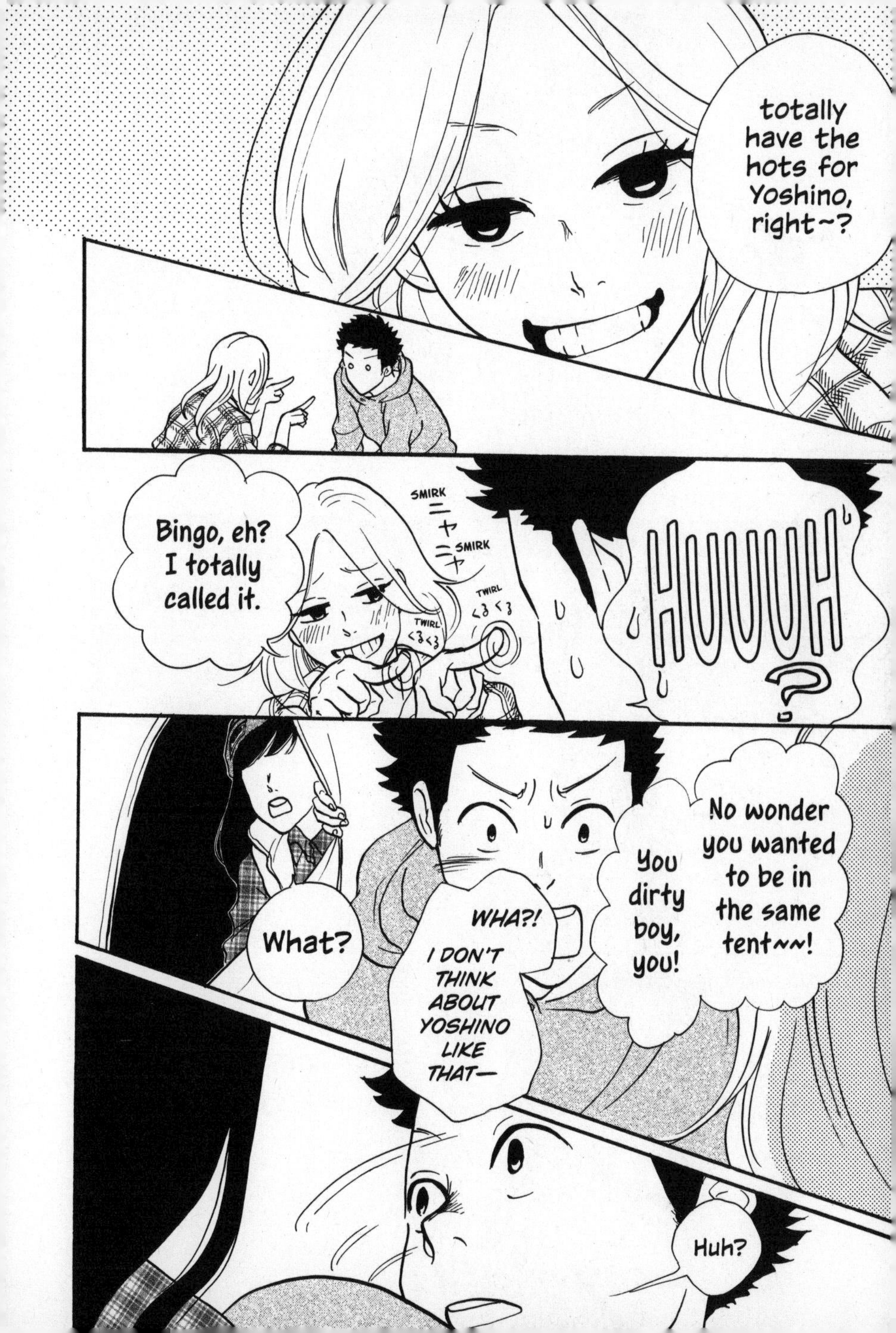
totally have the hots for Yoshino, right~?
HUUUH?
SMIRK ニヤ
SMIRK ニヤ
TWIRL くるくる
TWIRL くるくる
Bingo, eh? I totally called it.
No wonder you wanted to be in the same tent~~!
You dirty boy, you!
WHA?!
I DON'T THINK ABOUT YOSHINO LIKE THAT—
What?
Huh?

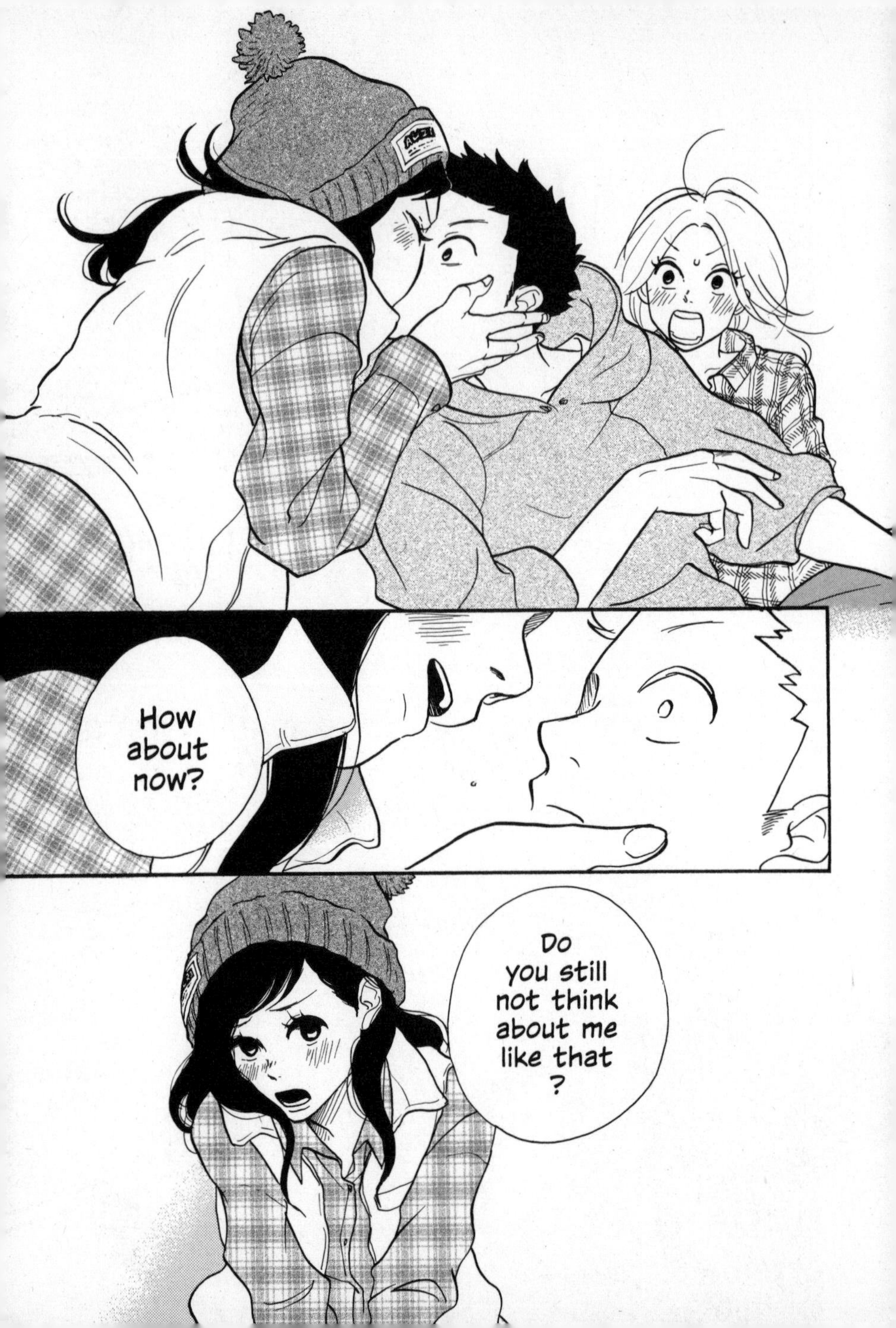
How about now?
Do you still not think about me like that?

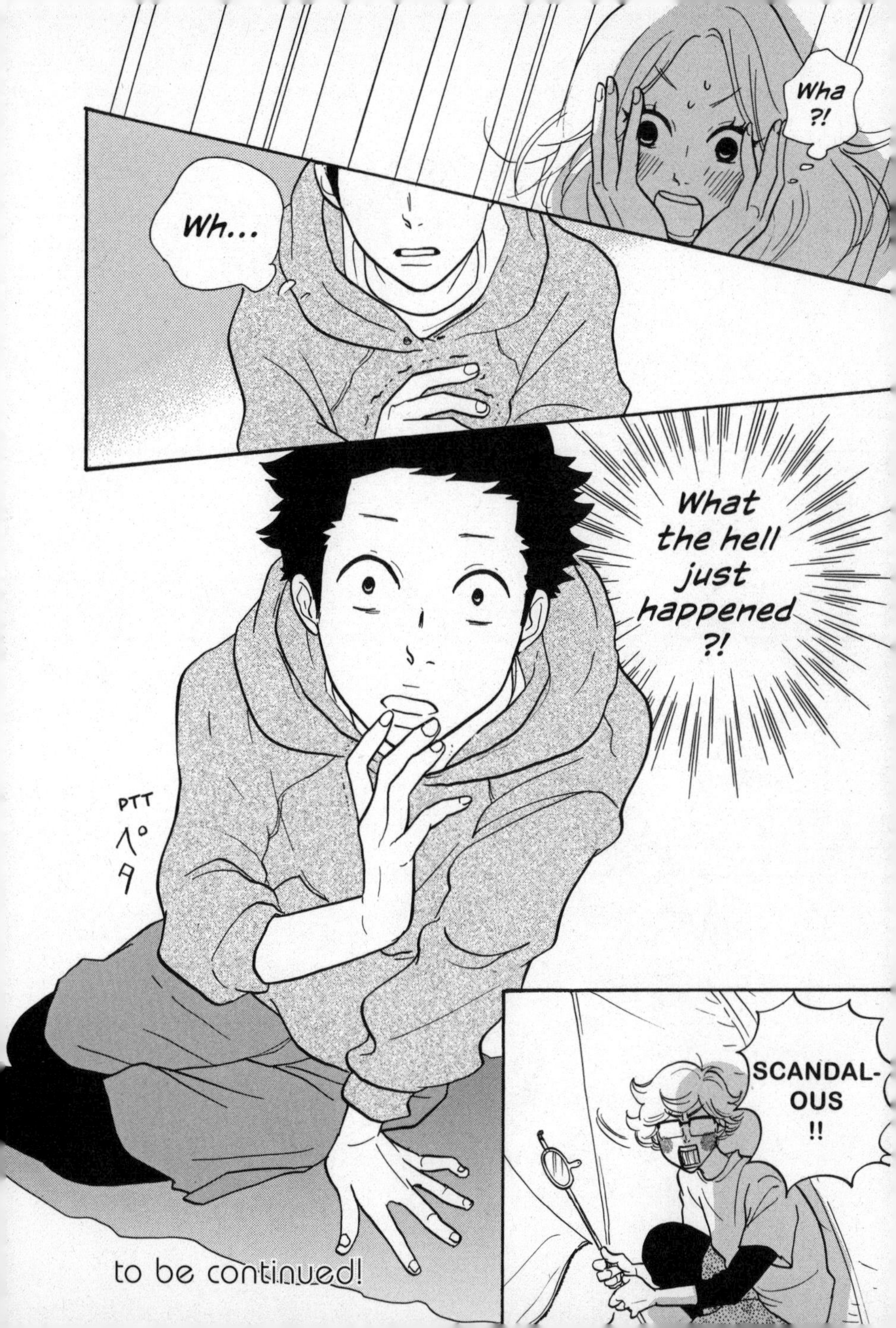
Wha ?!
Wh...
What the hell just happened ?!
PTT
SCANDAL-OUS !!
to be continued!

Looks like we got to meet again in the
pages of The Delinquent Housewife Vol. 2!
I'm very happy. I hope we'll see each other
again at the end of volume 3!

05/2016 Nemu Yoko

BRING
ON
THE
DiRT

SPECIAL THANKS

Tagucchan   Tsune-chan
Nomachin   Yuchika-chan
My editor, Domechin

And the book designer,
Niikami-sama

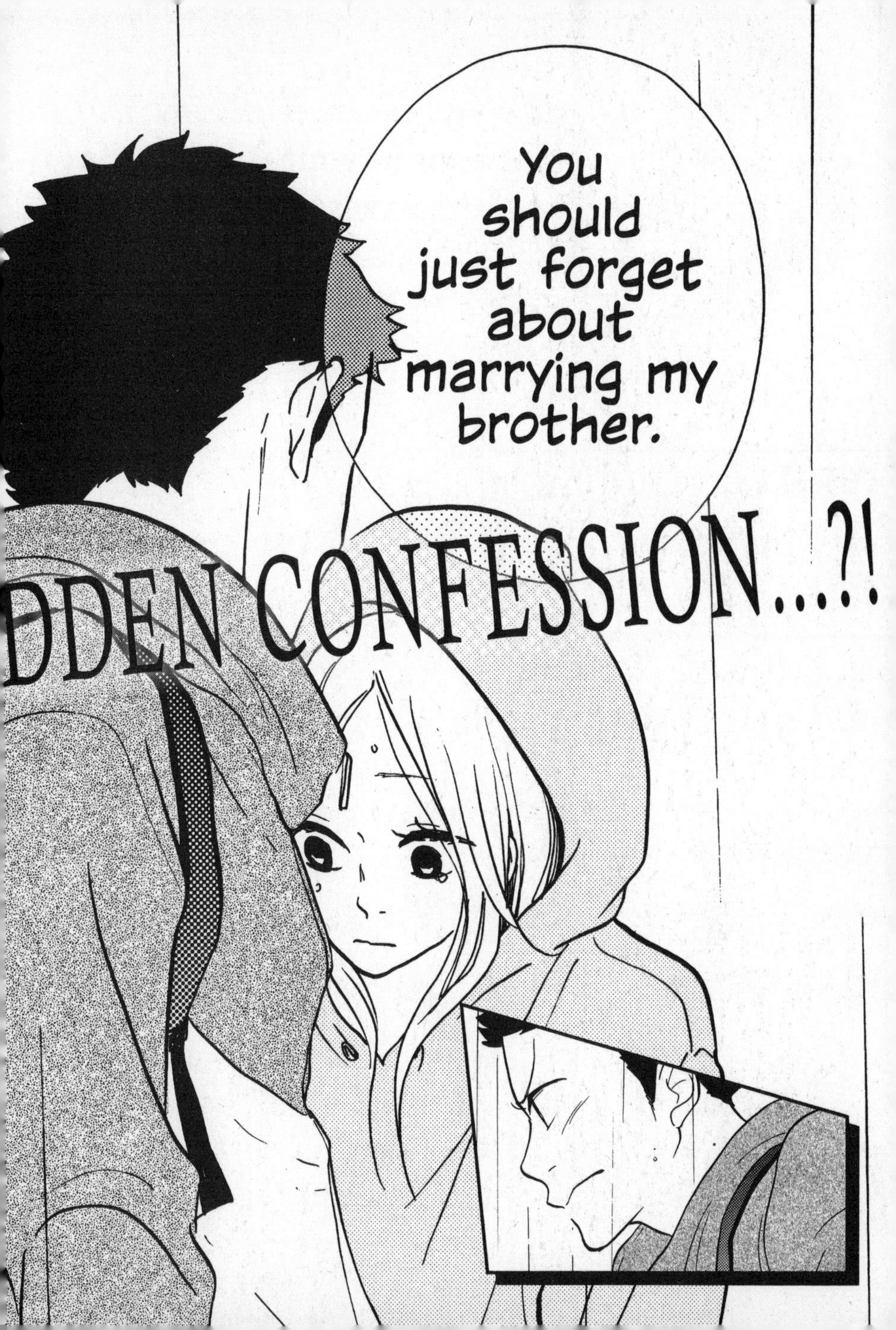
You should just forget about marrying my brother.
DDEN CONFESSION...?!

...No way...

Dai swings between opening the door to youthful romance with his classmate Yoshino and clinging to his unrequited crush on his brother's wife... but in the end, he can't lie to his heart!!

NO LONGER ABLE TO HOLD BACK...
DAI MAKES A FORBI

Don't tell anyone, okay?

You won't be able to look away from this love story as the pace speeds up!

VOLUME 3
ON SALE JANUARY 2019!!!

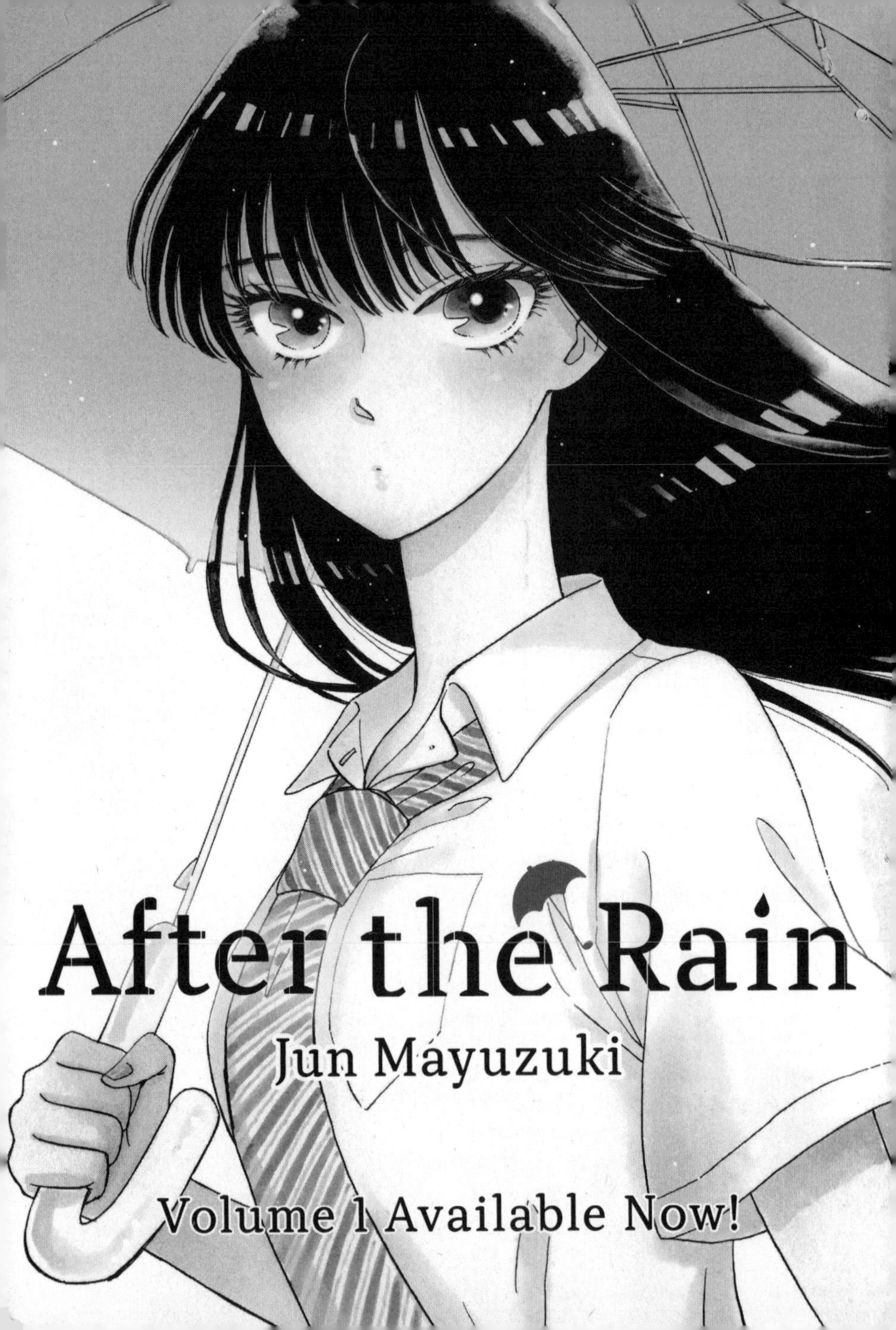
After the Rain
Jun Mayuzuki
Volume 1 Available Now!

The Delinquent Housewife! 2

Translation: David Musto
Production: Risa Cho
           Eve Grandt

FUTSUTSUKA NA YOME DESUGA! Vol. 2
by Nemu Yoko

© 2016 Nemu Yoko
All rights reserved.
Original Japanese edition published by SHOGAKUKAN.
English translation rights in the United States of America and Canada
arranged with SHOGAKUKAN through Tuttle-Mori Agency, Inc.

Translation provided by Vertical Comics, 2018
Published by Vertical Comics, an imprint of Vertical, Inc., New York

Originally published in Japanese as *Futsutsuka Na Yome Desuga!* 2 by Shogakukan, 2016
Futsutsuka Na Yome Desuga! serialized in *Shuukan Biggu Komikku Supirittsu*,
Shogakukan, 2016

This is a work of fiction.

ISBN: 978-1-947194-23-6

Manufactured in the United States of America

First Edition

Vertical, Inc.
451 Park Avenue South
7th Floor
New York, NY 10016
www.vertical-comics.com

Vertical books are distributed through Penguin-Random House Publisher Services.

If you enjoyed Mitsurou Kubo's *AGAIN!!*, then you'll like...

MOTEKI

Love Strikes!

Yukiyo Fujimoto's life has been in a rut. He is about to turn 30 and has never held a steady job or had a girlfriend. When the prospects for hope seem to be at their lowest, out of the blue he is contacted by several women from his past! Yukiyo may seem to have more romantic options than he can handle, but is he ready for love? The stage for love might be set, but the time might only be ripe for him to finally grow up!

Volume 1 & 2 Available Now!

Vol. 1 | 438 pages | $18.95 U.S./ 19.95 CAN | ISBN 9781945054808

Vol. 2 | 492 pages | $20.95 U.S./ 22.95 CAN | ISBN 9781945054815

The Basis for the Hit Anime Series!

"After the Rain takes a prickly premise and gives
us a story about two people with broken
dreams that just might be mendable."
— *Japan Times*

Akira Tachibana is a reserved high
school student who was the star of
the track and field team but had to
quit when she got injured. Sidelined
and depressed, Akira stops in at a
family restaurant one rainy day, and
after the manager—a 45-year-old man
with a young son—serves her free
coffee, she is smitten, and soon takes
a part-time job at the restaurant.

Despite the age gap, Akira is drawn
to his kind nature, and little by little,
the two begin to understand each
other. One day, she decides to finally
tell her manager how she feels... but
how will he react?

KOI WA AMEAGARI NO YONI © 2015 Jun MAYUZUKI / SHOGAKUKAN